The Knife and Fork Man

Redrup "Alpha"-powered Avro Gosport over Red Tarn, Helvellyn

The Knife and Fork Man

The Life and Work of

Charles Benjamin Redrup

Professor William Fairney
FREng BSc FEng FIET

First published 2007

PUBLISHED IN THE UNITED KINGDOM BY:

Diesel Publishing
2, The Tithe Barn
High Street
Hawkesbury Upton
Badminton
South Gloucestershire GL9 1AY

www. fairdiesel.co.uk

British Library Cataloguing in Publication Data.
A catalogue record for this book is available from the British Library.

ISBN 978 0 9554455 0 7

Design by Sally Mundy

Printed and bound by Ta Kung Printing, Shenzhen, China

Contents

Foreword

Mechanical devices have always fascinated me, whether on land, at sea or in the air. It was my father's Meccano set which first sparked my interest, as a five-year old. Since then, speed and mechanical excellence has been an abiding interest.

This book has everything that an admirer of engineering of all kinds could ask for. It is the story of a man who had the good fortune to be born at the dawn of motor engineering, and was himself present at the birth of aero engine design. Charles Redrup took advantage of all this. His automotive engineering skills first brought him public attention, but he soon became a leading light in early British aircraft engines and later had an important part to play in the design and development of the Lancaster bomber. There are many great names in the annals of British engineering. Some did not make the headlines but nevertheless made a significant contribution to British engineering heritage. Charles Redrup was one of these unsung and largely unknown names.

He was a remarkably versatile engineering pioneer who could turn his inventive mind to almost any mechanical problem. His trademark was simplicity. Indeed, he was seemingly able to solve almost any form of mechanical problem. Later in life he turned his skills once more to motor cycles. Unlike the majority of his genre, some of his ideas are still very much in use as recognised best practise today.

Professor Bill Fairney, an expert in his field, has carried out an immense amount of research on a story of inventiveness and persistence. It is a veritable treasure trove of the life of an early British engineer, whose work came to the notice of many of the great names in UK engineering circles, but is otherwise largely unknown. I am astonished that the life of Charles Redrup has never before been told, and I commend it to you.

Air Marshal Ian Macfadyen, CB OBE
President, The Royal British Legion
October 2006

Acknowledgements

I have been able to draw on many sources to research the book and it is not possible to mention them all. For those not mentioned, my apologies and thanks. I have tried to locate the ownership of all the photographs but have not always been successful.

Tom Clements' history of Barry gives a good flavour of life at the turn of the 20th century and has helped understand the early life of Charles Redrup. The Clevedon Civic Society supplied much useful information about Richard Stephens and I express my thanks to Mrs Georgina Westlake, grand-daughter of Richard Stephens, for access to her extensive archive of papers and photographs. Thanks are also due to Robin Loder for granting access to the Leonardslee Museum where two of the Stephens cars are still kept in excellent condition.

I am most grateful to the Mortons Media Group Archives for permission to use extracts from their publications going back over one hundred years.

Thanks are due to Cambridge University Library and the Vickers Archives at the library. Several of the photographs are published with their permission. I am also grateful to the Avro Heritage Centre at Woodford Aerodrome and to Mr Peter Teagle in particular for access to their archives, and much personal knowledge about life at the A.V. Roe Company.

Mr Julian Temple, Aviation Curator at the Brooklands Museum Trust Limited, gave full access to the extensive library at Brooklands for which I give my thanks.

I am indebted to Mr Andy King, Curator of the Industrial Museum Trust at the Bristol Museum, Galleries and Archives, Industrial and Military History Collection. The museum contains a large collection of papers and drawings related to the bus engines which Charles Redrup developed for the Bristol Tramways and Carriage Company. Without the readily-granted access and use of this material, this book would not have been possible.

I am grateful to Mr Alan Jones, a former colleague of John Redrup, and to Mr Peter Nield for permission to use reproductions of their paintings in the book, and for much background information about John and the A.V.Roe Company.

My interest in Charles Redrup was roused when I was researching axial engines for my own company, FairDiesel Limited which is developing an axial diesel engine. The Redrup name kept recurring in reference books, albeit fleetingly. Imagine my surprise whilst visiting the Bristol Industrial Museum in the spring of 2005, when I came face to face with a Redrup bus engine. My curiosity was stimulated and I approached Andy King who gave me access to the Museum archives. I determined to find out more about Charles Redrup and a chance search of the World-Wide Web gave me the name of the Redrup historian, Frank Redrup of Stoneleigh.

After some initial hesitation, because her husband John had died only a few months previously, Frank put me in touch with Charles' daughter-in-law, Joan Redrup. When I visited Joan I was amazed to find that she had a wardrobe full of papers, photographs, drawings and blue-prints about Charles Redrup, going back over a hundred years, neatly filed in date order. John Redrup had started collecting material for a book about his father's life, but had only just started when he succumbed to ill-health. Joan had been a secretary and had put the papers in immaculate order. Joan and I quickly struck a chord and before the day was out it was agreed that I would try and complete John's work.

I have talked to many members of the Redrup family to form a picture of Charles the man but it is to Joan Redrup that my heartfelt thanks are extended, for her extensive knowledge of the family, her advice and her painstaking preparation and archiving of the material, which has made the writing of the book a pleasure.

Finally I give my thanks to my wife Linda, who has seen little of me for over eighteen months whilst I have been writing, but whose unerring support, encouragement and advice has helped me to keep my feet on the ground whilst my head has been in the clouds.

William Fairney
Hawkesbury Upton
September 2006

Prologue
The Landing

Its engine purring smoothly, the Avro Gosport banked steeply over the mountain in the expert hands of its pilot John Leeming. Turning into the wind the aircraft buffeted and reared in the turbulence rolling off Helvellyn. His passenger, the ace Australian flyer Bert Hinkler, craned his neck out of the cockpit looking for the cleared area a few hundred feet below the summit. this was their third attempt to land on the mountain, and weather conditions today were ideal - or almost so.

John F. Leeming, a renowned glider and powered aircraft pilot was also a visionary, and had started a campaign in 1926 to build for the city of Manchester its own commercial airfield. He hoped to draw attention to the lack of such facilities by pulling off the spectacular feat of landing an aircraft on Helvellyn, the highest mountain in the Lake District. During the previous week he and his colleagues had trailed up the mountain and found a fairly flat spot just below the summit. They had dragged the rocks to one side to clear a narrow strip aligned with the prevailing westerly wind. The length of the strip seemed impossibly small, but Leeming judged that the undercarriage would enable him to land firmly on the ground with only a short landing run.

The aircraft was an Avro 585, a variant of the famous and ubiquitous Avro 504K, and named the Gosport. The variant was fitted with an engine designed by a recent recruit to Avro, Charles Benjamin Redrup. It was a five-cylinder radial which incorporated several novel features. These enabled a very smooth power output to be obtained, at a considerable weight saving compared to the engines they had been using up to this time.

Even in 1926 aircraft performance was marginal and totally dependent on the engine and its power to weight ratio. A much stronger lever-type undercarriage had been designed by George Dowty for the Avro 504N, which replaced the flimsier skid undercarriage used up until then on 504K variants. Leeming had seen that the weight saved by the new engine could be used with the stronger undercarriage to enable a short-field landing on rough ground.

"Sideslip a little to the left!" Hinkler shouted over the noise of the slipstream, guiding Leeming westwards below the summit towards the cleared area for an initial flyby. Reducing power, the aircraft nosed towards the ground but Leeming noticed that despite reducing his airspeed, the speed over the ground was increasing. At this height, because of the strange airflow curling around the summit, the wind was actually behind him, from the north-east. He opened up the throttle, and whilst climbing away again from the strip, Hinkler looked back to assess the situation. He realised that they could not turn to land into the wind because the cleared strip, on a rocky ledge, had an obstructed approach from that direction. On the very peak of the mountain, sheltering behind a small cairn, he saw a speck-like figure, watching, mesmerised as they circled once again. They knew from their previous climb up Helvellyn that there was a small, flat but narrow area at the very top, but it was not aligned with the prevailing wind. However, with the current wind conditions it was just possible to approach the peak into wind. "The wind up here is more easterly, let's take a look at the summit," Hinkler shouted to Leeming through the Gosport Tube over the roar of the slipstream. Leeming banked round once again, this time towards the east over the peak to assess the new landing area.

As they passed the black-clad figure on the top of the mountain Hinkler could clearly make out his walking gear and cane. The head wind was so strong that the aircraft seemed virtually stationary as they sailed past almost at walking pace. Leeming could see the surface of the mountain top, and was relieved to see it clear of stones. He remembered as a child climbing the mountain, and throwing small stones over the edge. Generations of children and walkers must have scoured the surface clean. "It looks a goer" the Australian shouted to Leeming, realising that a landing on the peak was possible, and Leeming gave a thumbs-up sign in agreement.

Swooping back up, Leeming circled the area into an elliptical approach pattern. He gradually reduced power and the aircraft slowed and nosed up into its landing attitude. As the speed washed off the controls became more sluggish and Leeming needed to correct with large inputs to the rudder. At these speeds use of aileron was not only ineffective but dangerous as a stall could result. The aircraft started to sink rapidly as the drag increased and Leeming corrected with a boost in power. The engine responded superbly and the Gosport inched forward against the wind, buffeted by the gusts around the mountain peak, but staying on track for the small flat area. As the aircraft touched the ground at a groundspeed of only about fifteen miles per hour, it bounced and lurched as Leeming cut the throttle. Thankfully the sturdy Gosport stopped in a very short distance, but still disturbingly close to the sheer Striding Edge of the mountain. Because of the upslope, Leeming had to open the throttle slightly to stop the Gosport rolling backwards.

Clambering out of the aircraft Hinkler immediately searched around for stones to put around the wheels to secure the aircraft against the gusting wind so that the Gosport would not roll back down the slope of the mountain. As he did so he was helped by an incredulous young man who came from behind the cairn and congratulated them on their feat. He was the walker they had seen on the mountain from the air and turned out to be E. R. Dodds, Professor of Greek at Birmingham University, on a lone walking tour of the peaks. Bert took some photographs and they improvised a certificate from an old bill which the professor found in his pocket. This he readily signed, confirming their feat of landing on Helvellyn.

Soon it was time to leave but they had a problem because there were only about thirty yards available in front and they did not dare to remove the stones from the wheels in case the Gosport rolled backwards. So together they pointed the aircraft into the wind and Leeming climbed into the cockpit to adjust the engine mixture and ignition for take-off. With the professor steadying one wing, Hinkler removed the stones and climbed aboard. Adjusting his goggles, Leeming pushed the throttle wide open and the aircraft surged forward against the wind. The Gosport reached the sheer edge of the mountain barely achieving flying speed and dived over Striding Edge towards Red Tarn. As the wings bit the air the aircraft steadied, then soared upwards under the smooth power of the Redrup radial engine.

Chapter 1
The Early Years

Charles Benjamin Redrup, who was in due course to become an outstanding and innovative engineer, was born on October 28th 1878 at Newport in Monmouthshire and spent his early years in South Wales. However this branch of the Redrup family did not originate in Wales. Redrups can be traced back to the Rudroppe brothers of Cheshire in the first half of the 16th century. All present-day Redrups, Redrops, Redropes and a variety of other spellings, are descendents of the two brothers, Richard and Robert Rudroppe. Their father, also Richard, was born in Bunbury in Cheshire in 1537 and became Vicar of Penn in Buckinghamshire. He died in 1614 after retiring from his living in 1607. The Redrup family historian, Frank Redrup of Stoneleigh in Surrey relates that when Richard the elder died, his elder son Richard inherited all his wealth and Robert got nothing.

In 1680 Richard the younger's son, also called Richard, Charles Redrup's ancestor, was indicted at Quarter Sessions for assaulting Sir Dennis Hampson and was fined five pounds. No reason is given for the assault but Richard made a representation, which was then the equivalent of our present-day appeal and the fine was reduced to one pound, which was the standard fine for assault on a man. The standard fine for an assault on a woman was only 3 shillings and 4 pence! (17 new pence). Hampson was a magistrate and later became Sheriff of Buckinghamshire, which might account for the severity of the original five pounds fine.

Since that time the two halves of the family have been called the Rich and the Pauper lines, although the fortunes of both sides of the family have waxed and waned several times in the meantime. Charles Benjamin Redrup's grandfather, another Charles Redrup, of Great Kimble in Buckinghamshire was from the Rich side. He became the landlord of the Red Lion Inn in Soham, Cambridgeshire in the early 1830's and owned other property and land. He married a local girl Elizabeth Elsdon in Soham in 1832 and they had five children over the next eleven years. The youngest of his sons, Harry Redrup, was born in 1846 at Soham. When he was old enough, Harry established himself in Soham in the trade of hairdresser and wig-maker. Despite this somewhat anchored profession he spent his weekends driving a pony and trap, venturing to many places around the locality. His travels must have taken him beyond the county boundaries for in 1874 he married Elizabeth Mary Ashman from Bracknell, in her local parish church. They moved to the High Street in Newport, South Wales the following year where he continued his trade.

Plate 1-1 Harry and Elizabeth Redrup

Over the next few years Harry and Elizabeth (Plate 1-1) had five sons and five daughters in their home at Villena Cottage, of which Charles Benjamin was the eldest. Harry had inherited land and property which provided him with a good income and so he was able to give his children a good private education. During his childhood Charles showed an interest in all things scientific. By the time he was twelve he was experimenting with a number of electrical and mechanical devices and it was during one of these experiments with a gas-fired burner that the vessel he was heating exploded and a fragment of glass hit him in the left eye. His father, whose occupation as a hairdresser still retained some remnants of the tradition of barber and surgeon, rendered immediate first aid whilst Charles bravely submitted to his ministrations. The local hospital removed the fragment of glass but Charles' vision from his left eye was left permanently impaired. Despite this setback he was more determined than ever to pursue a life in the fields of science and engineering.

With the rapid growth of the port facilities at Barry in the mid-1880s Harry saw the opportunity for expansion and moved his growing family and business to 70, Main Street in Barry, where he was soon employing a number of assistants. Charles Benjamin was enthralled by the new world around him and spent hours in the busy Barry docks observing the ships and the new railway systems built to serve them. Although his father had a good income from his properties and his trade, Charles was not keen to stay on longer at school once he reached the age of fourteen, the then school-leaving age. He wanted passionately to engage with the developing industries as soon as possible.

Harry knew that Charles had the aptitude and ability to go on to higher education and this resulted in extensive family discussion. Eventually Charles prevailed and his father, who cut the hair and made wigs for some of the most influential citizens in the town, was able to arrange for him to be apprenticed to the Great Western Railway for five years as a Premium Engineering Apprentice. There Charles received a first class engineering education and with his natural aptitude to all things mechanical he learnt all aspects of design, drawing, metallurgy, machining, pattern-making, casting and production methods. As well as spending time in the engineering workshops he travelled the network routes as a maintenance assistant. He also acquired a considerable knowledge of electrical engineering which was to stand him in good stead in his future career.

In about 1891 Harry Redrup moved his hairdressing business to 2, Jewel Street, Barry. A few years later he bought a house for Charles who was still an apprentice but was dabbling in engineering matters at home. The house was just around the corner at number 22, Guthrie Street and Charles built for himself a workshop, the significant features of which were a lathe and other simple machine tools. In this workshop he made a variety of engines in his spare time. It is remarkable that Charles Redrup was to use his home workshops throughout his life to make very intricate engines, and that he did this with the use of only one good eye.

He built a small steam engine which gave very smooth running, which was to become a major objective of all Redrup designs. Having tested the steam engine very thoroughly and found excellent performance, he decided to carry out a "flat-out" test, and screwed down the safety relief valve on the boiler. The engine output rose dramatically but the inevitable occurred and the boiler exploded on spectacular fashion, although no-one was hurt. Not surprisingly, nothing remains of this engine.

The railway apprenticeship served him well, for when it was completed in the spring of 1897 he signed-on to serve as an Assistant to the Chief Engineer of a cargo ship on a voyage from Cardiff to Philadelphia. His account records that the ship battled force nine gales and hurricanes during the two week journey, and despite being extremely seasick, he attended to the engines and equipment without fail. About six days into the voyage the ship met increasingly heavy seas and the next day was in the centre of a force ten gale. The crew brought the ship around to face into the wind but during one particularly heavy swell the ship pitched to such an extent that the screws came right out of the water and the engines started to race. As the stern of the ship crashed back down onto the swell the engines stalled under the excessive load, the boiler relief valves screamed open as the pressure rose above the critical safety level, and the boilers flamed out.

Despite being extremely seasick Charles and his crew set about re-lighting the boilers in the violently rocking bowels of the ship. Re-starting the engines was a long and complicated procedure as all the boiler and engine auxiliaries were driven by steam or electricity derived from the main engines. It was first of all necessary to hand-start a small petrol-driven generator, which provided power to excite a larger generator. Once this had started, loads could be progressively added to drive pumps and fans. The furnaces had to be cleared of ash and part-burnt coal by the stokers before the chain-grates could be started and the furnace re-lit. Some steam pressure was eventually restored and Charles was able to start up one of the engines once again. Once sufficient steam pressure had been raised he was able to advise the captain that power was now fully restored.

Relieved to arrive in Philadelphia, Charles was disconcerted to find that the turn-round was very rapid, and before he had time to recover from his sickness the ship set sail for the return voyage. Fortunately the conditions were less onerous, but on his return to Cardiff, Charles decided that the sea was not for him, and he resolved never to take to the water again. He did however have to relent on this resolution later in life, but for strictly business reasons!

With a good engineering training behind him, and more experience in his young life than he could wish for, Charles obtained employment in more stable territory through a family connection and obtained a place as after-sales engineer with Richard Stephens of Clevedon, Somerset. Stephens was a bicycle repairer who had branched out and designed and patented a car based on two bicycle-type frames linked together by tubular bars. He also designed the engine and gearbox.

Richard Stephens was born in Cwmbran near Pontypool in South Wales in 1856 and like many in that part of Wales went down the coal mines as a very young man. He became an engine driver at the Little Pit at Nantyglo and then trained as a mining engineer. When he was in his early twenties he went to Australia where he continued his career. He was engaged to a Mary Ann Masters, a farmer's daughter from Frome in Somerset and shortly after emigrating he sent for her and they were married in Paddington, Victoria, New South Wales in 1878. They returned to South Wales in 1882 but after a short time emigrated again, this time to Canada where Stephens was again in demand for his mining skills, but also engaged in seal-hunting and fur-collecting.

Plate 1-2

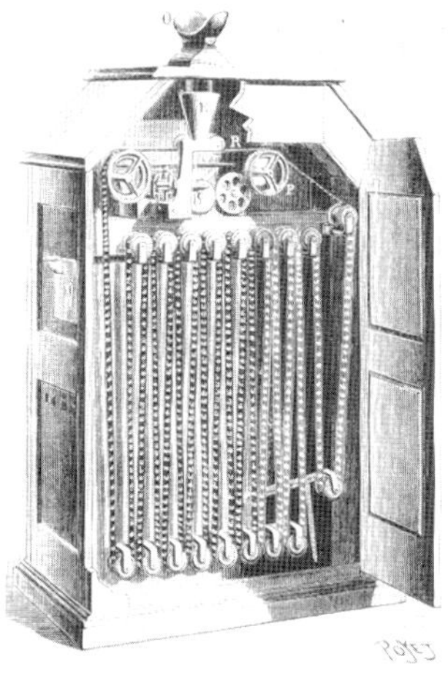

Plate 1-3

Their next move was in the following year to the United States of America. Here he became friendly with Thomas Edison whose wax-cylinder Phonograph (Plate 1-2), was just becoming available as a practical domestic machine and was being licensed for hire by one of Edison's business associates, Jesse H Lippincott.

Stephens also saw Edison's pioneering work on motion pictures. In 1888 Edison had filed a preliminary patent for a moving picture machine based on a rotating cylinder with multiple pictures printed on it. By 1889 he had a prototype machine working but the length of the performance was limited by the cylinder diameter and so he set to work developing a version based on a forty-seven foot long strip of celluloid film, about thirty-five millimetres wide. (Plate 1-3). The strip had perforations down each side for transporting the film, and this was the basis of the 35mm film used worldwide today for still and moving film production. Although the first model of the machine was completed in 1889 he was still not satisfied with it and a modified machine was perfected in 1891. The first public demonstrations were not given in America until 1894. Richard Stephens was fascinated by the Kinetoscope as it was called and when he and Mary had to return to England late in 1889 because of her declining health he brought with him the discarded prototype film Kinetoscope. Edison had licensed it to him to demonstrate in the United Kingdom in anticipation of achieving advanced publicity. Stephens also brought a Phonograph and a license to hire it out in the United Kingdom.

Richard set up home in premises in The Triangle in the centre of Clevedon, Somerset and started to give demonstrations of the Phonograph and Kinetoscope. He travelled all over the country with the two machines and carried with him a number of recordings including some of speeches by Gladstone and Sir William Harcourt, the then Chancellor of the Exchequer. He would hire out the Phonograph for one pound per hour. He also had a limited number of blank wax cylinders and would make recordings of local celebrities. On a visit back to Nantyglo he recorded the voice of a young boy elocutionist, Ben Jelley, who had already won over fifty prizes at Eisteddfods. The record of a recitation of "Rather Warm" was reproduced by Richard Stephens and sold widely at the time around the country. He also had recordings of poems recited by Lord Alfred Tennyson, of which the most famous is the 1890 recording of "The Charge of the Light Brigade".

Stephens carried out similar demonstrations of the Kinetoscope and in a 1890 newspaper report of a demonstration at Number Two, Park Street in Bristol, the machine is described as being a pillar-like cabinet with a small slit or window in the top through which the viewer peers. (Plate 1-4). The machine showed a number of scenes each said to consist of about two thousand photographs displayed at forty-six frames per second. Scenes of "Buffalo Bill and his Repeating Rifle " and "A Mexican Knife Duel", were shown and another scene said to be available was "Bertoldi, The Celebrated Contortionist" The whole contrivance was described as "a mysterious wonder that had to be seen to be believed". Thomas Edison had sold his phonograph companies to Jesse Lippincott in 1888 who marketed the machine primarily for hire. Lippincott became ill in 1890 and was unable to attend to the business which fell into debt. Edison bought back the companies but did not have the time to operate them as a hire business and decided to concentrate on outright sales. When Richard Stephens learnt of this he therefore ceased to pursue the hire business any further.

Plate 1-4 The Edison Kinetoscope

Whilst in the United States Stephens had seen developments in bicycle manufacture which made use of lightweight tubular welded steel frames. He therefore set himself up as a bicycle manufacturer and repairer, purchasing additional property on the Triangle in Clevedon. He was well acquainted with the local Squire, Sir Edmund Elton who helped finance his enterprises. Elton was however also a significant inventor in his own right. Over the next few years between them they patented several bicycle accessories including "The Stephens Detachable Ladies Dress Guard Clip" and "The Elton Stephens Rim Brake." The design of this brake is the now universal calliper brake which is renowned for its simple self-centering feature which automatically balances the brake force on each rim. These items were exhibited at the Crystal Palace Exhibition in 1897. The two inventors were also credited with the invention of the Elton Stephens Automatic Gas-Lamp Lighter. From about 1895 Richard and his wife Mary lived and kept tearooms at No. 12, The Triangle. Whilst Richard operated his cycle business from the larger premises at No. 9, The Triangle his wife ran the teashop business. At the turn of the century the Triangle was the centre of the town with the clock tower set in a little sedate area with houses and shops on three sides. (Plate 1-5).

Plate 1-5 Clevedon Triangle

In 1897 with the backing of Sir Edmund Elton, Stephens started developing his first motor car and produced the prototype a year later, with Dogcart style seating. It was the first all-British car to be built. This vehicle, AE 174 was pictured and described in the Autocar magazine in October 1899. Dogcart style seating is a back-to-back arrangement with the driver and front passenger facing forward and the passengers behind facing back, and was a practical solution for vehicles using a rear mounted engine. (Plate 1-6). In this photograph Richard Stephens and Mary are seen in the driving seats with daughter Ada and son Richard on the rear seat and youngest son Ewart on the front seat.

Plate 1-6 Richard Stephens First Motor Vehicle

The dog-cart arrangement had been used by other pioneer motor car manufacturers previously. In front of the driver was the storage compartment for batteries and tools with a bench seat suitable for a child or as a place to stow waterproof clothing. The engine was a flat twin-cylinder of 2,000cc capacity, designed and built by Stephens, arranged transversely across the back of the car. (Plate 1-7). It had a bore of 3.75 inches (95 mm), a stroke of 6 inches (152 mm) and was rated at 8 horse-power. (6 kw). Drive was by pulley and belts giving two forward speeds. Reverse gear was "passenger-assisted manual", that is to say, hand-pushed! The engine was high-revving and could exceed 2000rpm, giving a bottom gear speed of about 12mph, and a potential top speed of nearly 40 mph. An average speed of 30 mph (on good roads) was typical which was very fast for an early car. Steering was by a bar or tiller arrangement connected to the front wheels through an adjustable chain to a bevel and worm. The car was fitted with a very advanced independent front suspension running on cup and cone bearings which Stephens patented and gave a very comfortable ride, even over Clevedon's rough road surfaces, where the manholes protruded several inches into the air. The rear wheels were of slightly larger diameter and used semi-elliptical suspension for the solid axle. Owing to the position of the crankshaft in relation to the off-side rear wheel the starting handle had to pass through the spokes.

Plate 1-7 Four-cylinder Stephens Engine

Wire wheels were fitted to the prototype although production models had wooden wheels because the rough roads played havoc with wire spokes. Brakes could be applied either by foot or manually and could stop the vehicle in its own length. The prototype car was painted in a dark chocolate colour with red and yellow trim lines and furnished with plush red cushions. The metalwork was all plated and brightly polished. The prototype car was produced in great secrecy and all the early trial runs were carried out at night. Initially ignition was by hot tubes located under the passenger seat. On one of these nocturnal runs there was some excitement when the seat caught fire and the flames had to be extinguished by rubbing the upholstery on the damp grass verge! This system was soon abandoned in favour of electrical ignition but this was at first unreliable and required much testing at night to perfect.

Clevedon at the turn of the century was a mixture of seaside resort for the gentility and a retirement refuge for the wealthy. The Mendip Hills extend in a line across Somerset and meet the Bristol Channel at Clevedon and Weston-Super-Mare. Located on the side of a cliff on the sunny northern coast of Somerset Clevedon enjoys lovely views over the Bristol Channel. The warmth of the Gulf Stream combined in summer with warm south-westerly breezes makes it an ideal refuge for the retired and those recovering from illness. The residents would walk along the promenade and down the pier, or if incapacitated, would be pushed in their bath chairs by their family or retainers.

The graceful pier that extends into the Bristol Channel is considered to be the best preserved example of its architectural type. It has recently been restored to its full Victorian splendour, and has been listed Grade I by English Heritage. Clevedon developed as a resort for Bristol from around 1795, but it was the arrival of a railway in 1847 that led to hopes for its rapid development. It was thought that a new pier would not only provide an addition to the resort, but also a jetty to enable steamers to ferry passengers to South Wales. There were formidable problems to be overcome, with a tidal range of 47ft (14.2 metres), the second highest in the world) and huge currents, but addressing them resulted in the pier's very slender and elegant style. When it was opened in 1869 the pier was 840 ft (255 metres) long, with a six-level landing stage at its end. From this pier a ferry ran to Briton Ferry on the mouth of the river Neath in South Wales, which was an obvious destination being only thirteen miles across the water .

Richard Stephens was soon a successful business man with many customers. He needed an engineer to provide after-sales service, for automobiles were still very temperamental in the early years of motoring. Charles Redrup's responsibilities were to resolve any problems which arose when customers had taken delivery of their new cars, but he soon found himself involved in the engineering design work, together with Stephens' son Dick and a group of apprentices which Richard Stephens employed. (Plate 1-8). One of Charles' close friends, Archie Binding, seen here on the right, later joined with a partner to

Plate 1-8 Richard Stephens and his Apprentices

form Binding & Payne, motor engineers of Clevedon and lived to be well over a hundred. Richard Stephens' home was very lively as he always had friends or relatives staying. He and his wife Mary had three sons and three daughters as well as a niece staying with them, (Plate 1-9), and treated the employees like family members. In addition to this they also fostered a number of homeless children.

Plate 1-9 The Stephens Family

Charles commuted to Clevedon daily from Barry, using the ferryboat from Briton Pier, having to overcome his dislike of water in the process! The ferry was the only means of crossing the Bristol Channel to avoid the long road journey up to Gloucester, where the first road bridge crossed the Severn. It was not until 1966 that the first Severn suspension bridge was built to link Chepstow to Filton.

Plate 1-10 Charles Redrup Driving Tourists at Burrington Coombe, Somerset

Stephens was soon driving his cars around Clevedon and obtained a license to ply for hire around the town. He also taught Charles Redrup and his own son, also named Richard but always known as Dick, to drive and they would tour customers around the surrounding countryside. (Plate 1-10). Wells, Cheddar Gorge and Burrington Coombe were favourite destinations. This photograph shows Charles Redrup driving a party at Burrington Coombe, a favourite tourist spot in the Mendips. The round trip to Cheddar cost one pound and to Wells one pound ten shillings. Stephens obtained a contract with the Great Western Railway to drive their customers to and from Clevedon station to various destinations and painted all his vehicles in their chocolate brown and cream livery. The return journey cost two shillings per person. Orders for Stephens' cars started to come in from private customers and the first one was built for a Mr Byrom of Park Street, Bath.

Plate 1-11 Bath's First Motorised Hackney Carriage

Close to Clevedon, the City of Bath was also a hilly place, frequented by visitors to the Spa and inhabited by wealthy merchants, landowners and gentry. It was a retirement resort for the elderly and indeed, the bath chair gets its name from the city. Richard Stephens realised that the hilly streets of Clevedon and Bath were well suited to motorised travel and set out to develop these markets. A friend of Byrom's in Bath, John Hunt, who ran a horse-drawn hackney carriage business, heard of the Stephens cars and visited the works in Clevedon to see Byrom's car being built. He ordered a larger version of the car for use as a taxi. The four-seater design was therefore followed by a mechanically-similar but slightly larger 6 seater, AE 341. Dick Stephens delivered Mr Byrom's car in spring 1900 and as it drove through the city it was derided by the hackney carriage drivers as a seven-day wonder. John Hunt applied to the Watch Committee in Bath for a Hackney Carriage license and this was strongly opposed by the horse-drawn hackney drivers. However Richard Stephens junior, although only sixteen, gave Hunt driving lessons and in May 1900 drove the new vehicle to Bath to demonstrate it to the Watch Committee. He vouched to the Committee for Hunt's ability to drive and they were so enthralled that the license was granted without further ado. (Plate 1-11). It was the first motorised hackney carriage to ply for hire on the streets of Bath. (The first hackney carriages were licensed in 1662, and were at the time literally horse-drawn carriages. The name derives not from Hackney in London, but from the French word 'haquenée', referring to the doddery old horse that was pulling it!).

Hunt had the motorised carriage field to himself in Bath for four years and established himself as Hunt's Garage in Henrietta Street, just off Grove Street. When he died in 1936 his two sons F J and A W Hunt carried on the business. In 1956 John Hunt junior met up with Dick Stephens at the Bath Recreation Ground for the Abbey Week Concourse d'Elegance. He recalled being taught by his father how to drive horses, and later, the motor cabs.

AE 341 was later sold back to Stephens and joined a fleet of small omnibuses and taxis that Richard Stephens had established around Clevedon. Charles Redrup was a very presentable young man and as well chauffeuring customers around the local beauty spots Stephens occasionally used him to drive his buses. Stephens ran his fleet of Hackneys (Plate 1-12) from his works on the Triangle at Clevedon, and obtained contracts to run his buses from Clevedon to Portishead. (Plate 1-13).

Plate 1-12 Richard Stephens Works at Clevedon

As the Stephens products achieved sales further afield Charles found himself travelling more and more to service customers' vehicles and for the more serious work requiring engine overhaul his mentor invented the "Stephens Folding Engine Stand" which Charles would carry about in the car which Stephens provided for the purpose. In 1907, when the Great Western Railway reached Clevedon Stephens sold off most of his fleet and purchased *a* fleet of Ford motor taxis which he continued to run for a few more years. Richard Stephens also liked driving more powerful cars and in 1910 he had a lucky escape when he overturned a sixty horse-power Napier tourer. (Plate 1-14). His inventive genius was again brought to bear when motor vehicles became converted for use as hospital transportation and he invented a folding frame, the "Stephens Stretcher-Carrier For Ambulances."

Plate 1-13 Stephens Hackneys at Portishead Station, 1902

When AE 341 was taken out of service in 1907 the engine was removed and loaned to the Science Museum. The chassis was literally cut up with a hack-saw and the pieces stored in tea chests. Luckily Dick Stephens kept and regularly used his father's prototype of 1898, and also kept the remaining parts of the 1900 six-seater in store.

Richard Stephens' cars were very popular and he produced several versions with a variety of seating arrangements. The two buses he made, or "Wagonettes" as he called them, had a nine-seat arrangement with two benches running the length of the rear carriage on either side with foot space between them. Stephens continued his motor engineering business with his son Dick until 1907 when Dick moved the business to Upper Norwood in London. Mary still ran the tearooms at their home in No. 12, The Triangle Whilst Richard ran the bus and taxi services. Altogether Richard Stephens manufactured a total of about twelve vehicles. (Plate 1-15).

After the car, Richard Stephens' most famous invention was probably the Stephens Adjustable Brake Shoe for Motor-Cars, now known as the Clevedon brake, which operated on the same principle as the calliper bicycle brake invention. A model of the Clevedon Brake is on permanent exhibition in the Science Museum. Richard retired in 1919 and he and Mary (Plate 1-16) moved to Upper Norwood to be close to Dick and his wife Lily. Mary died in 1922 and in 1924 Richard remarried. His second wife was Florence Steane who had been headmistress of the Grange Street Girls School in Burton-on-Trent and they went to live in Hove, Sussex. In 1927 the first "Old Crocks Race" was run between the "Daily Sketch" offices in Fleet Street and Olympia. A contemporary photograph shows an elderly Richard Stephens driving one of his vehicles, probably AE 174, along the route.

Plate 1-14 Richard Stephens had a Lucky Escape from this Napier Tourer when it Overturned

The vehicle came first in the race winning the gold medal and Richard Stephens' grand-daughter Georgina Westlake still has the medal. The photograph shows Richard Stephens and Dick with the same vehicle on the 1931 London to Eastbourne run with a contemporary number plate. (Plate 1-17).

Richard Stephens died after a short illness in February 1932 and he was buried at Elmers End cemetery. Dick Stephens continued to run the prototype car and regularly entered rallies and runs for vintage and veteran vehicles. At the beginning of the 1951 London to Brighton Run

Plate 1-15 Stephens Hackney Carriages on Clevedon Triangle

Plate 1-16 Richard and Mary Stephens

in Hyde Park the crankshaft broke close to the flywheel. As the weather was very wet this was probably no bad thing, but Dick traced the failure back to an incident twenty years earlier when the back main tube of the frame was broken. Owing to the considerable amount of work involved in fitting a new tube the old one was repaired with the result that the extension tube carrying the driving pulleys was subjected to continual flexing. The effect of this prolonged cycling was to cause a fatigue failure of the crankshaft. A complete and proper repair was then carried out to the frame and a new crankshaft fitted.

Plate 1-17-The 1931 London to Eastbourne Run

Dick eventually became too old to continue with the car and in 1969 Robin Loder who had a motor museum at his property in Leonardslee Gardens in Horsham, Sussex purchased the complete prototype through Sotheby's for two thousand six hundred pounds. He also purchased the cut-up pieces of the hackney vehicle AE 341 and was able to recover the original Stephens engine from the Science Museum. He was immediately certain that it was the correct engine, for the hacksaw cuts on the engine frame precisely matched those on the car frames! Today both the 1898 prototype AE 174 and the 1900 six-seater AE 341, once

Plate 1-18 The Stephens Prototype Vehicle AE 174 in the Robin Loder Museum, Leonardslee

Plate 1-19 The 1900 Six-seater at Leonardslee

again reunited with its engine, are kept in immaculate condition in Robin Loder's museum, now tended by his children. (Plates 1-18 and 1-19).

The cars appeared in the film Genevieve and are often to be seen on the London to Brighton Run where they regularly come in ahead of the field owing to their high speed and reliability. AE 174 came first in the 1960 run (Plate 1-20) and in 1987 Robin Loder and Richard Stephens' grand-daughter Georgina Westlake rode AE 174 to second place in the run. In the summer of 2006 a Cavalcade of old vehicles took place in Clevedon and Robin Loder took both vehicles on the run. (See colour plate C1).

Richard Stephens wife Mary, formerly Masters, had a sister Elizabeth, who in 1882 married a mining engineer John Stacey in Pontypridd, South Wales. John and Elizabeth lived in Swansea and had three daughters, the eldest Jessie, being born in the summer of 1883 at Coedpenmain Road, Pontypridd. The growing family soon moved to Swansea, living in Clifton Row. John Stacey had established a reputation as an expert in deep mining and had already travelled extensively overseas as a consultant engineer specialising in hard rock mining. (Plate 1-21).

In 1888 he was offered the position as a consultant to a South African diamond mining company. Leaving his family of Elizabeth and three daughters behind in Swansea, he went to South Africa to take up his engagement. Unfortunately he had only been there a short time when he caught yellow fever. The prognosis at that time was very poor and Stacey soon succumbed to the disease. Back in South Wales, as was

Plate 1-20 Victory in the 1960 London to Brighton Run

often the practice in those days, the childrens' upbringing was farmed out to relatives, and the eldest, Jessie, who was only five at the time, went to live with her aunt Mary in Clevedon. The other daughters stayed in South Wales, but never lost contact with their sister. So it came about that in 1897 the nineteen-year-old Charles Redrup (see colour plate C2) met fourteen year-old Jessie Stacey, the pretty niece of Mary and Richard Stephens.

Plate 1-21 John and Mary Stacey

Chapter 2
The Rotary

Charles was by now a dynamic and personable young man and determined to make his way in the world. He experimented with various petrol engine designs and his first private venture, in 1901, was to fit a small home-built single-cylinder engine to a bicycle. (Plate 2-1). This was a motorised cycle of original design, where instead of a belt drive to a large pulley on the rear wheel, had a shaft drive. This was to be a feature of many of his later designs. Charles used his home-built motorcycle to commute to Clevedon at each end of the ferry trip, and to visit Richard Stephens' customers until Stephens started to provide him with a car. Perhaps Charles Redrup was the first motorised commercial traveller!

Plate 2-1 The First Redrup Motor-Cycle

One of the Stephens customers was William Graham, (later Sir William), the Assistant Manager of the Tyneside Engine Company which had a works based at Barry Dock, and Charles Redrup soon came to his attention because of his expertise with motor vehicles and engines. In 1902 Charles was recruited by Graham and appointed as their expert motor engineer in charge of the transport section, and also, because of his electrical engineering expertise, of all their electrical plant. Despite this appointment Charles still kept up his friendship with Richard Stephens, and, in particular, his niece Jessie.

Encouraged by the success of the motorcycle engine Charles decided to strike out with his own company, or at least, a partnership. After just a short stay with the Tyneside Engine Company, he left them later in 1902 to link up with a neighbouring building contractor, W Alban Richards. Richards' father Thomas Richards, who had started life as an Iron Weigher in a mine near Michaelston just north of Barry, had become a wealthy landowner and was now a neighbour of Charles Redrup, having a blacksmith's shop in Lower Guthrie Street, Barry. Charles and Alban, whose building and contracting business was in nearby Kendrick Street set up the Barry Motor Company. With offices based at Alban's home in Ton Pentre Pontpridd and a works at Kendrick Street, their objective was to manufacture and sell a supercharged rotary engine which Charles had invented. This concept was very revolutionary for its time and Charles patented it in 1904.

Rotary engines were to become very common in aircraft applications, especially by the French during the First World War, but of course in 1902 the Wright brothers had not yet undertaken their first powered flight. The invention in 1861 by the German engineer Gustav Otto of the internal combustion engine led immediately to the Belgian engineer Etienne Lenoir driving his first self-propelled vehicle along a track sometime later in the same year. Development of the internal combustion engine advanced very rapidly as ignition and carburettor systems were improved and power outputs increased accordingly. However the low "knock" resistance of fuel then available (the term 'Octane Rating' had not been coined at this time), meant that low compression ratios had to be used, typically only four, compared to today's ratios of ten to eleven, and so the thermodynamic efficiencies were low, of the order of 25 percent. Lenoir's first internal-combustion engined vehicle of 1861 produced its own fuel. Drawings of it in action show that it had a coal fire with a chimney! However, unlike the steam engine where the coal fire was used to boil water, in Lenoir's case it was apparently used to create a hydrocarbon gas to power the internal-combustion engine.

There were four major problems for early internal-combustion engine designers.

Firstly for fuel, town gas was ideal in a fixed installation such as a factory, but, as Lenoir discovered, it was not a practical solution when on the move. Converting a liquid and highly volatile hydrocarbon into a combustible vapour was a different challenge. Certainly the Bonnet car of circa 1883, owing maybe something to Lenoir in its design, used a simple vaporizer to some effect.

Secondly, for ignition a hot tube was initially used, with the attendant problems of using external pressurised petrol for the burners and the consequent risk of the whole thing catching fire. Sparking plugs were very unreliable, and, combined with the corrosive problems of lead-sulphuric acid accumulators in glass jars, electrical ignition systems were not initially popular. The risk of acid spillage was too great in a not very vibration-free piece of machinery.

Thirdly, further reasons for using low compression ratios were that higher compressions needed better piston rings and better lubrication, still in their infancy at that time. Also if electric ignition was used, higher compressions required a higher voltage to produce a spark. When mechanical losses and transmission efficiencies were taken into account, overall efficiency was less than twenty percent.

Fourthly, low efficiency meant that large quantities of waste heat were generated. Overheating was frequent with the consequent distortion of cylinders and seizing of engines. Thus as power outputs increased, larger and larger amounts of waste heat had to be rejected to the atmosphere. Water cooling was introduced very early on, but the weight, cost and reliability were significant penalties in applications such as industrial drives, motorcycles and later on, aircraft.

For aircraft engines in particular, there was a fifth problem. The low efficiency of the early engines coupled with the need to limit propeller speed to below about 2,800 rpm meant that to achieve the high power outputs required, the power pulses were large and of low frequency. In addition to the inertia of the propeller, they needed a flywheel to carry the pistons over into the next compression cycle, and flywheels were just dead weight.

The rotary engine however was an air-cooled engine, büt obtained cooling by having the crankshaft fixed to the frame and rotating the whole of the cylinder block in the air stream. The drive shaft, or propeller in the case of aircraft, was fixed to the cylinder block and rotated with it. Thus the whole of the cylinder block and propeller acted as a flywheel and produced smoother running.

The prototype rotary-engined motor-cycle arrangement produced by Charles had the cylinder block whirling between the driver's legs. (Plate 2-2). The engine had two cylinders and these rotated on the same axis as the bicycle pedals and clanger gear, which were retained in the prototype machine. The engine was very ahead of its time, in that it was fitted with what were in effect superchargers for each cylinder. (Plate 2-3).

The bottom of each cylinder B was connected to the crankcase to which the carburettor was mounted. As each piston moved radially outwards air

Plate 2-2 Prototype Redrup Rotary Motor-Cycle

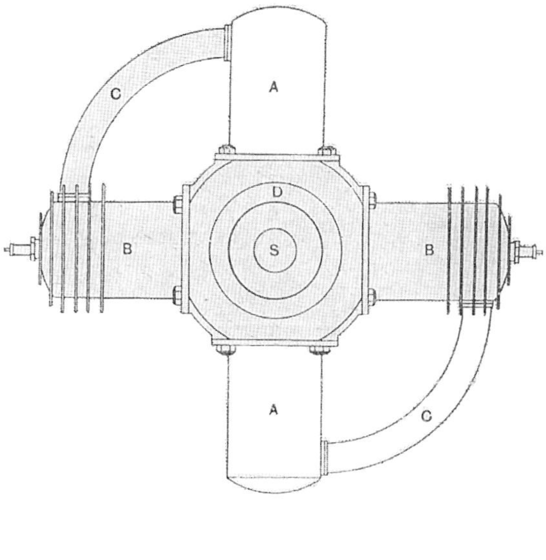

Plate 2-3 The "Barry" Engine

was drawn into the crankcase and cylinders via the carburettor. On the piston down-stroke this fuel-charged air was driven, via a rotary valve into one or other cylinder head. Thus each cylinder received a double-charge of air. Whilst one cylinder fired, the other was on its induction stroke. The waste gases then escaped via further ports in the rotary valve into the two silencers A, arranged in the same plane as the cylinders. The drive was from a pulley D through a wide belt driving a large pulley attached to the rear wheel of the motorcycle. There was no flywheel, the mass of the engine revolving at high speed forming its own flywheel.

There was a firing stroke for each revolution of the engine, the charge being forced into a chamber each time the pistons approach one another. The silencer was fitted exactly opposite to the gas storage reservoir, being of the same weight, and so balanced the weight of this reservoir when the whole mechanism was revolving. The method of ignition was by induction coil and battery. The centre portion of the revolving mass was used as a contact breaker plate, contact being made behind the plate by a metal segment let into a fixed but adjustable insulated disc. This disc was mounted around the fixed shaft and by moving the disc clockwise or anti-clockwise the ignition could be advanced or retarded. The engine, silencer, gas reservoir, in fact, the whole revolving part with the exception of the pulley, was enclosed in an aluminium case.

Plate 2-4 The Engine in Situ

The original engine suffered from a number of minor problems. The sparking plugs were let into the sides of the cylinder heads and the leads would sometimes catch on the casing under the effects of centrifugal force. To cure this the engine was lowered on the frame and the plugs were fitted into an elbow on the cylinder head, thus reducing the radius and shortening the leads. (Plate 2-4). In addition the speed of early models was restricted to about 500 rpm as the valves would lift under centrifugal force. The improved model had valves fitted with balance weights raising the speed to 2000 rpm. Greater cooling was provided by holes bored in the aluminium casing. (Plate 2-5). The engine gave a very high power to weight ratio for its time of 3.75 pounds per horse-power (2.3kg per kw). A very smooth and vibration-free drive was obtained. The total weight of the engine was about 15 pounds (6.5kg) and the mass of the complete machine was about 70 pounds (32kg).

Plate 2-5 The Production Version of the "Barry" Motor-Cycle

This inertia effect is a particular feature of the laws of physics, and not fully understood to this day. Until 1887 physicists thought that the sun and its planets floated through a fixed yet invisible "ether", which did not drag on moving bodies, yet gave a suitable medium through which light could travel. It was motion relative to this "ether" through which rotating bodies were supposed to experience inertia. It was also thought that light would travel at different speeds relative to moving bodies such as the earth, depending on which direction the body was moving relative to the "ether". In 1887 two physicists, Michelson and Morley carried out very sensitive experiments which showed conclusively that light travelled at a fixed velocity, no matter which direction the earth was travelling. This result was so counter-intuitive that physics was thrown into a quandary. It was not until Albert Einstein published his revolutionary paper on Relativity in 1905 that it became clear that the concept of the "ether" as a physical medium was superfluous. Einstein showed that the "ether" was time itself and that bodies moved relative to each other in an indivisible medium of "space-time".

But where did this leave rotational inertia? In this fixed framework of space-time, a body such as a flywheel or a rotary engine, acts against the gravitational fields of all the distant stars and galaxies. Though these fields are infinitesimally weak, they act on the elements of a flywheel to produce inertia. This realisation leads to the fact that as the universe slowly expands, these gravitational forces will inexorably weaken, and the effects of inertia will gradually diminish. The universe is currently thought to be about thirteen billion years old. In another thirteen billion years the inertia effect will be only one quarter as strong, so the Barry engine will probably then require a flywheel!

Plate 2-6 The "Barry" Motor-Cycles at the Burners Hall Exhibition

In the autumn of 1904 two models of the refined version of this motorcycle manufactured by the Barry Motor Company were exhibited (Plate 2-6 and colour plate C3) at the Stanley Exhibition in Burners Hall in London, and excited a lot of interest. Called "The Barry", one engine was on static display and the other gave live demonstrations outside. In one of these machines the pedals and clanger gear were dispensed with. With no additional flywheel, unlike rival motorcycle engines the motorcycle excited a lot of interest. At the exhibition leaflets were distributed advertising engines for sale ranging from three horse-power at sixteen guineas to six horse-power at twenty-six guineas. Larger sizes would be quoted on application. (Plate 2-7).

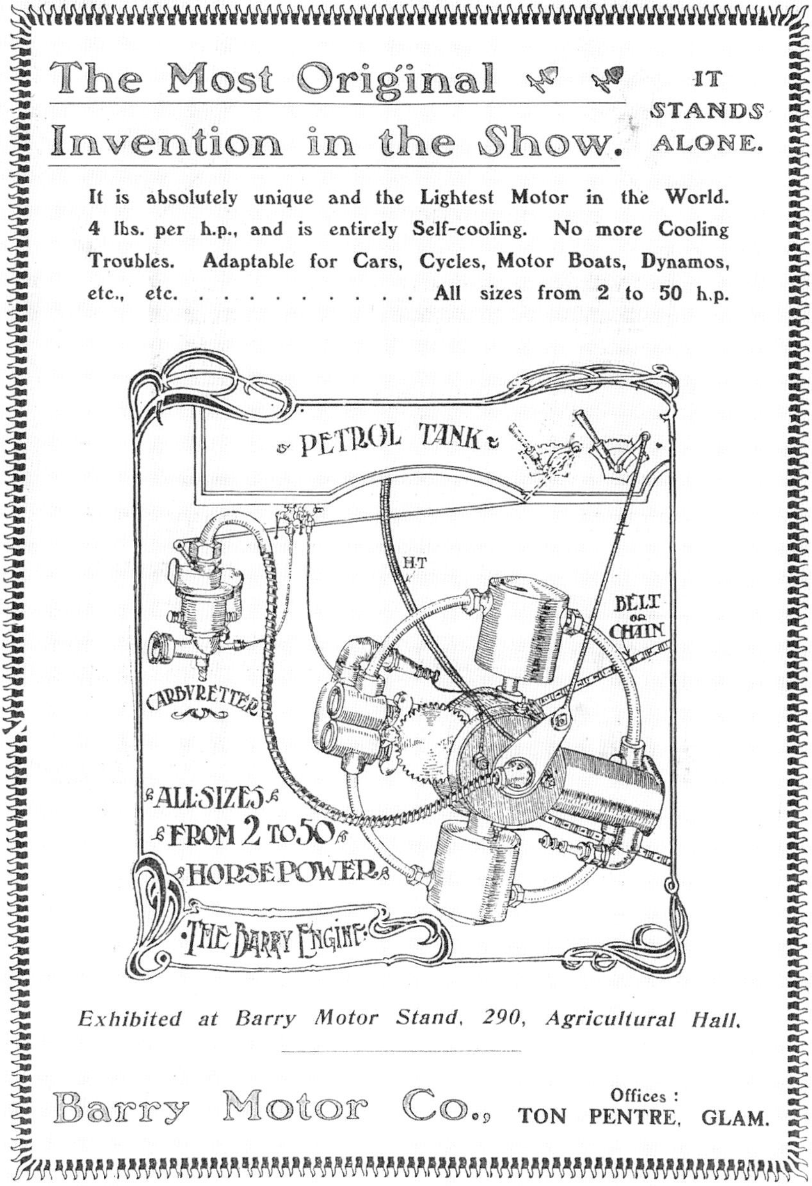

Plate 2-7 The Burners Hall Brochure

The brochure states that engines were available from two to fifty horse-power. It is unlikely that the fifty horse-power version had been made at that time, but it is known that at least one engine of this size was used later in the decade. A "Power Increaser" was also advertised to be retro-fitted to existing engines for five or six guineas depending on engine size and was probably a primitive super-charger. The Kendrick Street factory expanded to Britton's Yard on Gladstone Road In Barry and a considerable number of these motorcycles were manufactured over the next six years.

Also on display at the Burners Hall exhibition was an invention by two brothers from Llanelli in Wales, Thomas and Walter Davies. They were cycle makers, but following the development of the motor car, they were often asked to repair tyres and wheels. They seized on a market opportunity as car manufacturers in those days did not supply spare wheels. If you got a puncture you had to remove the wheel, lever off the tyre, fit a new tube or repair the old one and replace the wheel. Then it was necessary to pump the tyre up to at least forty pounds per square inch on a small car, and as much as seventy psi on a larger or more powerful car. This caused serious delays, and punctures were considered the most expensive part of the budget in early motoring.

The Davies brothers decided to fill the gap by supplying spare wheels of their own design. However it was not practicable to supply wheels to the design of every motor vehicle, so they designed a 'universal' wheel which consisted of a rim fitted with a pneumatic tyre, and three stout arms fitted with clamps, so the wheel could be clamped to the side of the punctured existing wheel and give a get-you-home capability. This is probably the original "bolt-on" goody! When inflated, the tyre on this wheel was slightly larger in diameter than the deflated wheel that was punctured. With a small range of rims of different diameters, the brothers could cover a wide range of vehicle wheel sizes. (See colour plate C4).

In 1904 they set up a factory in Stepney Street, Llanelli, and named the wheel after the factory. The wheels were highly successful and they were soon producing two thousand of them a month. The benefit to the economy of the town was such that their wheel was incorporated into the Llanelli Town Coat of Arms. They eventually closed their works in Llanelli and opened up a larger factory in Walthamstow. The wheels were exported all over the world and in many ex-colonial countries to this day the word 'stepney' means spare, or replacement. In India today, the spare wheel is still referred to as 'The stepney', and "the stepney" is also used to refer to an extra-marital lover! In Malta, the spare wheel is called "is-stepney". The author, whilst on holiday in Switzerland met a

Mauritian missionary, who, when asked what he kept in the boot of his car, replied "Only the stepney." In Edwardian times a Music Hall sketch did the rounds in which the character says "... I looked into her eyes - or rather eye, as the other was just a Stepney". Stepney is still used in parts of the UK as a reference to a glass eye!

The car manufacturers were slow to catch on to the market opportunity of 'optional extras' such as spare wheels, and it wasn't until 1922 that the brothers changed the name of the company to Stepney Tyres Limited, and ceased wheel production.

Richard Stephens learnt about the spare wheel when Charles Redrup saw it at the 1904 Burners Hall exhibition. All Stephens' early cars had solid rubber tyres which did not puncture. However, he did use Stepneys on the Model T Fords which he used for his later Hackney Carriages. In 1910 his son Ewart was driving one of the Fords and was stopped by the police for speeding. His licence was a month out of date and he was fined fifteen shillings! (75p). (Plate 2-8).

Plate 2-8 Ewart and the Model "T" Ford with Stepney Spare Wheel

Punctures in those days must have been frequent. A contemporary bus timetable of Richard Stephens states "The Time Table shows the times at which the Cars may be expected to arrive and depart, but their arrival or departure at the times stated is not guaranteed, nor do the Proprietors hold themselves responsible for delay, or any consequence arising

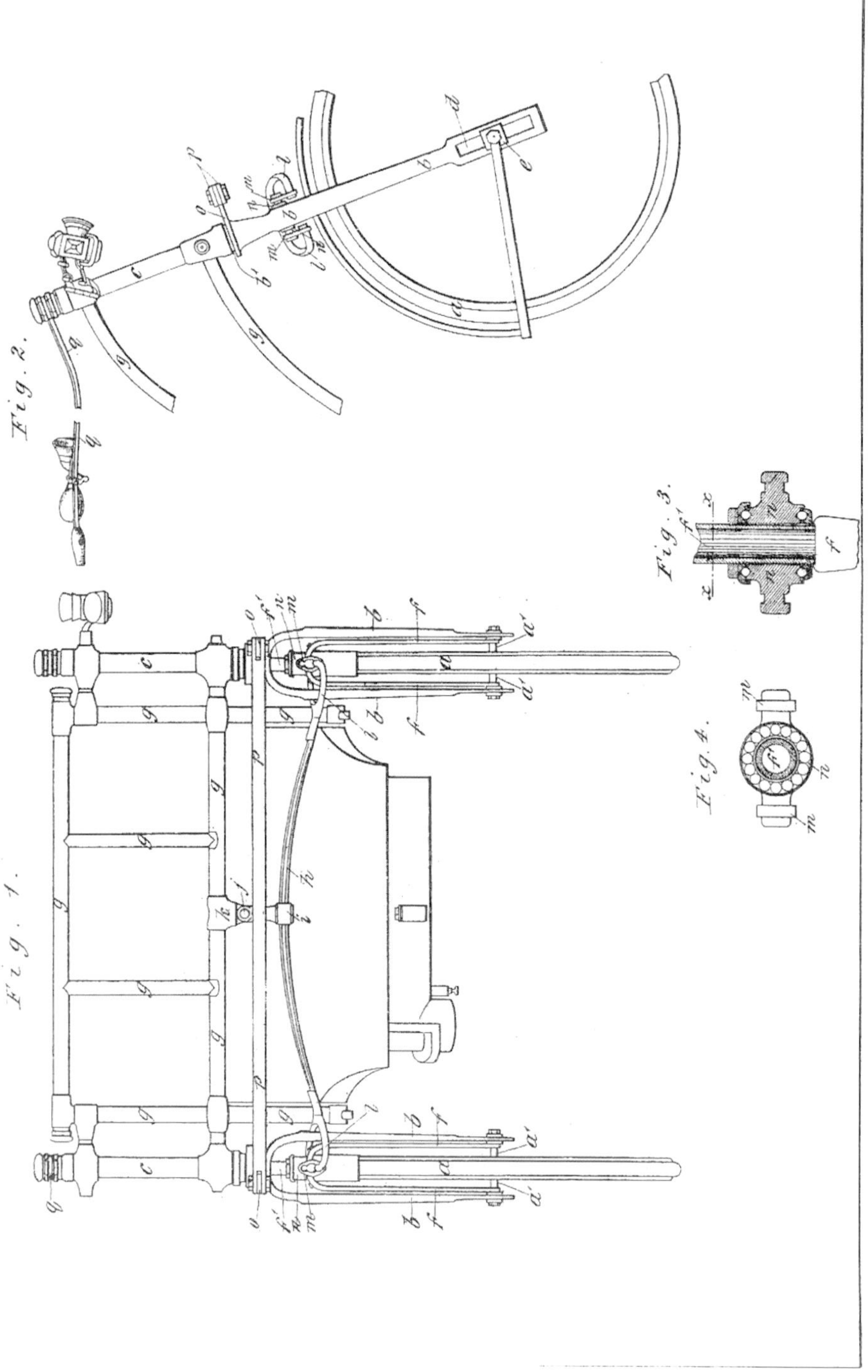

Plate 2-9 Stephens Patent Suspension

therefrom." Stephens' suspension was - and according to Robin Loder still is - excellent. Some authorities credit the 1898 Stephens as the first vehicle to have independent front suspension, as can be seen from his 1899 patent application. (Plate 2-9).

An American entrepreneur visitor at the 1904 Burners Hall exhibition, George Fairfax, became very interested in the Barry engine. He and his partner Thomas Abraham entered negotiations with the partners and eventually offered the company forty thousand pounds for the rights to the engine. They also asked Charles to go and work for their company in America where the engine would be manufactured. However Alban Richards' father who was backing the Barry Motor Company, said that if the Americans were asking forty thousand, it must be worth at least eighty and they should stick out for this.

Negotiations continued for some months, but a deal could not be struck, and Charles, loyal to his partner, turned down the offer of employment. This integrity, exhibited here early in his business career, was evident throughout his life. Charles Redrup, as we shall see later, probably lost a number of career opportunities because of his loyalty to other business partners.

Charles was very disappointed in the outcome as he had glimpsed the opportunities available in America during his very short turn-around in Philadelphia and been told about the country by Richard and Mary Stephens. He had hoped to go to a country where innovation was welcomed and encouraged and to start a new life there as he and Jessie Stacey had married the previous year, and settled in the house at 22, Guthrie Street. By the time the negotiations collapsed, their first child was on the way.

Over the turn of the century Richard Stephens' niece Jessie Stacey had grown from a gawky schoolgirl into a tall, elegant woman. Charles' frequent visits to Clevedon were, as much as anything, an excuse to see Jessie and they soon grew very close. When Charles opened up his business in Barry In 1902 Jessie came to live with his parents at Number two Jewel Street whilst they spent what little spare time they had refurbishing the Guthrie Street house. Charles and Jessie were married on July 1st 1903 in Cadoxton Parish Church, Barry. Richard Stephens gave Jessie away and the reception was held in Harry Redrup's home at Jewel Street.

Florence Madeleine Redrup, the first of Charles and Jessie's five daughters, was born on 21st September 1905, at the Guthrie Street house. As the family grew, the Redrups were to become very close.

Mealtimes would be followed by much debate, always interesting and intelligent, but never tedious. They were a religious family, and always went to church on Sundays. This devoutness rubbed off on several of their children in later years. They also spent evenings playing music and singing. Jessie remained close to her mother and two sisters, but her aunt Mary Stephens died in 1924.

Family life however was not all joy. Charles and Jessie's first son, Charles Beresford Redrup was born healthy in 1907. At that time smallpox was still a scourge and the recently developed vaccination against it had become compulsory. At the age of six months Charles junior was duly vaccinated, but developed a serious infection and died. Jessie resolved that none of her children would be exposed to such a risk again and when her later children were born, the last, Raymond in 1925, none were ever vaccinated.

Charles was well established in his modest workshop in the Guthrie Street home in Barry. His engineering philosophy was simplicity, for ease of production. All his original manufacturing work was done in his home workshop, and in later life he claimed that all his engines were made simply with little more than a knife and fork!

Barry was once the largest exporter of coal in the world, at one time exporting over 10 million tonnes of coal per year. The town thrived on the industry boom from the "Black Gold", which passed through Barry docks for many decades. The port has one of the largest tidal ranges in the world, which made it ideal for the construction of the docks in the late 19th Century and enabled the largest ships then extant to be berthed.

As the demand for South Wales coal grew, so the town of Barry grew to service it. But it was not the tradesmen who consciously furthered the development of Barry. It was the far sighted people who could look beyond what was happening at that time and visualise what could take place in the future. Although they gave the building of the town its initial impetus, David Davies and the other mine owners did not actually contribute to its future development. This was left to Mr T A Walker, the main contractor for the building of the docks, and others, business and professional people who contributed much to the town's development. Their motives were not completely altruistic but by their activities they attracted more people who wished to live in the town and thereby increased the value of their business interests. By their efforts they succeeded in placing Barry firmly on the map. They were not owners of shops or similar businesses and realised that visitors would not be attracted by Barry's shopping facilities, which were inferior to Cardiff and a lot of other towns. Instead the burgeoning holiday facilities at the sea front and beaches of Barry Island were to be one of the new sources of wealth and growth. New industries required new building, and Barry's own resources seemed at first inadequate.

To house a population that changed from less than 1,000 to over 30,000 in the space of a few years must have required one of the fastest building programmes ever undertaken. Bricks came from the Rhondda, Bristol, and Bridgewater and home-produced bricks were made at Cadoxton Moors, Coldbrook, and Dinas Powys brickworks. Surprisingly the main brick suppliers to the builders of Barry were the colliery owners. In the 1880's brickworks were established at many of the collieries as a very cost effective way of using the clay which was a waste product from the mines. The unsaleable coal tailings which had stood on spoil heaps for many years were used to fire the kilns.

The Barry Railway and Docks Company also owned a colliery at Llwnypia. In 1890 the colliery was producing 10,000 bricks per day, the process being carried out by the wives and daughters of the colliers. The production of these brickworks was originally intended for construction within the mines. However production was rapidly expanded to meet the ever increasing demands from Barry and Cardiff, and thousands of bricks were shipped daily. Bristol and Bridgewater imported coal from South Wales, and vessels on the return run brought bricks from Bristol, and chimney pots, ridging tiles and ornamental earthenware from Bridgewater. Slates were mainly from North Wales but a number were imported from Belgium. Blue Pennant flagstones for pavements came from Yorkshire and quarries attached to the Clydach and Llwnypia mines were the main suppliers of stone. Most of these pavings have now been replaced by concrete paving slabs or tarmac but many can still be seen in the pavements and back lanes of Cadoxton.

Before bricks came flooding into Barry, stone from local quarries and beaches was used for building. Much of this material was used for the building of earlier houses. Together with demand for bricks, timber was also in great demand. Small coasters could unload timber in Barry Harbour but by 1885 when the docks were taking larger vessels, red deals, spruce deals, pitch pine and oak, as well as flooring imported from Norway, Russia and America, were available in quantity for immediate delivery. So much timber was required by contractors that a Mr Meggitt built a timber mill within the docks. Timber could then be unloaded directly from the ships into the mill for processing. In the years after 1890 ships carrying timber from America, Norway, Gelfren, (Sweden) and Archangel were discharged at Barry. Meggitt went on to become one of the largest timber suppliers in South Wales,and surprisingly, was the only industry in Barry hit by bombs in the Second World War, producing a blaze that could be seen for miles around.

When in 1901 Albert Edward, eldest son of Queen Victoria assumed the throne a King Edward VII, it ushered in what was to become known as "The Edwardian Era". Properties built around this time are still being used as dwelling houses and business premises all over Barry. There are many fine examples in and about the High Street area. When the purposes for which many of the buildings were constructed altered or ceased, a great number were demolished. Some of these buildings had architectural features such that nowadays, many would have been listed and preserved. However the old bricks and timbers have been re-cycled several times and are still in use and in great demand for restoration projects where 'period' materials are needed.

Plate 2-10 Redrup Two-Cylinder "Reactionless" Aero Engine 1906

Comfortably settled in Barry, Charles Redrup continued his development work on engines in several parallel courses. He developed an early interest in rotary engines for aircraft applications and demonstrated a two-cylinder engine, based on the Barry motorcycle engine, to the Royal Balloon Factory at Farnborough in 1906. (Plate 2-10).

This engine differed however in that the crankshaft rotated in one direction whilst the engine block rotated in the opposite direction. Paddles, to represent propellers, were fitted to each rotating element and used to load the engine for bench tests. The concept resulted in an engine which produced no net torque reaction on the airframe, and was thus named the "Reactionless" engine.

The Balloon Factory had built its first semi-rigid airship, the Nulli Secundus, "Second to None", and were looking for a suitable engine. No records remain of the negotiations but eventually the airship was fitted with a 35 horse-power Antoinette V-8 engine. In a subsequent flight trial the airship was found to be underpowered and unable to return to her base due to headwinds and she was landed at Crystal Palace. She was subsequently damaged by high winds and had to be dismantled and returned to the Balloon Factory. She was rebuilt with more rigidity as Nulli Secundus II, (an oxymoron if there ever was one!), but proved unstable in flight trials and was eventually broken up.

In the early 1900s a Walter Welch was working for a cycle repair business in Bristol, the Nimrod Cycle Company. In 1903 he set up his own business in the Redcliffe area of Bristol, and marketed an automobile based on a dog-cart, the Nimrod Car, which was very similar to Richard Stephens' cars. At this time of rapid engineering development, much copying and perfecting of designs took place. In about 1910 Welch produced a car which used a large Barry engine of about fifty horse-power. One of these machines is in the Bristol Industrial Museum to this day, standing next to another of Charles Redrup's engines made twenty-five years later. (See colour plate C5).

In 2005 another engine came to light which is almost certainly a variant of the Barry engine. In that year the Motor Cycle Museum on the Isle of Man closed and its contents were sold off. John Caddick of Kingswood Bristol, home of the Douglas motor cycle, bought a two-cylinder rotary engine which had been in the museum for over forty years.(Plate 2-11). This engine has a double-throw crankshaft but the cylinders are directly in line and the connecting rods are bent to line up with the crank shaft big end bearings, rather like the Hickman conversion of the Lawrance C" engine of 1917. The engine has several features which signify it as a Redrup. The cylinders have holes in the top which connect to a slot in the side. This slot lines up with exhaust holes drilled in the side of the cylinder head casting. The air intake is via the fixed crankshaft to which is connected the carburettor, and goes directly into the crank case. As the pistons move together towards the crank shaft

Plate 2-11 Two-cylinder rotary engine

the crank case is pressurised by a non-return valve in the inlet pipe until the pistons uncover slots in the side of the cylinders, allowing the mixture to be forced under pressure into the cylinders and helping to scavenge the exhaust gases. As the pistons accelerate towards top dead centre some of the mixture escapes through the exhaust ports but these are quickly closed by the piston heads. On the firing stroke the pistons accelerate rapidly towards the bottom dead centre position and the exhaust gases escape through the side holes.

The location of the exhaust slot in the piston side is such that the cylinder pressure during expansion acts through the holes in the piston crown and the slot in the side of the piston to relieve the side-load on the piston from the connecting rod. This concern for side load is very typical of Charles Redrup and in later years he devised parallel-action mechanisms to relieve such loads on his much larger engines. The engine also has a commutator very similar to that used on the Barry engines for spark distribution to the plugs. The workmanship on the engine appears very similar to that of Redrup engines and it is likely that this machine was made in the Barry works.

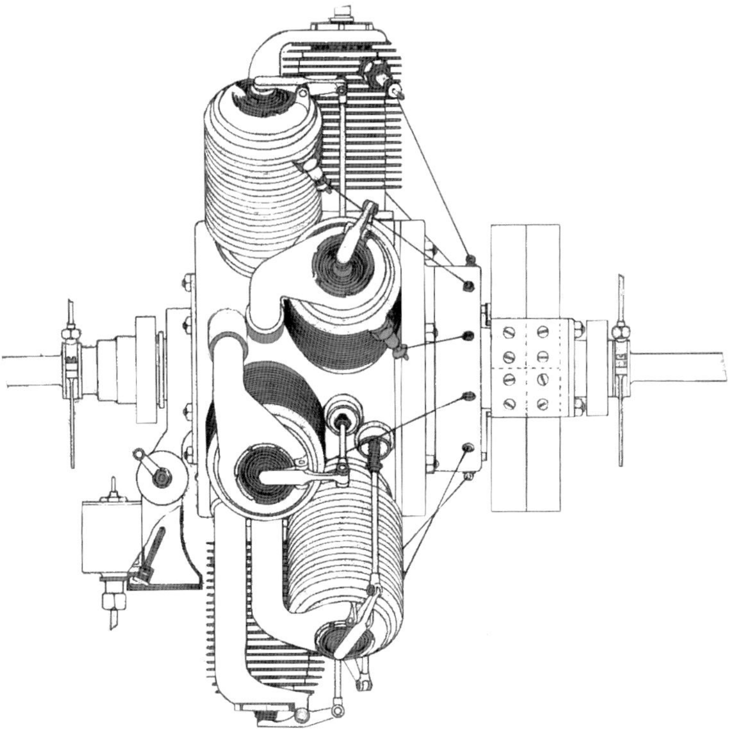

Plate 2-12 Ten-Cylinder Reactionless Engine

Charles' partnership with Alban Richards was at times somewhat strained. As with many engineers involved in a struggling business, Charles fought an ongoing battle with the accountants to maintain quality. In one 1907 memorandum which still exists, Charles is cross-examined by Richards about an employee;s timesheet. It appears he was not making piston rings fast enough. In another memo, more worryingly, Richard asks Charles to account for why he is using cast steel as opposed to mild steel for engines, bearing in mind that cast steel costs twice as much! Charles would have known that weight for weight, cast steel is much stronger and better suited to highly-stressed engine components. The precarious nature of the business must have been quite a strain on the Redrups, but in 1909 Charles and Jessie had additional mouths to feed in the form of twin daughters, Marjorie Constance, and Dorothy Maude.

Charles' interests continued to diverge down two distinct routes. As well as his motor cycles, he pursued further his interest in contra-rotating aero engines. In 1909 he had patented the rotary aircraft engine concept based on the contra-rotating principle and designed a much larger engine than the two-cylinder 1906 model. It was design-rated at fifty horsepower and had ten cylinders but was not built at this stage because of financial constraints. (Plate 2-12). In 1911 the Barry Motor Company faced severe financial difficulties and the partnership with Alban Richards came to an amicable end. Alban Richards returned to his building and contracting business whilst Charles, in conjunction with Joseph Stanfield, who had collaborated earlier in one of his sleeve-valve patents, and two financiers John Boyle and a Mr Christie set up a new company, the Gyroscopic Syndicate. This was established in 1911 and purchased the rights to the Barry Motor Company engines. At the same time, keeping his options open, Charles joined a Mr Thomas in a Daimler agency in Cardiff as Motor Engineer.

Chapter 3
Radial and Axial

The German engineer Gottlieb Daimler had a broadly based engineering background before establishing his own business with his long term friend and colleague Wilhelm Maybach in the 1880s. They had been experimenting with high speed petrol engines for some years and a prototype was fitted to a motor-cycle-type 2-wheeled vehicle with outriggers and then in 1886, a motor car. The Daimler designed engines were also used extensively in boats.

The demand for motor cars was not great and Gottlieb Daimler was more interested in the engines themselves as a means of propulsion for all forms of transport. A contemporary business analysis concluded that the world market for automobiles was limited to forty thousand vehicles because that was the number of households that could afford chauffeurs! The term "chauffeur"or "warmer" itself derives from the period when steam-driven cars were the rage, which required a period of fire-lighting and warming-up before the start of a journey. It was not until 1886 that a purpose-built Daimler chassis was fitted with a Daimler engine. Daimler who was 56 years old and Maybach in particular who was only 42, were interested in developing the "high speed" engine for the motor car and so in 1892 they set up their own experimental workshop. It was during this period that Maybach developed the float-chamber carburettor as we now know it, as a means of atomising the fuel which allowed much higher engine speeds to be attained.

Their Phoenix car was a more modern design and employed the layout pioneered by Panhard, with the engine mounted at the front. A 5.5-litre 24 horse-power 4-cylinder version, designed by Maybach, was driven by Emile Jellinek at the 1899 Nice Speed Week and won the Nice-Castellane Hillclimb in the touring car class. However Jellinek, who was the Daimler agent for Nice, concluded that the Daimler was not really suitable for competition with it's high chassis and short wheelbase. He therefore negotiated to take 36 cars from Daimler, modified to his own design on the understanding that he would have the sole rights for France, Belgium, Austria, Hungary and the USA. It was also agreed that these cars would be named after Jellinek's 11-year old daughter Mercedes. It was an inspired decision and by 1902 all Daimler cars except those in the UK and Austria were called by the Mercedes name.

The rights to Daimler designs in Britain were negotiated in 1891 by Frederick R Simms and whilst most engines were sold for marine use Simms was already very involved with the new Automobile industry. In 1895 he sold the company for £35,000 to H J Lawson who floated the company as the British Motor Syndicate for £150,000 on the stock-market just a few weeks later. From an old mill building at Foleshill in Coventry he undertook the manufacture of Daimler cars. Sims was mortified.

Reliability was a great selling point at this time and so the run from John O'Groats to Land's End in a Daimler at an average speed of 10mph by Henry Sturmey in October 1897 attracted considerable attention. Daimler went from strength to strength during the next decade when royal patronage came in the form of The Prince of Wales, soon to become king, who used Daimlers almost exclusively.

1908 saw a radical change of direction for Daimler when they dropped all the side-valve 4-cylinder engines in favour of the Knight sleeve valve patent. These engines had a double sleeve valve arrangement which worked concentrically between the pistons and the cylinder walls in place of the normal poppet valves. The sleeves had ports cut into them which lined up respectively with inlet and exhaust ports in the cylinder walls. The sleeves were reciprocated by gearing at half-engine speed so that one complete inlet-exhaust cycle was completed in two strokes of the piston. At a time when lubrication was somewhat hit and miss, the arrangement had the advantage that, even at top-dead-centre or bottom-dead-centre there was still relative motion between the sleeve and the piston so that the oil-film did not break down and wear was minimised.

A further benefit of this patented design was its quiet running, for which it became known as the "Silent Knight". The designer was an American named Charles Yale Knight and the royalties for his patent were high. This coupled with the cost of redesigning their entire range of cars brought Daimler to the brink of bankruptcy by 1910. The company was amalgamated with BSA (the Birmingham Small Arms Co.) in that year and this gave Daimler the financial backing required to become one of the best British car manufacturers. Daimler agencies were set up all around Britain and it was one of these new agencies that Charles Redrup joined in 1911.

The Daimler financing problems had been overcome but the Knight sleeve valve royalties were still high. Working in his own workshop

Plate 3-1 Three-cylinder Rotary "Reactionless" Aero Engine

Charles designed a four-cylinder sleeve-valved engine for which he made a patent application in 1911. This engine incorporated a single sleeve valve which got around the Knight patent. Whereas the Knight sleeve had two ports, one for inlet and one for exhaust, Charles' design had only one port which lined up with the inlet and exhaust ports in the cylinder sequentially. There was a significant problem with sleeve valves in that they had to be machined to a high degree of accuracy, as they fitted snugly inside the cylinders, and had the pistons running inside them. Heat distortion was a problem and could cause the engine to seize. The ports cut into the sleeve led to asymmetry and distortion. Reducing the number of ports made manufacture simpler and reduced distortion under heat load.

Charles was not only interested in engines and in partnership with a neighbouring carpenter, Arthur Richard Edwards, in 1910, he had patented a soft drinks re-usable bottle. This had a removable top in place of the neck and a glass stopper sealed in the top by the internal gas pressure. In usual bottles of the time the glass neck of the bottle was sealed by a glass ball, or "alley" and the bottle was opened by breaking off the neck. The alleys, often of brightly patterned glass, were usually retrieved by children and used as marbles. In Charles' design the neck could be broken off and the rest of the bottle re-used. It also acted as a filling device. In a later patent of 1912 he considerably simplified the design.

Meanwhile, working with the Gyroscopic Syndicate, having taken the 1910 two-cylinder engine to its limit of development, in 1911 he made a contra-rotating radial aero engine which had three-cylinders and an epicyclic gearbox. This was a single-propeller version of the "Reactionless" engine as it became called, in which the crankcase rotated in one direction and the propeller in the other. (Plate 3-1). Charles then went on to convert the small three-cylinder engine to operate with contra-rotating propellers. (Plate 3-2). This was demonstrated firstly in Cardiff and then to Captain B C Hucks of the Royal Flying Corps at Hendon in 1912 in a spectacular way. With the engine on its stand developing its rated ten horsepower, Charles gently lifted the engine and stand off the ground, leaning back at the same time to balance the engine thrust. This impressive demonstration of both light weight, Reactionless torque, good balance and smooth running impressed the onlookers.

Captain B C Hucks was famous for his invention of an aircraft engine starter. The flimsy structure, low power and weight restrictions on aircraft of the era meant that the penalty of an electric starter could not be justified. For engines below about 150 horse-power, hand-starting by flicking the propeller was practiced. For larger engines ever more ingenious methods were tried. The "bag starter" consisted of a stout linen bag which was fitted over the end of the propeller. A strong cord attached to the base of the bag was then hauled by one or more men to pull the engine over the compression. Invariably the engine would not start first time, so the bag had to be refitted and the procedure repeated. Usually centrifugal force threw the bag off the propeller once the engine started but occasionally the bag would foul and the cord would wrap itself around the propeller, snatching at the hands of the crew.

Plate 3-2 Contra-rotating Rotary "Reactionless" Engine

Captain Hucks mechanised the starting process by mounting a forked overhead drive shaft on the chassis of a vehicle. The shaft was driven by the engine through a second clutch and the forked end which incorporated a dogged coupling would be engaged with the propeller. The vehicle's engine would turn the aero engine over and once the engine started the forked end was thrown clear by the propeller. Hucks used a variety of chassis, mainly Model "T" Fords or Crossleys. Plate 3-3 shows a Hucks starter mounted on a Crossley chassis. A Model "T" Hucks starter has been in continuous use since the 1920s, and is now in regular use at the Shuttleworth Collection at Old Warden airfield in Bedfordshire. (See colour plate C6). It was at this time that Charles first became involved with Crossley Motors, which was to have a significant influence on his life in later years.

Plate 3-3 Hucks Starter Mounted on a Crossley Chassis

The Redrup Rotary-Radial engine was also demonstrated the following year to the re-created airship division of the Vickers armaments company. The Division had been dismantled in 1911 following the structural failure of their first airship, the Mayfly. With Pratt, the new chief designer and his young assistant Barnes Wallis the new division set about designing and building their first successful airship, His Majesty's Airship No.9, and they were searching for suitable engines. Charles demonstrated the contra-rotating Reactionless engine but it was far too small for the purpose and did not result in any orders. It did however alert Vickers to Charles' capabilities and as we shall see, he later went on to work with them. Towards the end of the First World War in 1917, an anonymous correspondent of *The Autocar* magazine, who had been instrumental in setting up these demonstrations, recalled the little engine, showing a drawing of his recollection of the display. (Plate 3-4).

—How the Redrup rotary engine was held while its balance was being demonstrated, the demonstrator leaning back to resist the pull of the propellers.

Plate 3-4 The 1917 "Autocar" Sketch Showing the Redrup radial Demonstration at Hendon

This engine was subsequently loaned to the Science Museum for several years and then was returned to its owner in 1961. It then passed to the famous motorcyclist Ken Blake and then on to Phil Collins. It was eventually purchased by Mr Christopher Musk of St Albans, who recently sold it to a collector in Holland. It is still in remarkable condition although the carburettor, magneto and distributor are missing. (Plate 3-5 and colour plate C8).

Plate 3-5 The 1912 Redrup Contra-rotating Rotary Aero Engine

The main block, which consisted of three cylinders equally spaced with the cylinder heads pointing radially outwards, rotated in one direction and the crank-shaft in the opposite direction, with each rotating component driving a propeller in opposite directions. The concept was that by mounting a propeller on each rotating component, this would result in an engine which produced no net torque on the airframe, and in particular, the differential action would automatically adjust the relative shaft speeds to balance out any slight difference in the pitches of the two propellers. One problem with the smaller aircraft engines is that the best crankshaft speed for engine efficiency is usually well above 3,000 rpm, whilst the propeller speed needs to be kept below about 2,800 rpm. To match these, gearing has to be incorporated with its attendant problems of wear, noise, weight and reliability. With the Reactionless engine, the relative crankshaft-to-cylinder rotational speed could be optimised for engine efficiency whilst the propellers, contra-rotating at half-engine speed, could operate at their optimum efficiency. This engine also had a novel feature in that the inlet and exhaust poppet valves were concentric!

Plate 3-6 Three-Cylinder Motor-Cycle Rotary "Reactionless" Engine

Late in 1912 Charles used the same basic engine for a modified motor cycle drive. (Plate 3-6). This engine, as compared to the Barry engine, had the rotational axis horizontally along the fore-aft axis of the motorcycle. The rotating cylinder block and the crankshaft were connected via an epicyclic gearbox to the rear wheel with one shaft on either side of the wheel. (Plate 3-7). A is the flywheel which is attached to the crank shaft, and rotates in an opposite direction to the crank case and cylinders. It is a casting arranged with blades to take the place of spokes which give a cooling effect to the cylinders and its size is designed to match the inertia of the rotating cylinder block. Two versions were produced, one with concentric poppet valves and one with sleeve valves.

Plate 3-7 shows a sectional drawing of the mechanism of the sleeve valve version. B shows the cylinders in section. These cylinders are turned out of solid steel and composed of outer casing, two hemi-

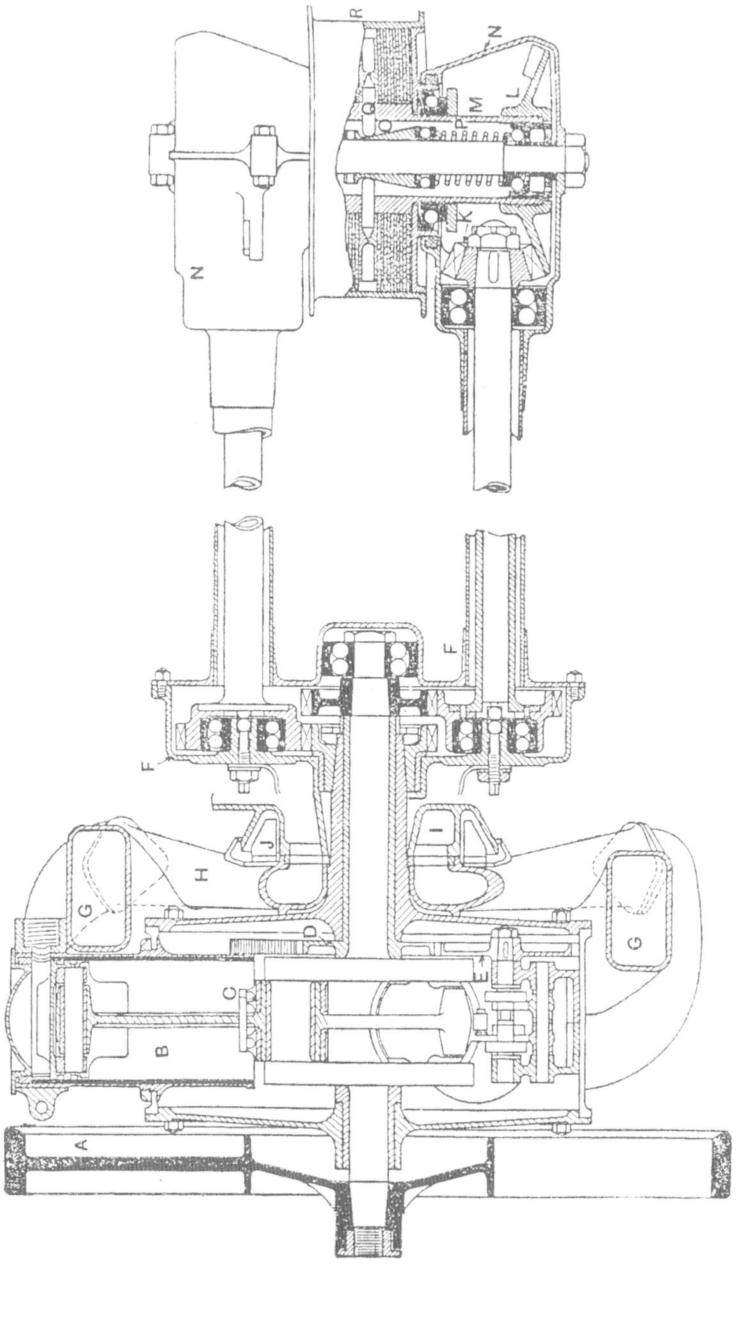

Plate 3-7 Plan View of 1912 Rotary Motor-Cycle Engine

cylindrical sleeve valves (Plate 3-8), and inner casing or cylinder proper, which are all secured to the cylinder head cap as shown. The particular features of the cylinders and valves are that they are extremely light, offering very little resistance, and owing to the special arrangement of the valve gear, the valves do not move under load, and their movement is very quick, giving immediate full port areas to the exhaust and induction gases. In the design of the pistons lightness had every consideration.

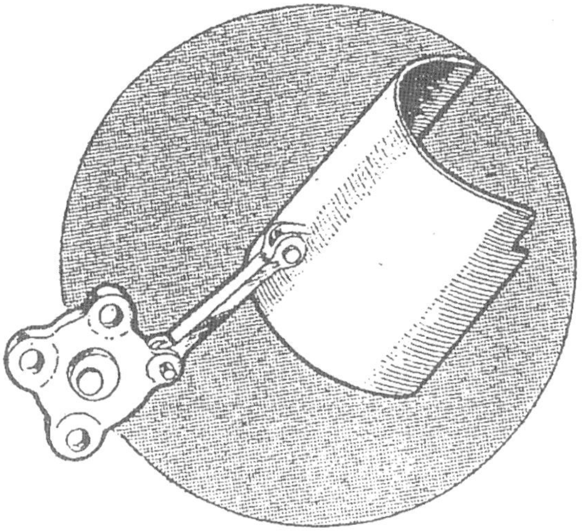

One of the sleeve valves and its rod which works on a cam.

Plate 3-8 Hemi-Cylindrical Sleeve-Valve

The three connecting rods are fastened to the crank pin by two phosphor bronze retaining rings C, which are held in position by two steel spring clips which are sprung over the crank pin and retaining rings and drawn together by a set pin with an efficient locking arrangement for the two set pins as shown. The crankshaft is of the ordinary balanced type.

D is a spur wheel with a long bush attached as shown, which runs into the gear box and has attached to it a lever which gives it a movement of approximately two inches. This is used for altering the setting of the valves for starting up, and is claimed to he an improvement on the then new decompression devices, which were at that time being fitted to some machines. The spur wheel meshes direct with the wheels E, of which there are three, one for each set of valve gear. This wheel is keyed on to the camshaft as shown, which runs in the two brackets which are bolted to the crank-case and carry the valve operating gear. There are four cams on the camshaft, one for operating the induction sleeve in an upward movement, and one for giving a downward movement of one cylinder, and the other pair do exactly the same for the exhaust valve of the other cylinder, doing away altogether with springs and giving a positive movement to the valves. With this arrangement three sets of valve gears placed in the space inside the crank case between the three cylinders do all the valve operating that is necessary, and forms a very compact arrangement which is always running in oil. The cams operate inside a rocking lever which is coupled to the lugs on the valves by a short connecting rod and gives the desired movement.

The crank case is built of three parts made from castings, one having a cylindrical drum with three flats which accommodate the cylinders and two covers with bearing bushes one for either side. One cover has an extended portion which runs into the gear case and carries a gear wheel which is geared into a pinion attached to the transmission shafts. The crankshaft also runs through into the gear case, and carries a similar toothed wheel which is meshed in a similar manner with the other transmission shaft. The crankshaft rotates in an anti-clockwise direction, and the crank case in the opposite direction, giving a movement to the transmission in the opposite direction and to the back wheel in the same direction. The gear case is supported to the frame of the machine by two stays going down from the crossbar. It is a crucible steel casting, made in two parts with the cover as shown. The one-half of the gear case F is brazed up solid to the two main bottom stays of the machine.

The transmission-shaft and crankshaft run on Skefko ball bearings, which are accommodated in the gear box, and the crank case runs on the long bush on the crankshaft. The other end of the engine runs also on a Skefko ball bearing, not shown, which is accommodated in a lug which is brazed to the frame. G is a rotary silencer which is-attached to the strap which encircles the cylinders and receives the induction and exhaust gases and H is a three-way pipe also attached to the cylinder strap, through which the induction gases pass to their respective cylinders. At the foot of this induction pipe a phosphor bronze face plate with apertures is accommodated forming a movable joint which works against the face of the stationary induction pipe coming from the carburettor.

On the stationary induction pipe I are fitted two brushes for transmitting the high-tension current from a Bosch magneto to the porcelain or ebonite ring J, which is fitted to the three-way induction pipe and receives three wires from contact pieces leading to their respective sparking plugs. Lubrication is provided for by means of a hollow crankshaft, through which oil is forced by a plunger pump through the crank pin, which lubricates the big end and from thence falls into the crank case, where it lubricates the valve gear and other mechanisms. It also passes through the two crank webs and lubricates the main bearings. The gear case is lubricated in the ordinary method by grease being forced in by a Stauffer lubricator.

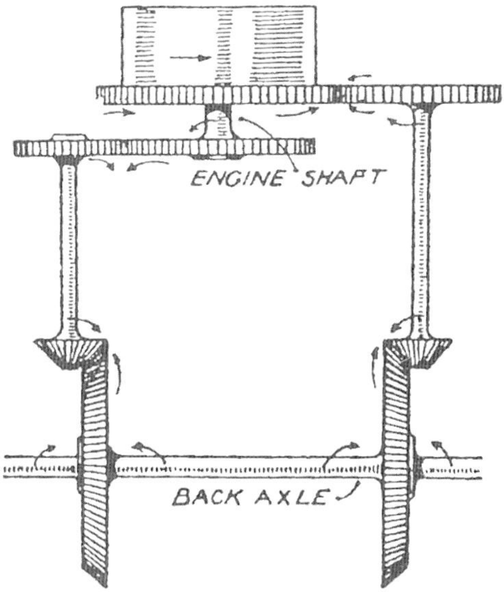

Plate 3-9 Twin Drive to Rear Axle

The drive from the gear case is taken up by two bevel pinions K, keyed on to the two transmission rods. These are meshed into two crown wheels L attached to sleeve M, on which are fastened a set of plates which are accommodated in the main hub and run between other plates fastened to the main hub in accordance with the ideas of the ordinary plate clutch methods. All these gears are enclosed in a bevel gear case casting N, which is brazed on to the back stays of the machine. The clutch is operated by a Bowden wire, which when in tension pulls the collar 0 against a spring P and so allows the wedge pins Q to fall down and the plates to be disengaged. When the Bowden wire is not in tension the spring P comes into operation, forcing the taper collar 0 inwards, which in turn forces the wedge pins Q between the two discs so engaging the plates attached to the sleeve M and the main hub. It will be noted that ball bearings are used throughout in the back hub. Attached to the main drum R is the back rim, which built up with tangent spokes in the usual method. Plate 3-9 shows a diagrammatic representation of how the drives from rotating cylinder block and crankshaft respectively are geared to the road wheel.

The engine was run on a test demonstration for a period of two hours at 4,000 r.p.m. on a stand, that is to say with the cylinders revolving 2,000 r.p.m. in one direction and the flywheel 2,000 in the other, which they did perfectly satisfactorily, "without undue heating or breakdown of any kind, and the lubrication through-out was perfect." As was reported in a contemporary magazine. The engine was very compact, of total capacity 300ccs and weighing only 4.5 kilos. (Ten pounds). Its output was measured at well over six brake horsepower (4.5kw) and the contra-rotating mechanical arrangement was very well balanced and vibration free. At this era of engine development, a power-to-weight ratio of 1.67 pounds per horse-power was exceptionally good.

In 1912 Charles and Jessie's family enlarged again when their fourth daughter, Violet Muriel was born. Charles was not very domesticated, being immersed in his projects, but Jessie (See colour plate C7) more than made up for this by her organised approach. Although only seven years old, Florence, the eldest was already being a great help to her mother in tending to the younger sisters.

Charles' next development was to build the straight-four cylinder engine with single sleeve valves which operated by part rotation and part axial motion in the cylinders for which he had made a patent application. His development of the single-port sleeve valve was not however unique as several people were working towards similar goals at the time, and his patent application was beaten to the post by Argyll Motors Ltd, whose patent in the name of Burt and McCollum was filed only two days earlier. The year 1911 was a year of technical innovation for Argylls with the introduction of four-wheel braking and, on their 15 - 30 hp models the single-sleeve-valve engine. This engine was designed by Glasgow Baillie Mr Peter Burt and developed by the Argyle engineers headed by Archibald Niven. A Canadian J K McCollum who was working on a similar design was included in the patent to avoid litigation.

Charles went to work with his brother Alfred, John Boyle and his engineer brother Henry Kirk Boyle to re-design the valvegear and their patent was eventually granted the following year. (Patent 19,859, 1912).

With the assistance of Crossley Motors Charles fitted his modified four-cylinder engine to a Bull-nosed Morris Oxford car in 1913. (Plate 3-10). The origins of this car are interesting. The registration, H-2558 is a Middlesex County Council registration, but the H-series ended in 1912. The Morris Oxford was not produced until 1913, and the production models were fitted with "Artillery" style wheels. The wire wheels shown on Charles' car were only used on one or two models which have not been traced. It seems likely that Charles obtained one of these models and transferred the registration from an older car. Charles went on to use this design of sleeve-valve in several of his later engines.

Meanwhile C Y Knight had also filed a patent for a single-sleeve valve engine, although he had not actually made one at the time. Argylls were taken to court but they were able to prove that the new Knight patent was unworkable. Though they won their case and subsequent appeal, it cost them a huge sum which undoubtedly precipitated the impending financial problems. The new engine was very successful and partly because of the precedent of Daimler's previous successful use of the Knight double-sleeve valve and partly because of the competition successes which the new engine achieved, it was confidently received. However sales did not cover costs and the company went into liquidation and their factory was sold to the Admiralty for £153,000. The Burt-McCollum single-sleeve valve patents were sold to Wallace

Plate 3-10 Charles Redrup Driving his Sleeve-Valve Engined Bullnose Morris

(Glasgow) Ltd who made a few engines before selling the patents to Continental Motors in Detroit. This design was taken up by Roy Fedden, the fiercesome engine designer of the Bristol Aircraft Company, who went on to design a large range of sleeve valve radial engines in the 1920's onwards.

Charles always maintained diverse interest in all kinds of engine and about 1911 he started to investigate "axial" type engines in which the cylinders are arranged around the drive-shaft rather like the barrel of a revolver. Various designs are used to translate this axial motion to rotary, either by using an angled "swash-plate", or cams, or a "wobble-plate". In 1911 a barrel-type four-stroke air-cooled rotary engine was patented and placed on the market by the Macomber Rotary Engine Company of Los Angeles, California. The engine had seven cylinders of 7.00 inches (179 mm) bore and 4.25 inches (108 mm) stroke, with cylinder axes parallel to the central shaft. (Plate 3-11). The length of stroke and the compression ratio could be varied by changing the angle of the swash-plate by means of a rack and pinion.

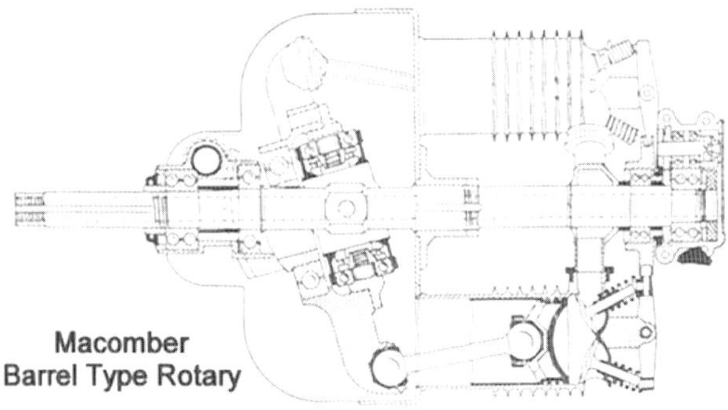

Plate 3-11 Macomber Swash-Plate Rotary Engine of 1911

The engine was a rotary type in which the whole engine revolved with the exception of the casings at either end. Ball and socket joints at each end of the connecting rods joined the pistons to the swash-plate, which revolved with the cylinders. Each pair of valves was operated from a single rocker pivoted between the two with one end sliding in a grooved four-lobed cam located on the central shaft and running in the same direction. Ignition was provided by a Bosch magneto that was operated directly by the cam gears. The high tension was taken by wire to a stationary electrode on the top of the bearing case, from which the spark leapt to the spark plugs as the cylinder heads passed within one-sixteenth of an inch (1.5mm) of it. Fifty horse-power (37.3kw) was developed and the complete weight was 230 pounds (105kg). The engine was less than 20 inches in diameter and 29 inches long. (0.5m by 0.75m).

Charles did not consider this arrangement very satisfactory owing to the large sliding areas and consequent friction, so instead he came up with an alternative static cylinder-block arrangement which used an angled or "Z" section of shaft which ran in a journal in a spider to which the pistons were attached. In this arrangement the cylinder block and pistons were stationary and the shaft rotated. The Gyroscopic Syndicate did not have the funds to develop more than one product at a time so Charles started to draft out engine designs based on the axial principle in his spare time.

Plate 3-12 Seven-Cylinder 1912 Redrup Radial Aero Engine

Charles continued to develop his aero engines by building in 1912 a seven-cylinder 35 horse-power (26kw) fixed radial engine. (Plate 3-12). Whilst fully committed to continuing his development of the ten-cylinder Reactionless engine when funding permitted, he was beginning to see that, if only the cooling problems could be solved, fixed-cylinder engines could have advantages over the mass of whirling cylinders inherent in the rotary engine concept. In May 1912 members of the Gyroscopic Syndicate went to Farnborough to discuss with Samuel Cody the installation of this engine in his Cathedral biplane.

Stories of a man-carrying heavier than air aircraft, emanating from The United States in 1903 were met with scepticism by the British government, and this was not helped by the almost paranoiac secrecy of the Wright brothers. The government entered negotiations with the Wright brothers but these were protracted and inconclusive. It was not until the brothers themselves came to England in 1908 and made some spectacular and obviously very well-controlled flights that the military started to take an interest.

Samuel Franklin Cody, (Plate 3-13), was a colourful character who came from America during the 1900's to develop a man-carrying kite. His American origins are vague but his original name was Franklin Cowdery. It seems probable that in coming to England he was cashing in on the fame of William Cody, "Buffalo Bill", who was a famous rodeo rider and crack-shot. In America Cowdery was also a cowboy and a sharp-shooter, having competed with Annie Oakley in shooting competitions. With his wife Maud he toured rodeos as a stunt rider act. He worked on man-carrying kites with the American government in Massachusetts in the 1890's and

Plate 3-13 Samuel Franklin Cody

on coming to England as Sam Cody with his daredevil act, he also demonstrated various models of kite to the British Military as Air-Observation machines. His tethered kites were very successful and a record altitude of 3,400 feet was established in one of his designs. He succeeded in selling kites to the military and earned a living for a short time training the Army to fly them at Aldershot. He designed man-carrying gliders and successfully flew one at Crystal Palace in 1905.

Cody then turned his attention to powered flight, and fitted a 12 horse-power (9kw) engine to one of his gliders. This was flown in 1907 at the Royal Balloon Factory at Farnborough, where he made a short powered flight over Laffans Plain. With Army support he then designed and built a machine specifically for powered flight, the British Army Aeroplane No. 1 and flew it at Farnborough during September and October 1908. On 16th October in this machine he made what was subsequently recognised as the first controlled, powered flight in England, over a distance of 1,390 feet. At the end of the flight whilst turning to avoid a clump of trees, the wing touched the ground and sustained some damage. During its early years the Factory was subjected to criticism in Parliament for manufacturing aircraft as there was considerable hostility from private venturers to what they saw as unfair competition. It came as no surprise therefore when the next day, *The Times,* whose correspondent was one of the critics, in publishing a full account of this historic flight, headlined the article as "The Army Aeroplane - Accident at Farnborough"!

Cody went on over the next few years to break distance and duration records and in 1910 built a new, huge biplane called "The Cathedral", based on a Wright Brothers design. With this he entered the Round-England Race in that year. It was the only British-built entry to complete, and came fourth. For the autumn of 1912 the British Army organised Military Trials on Salisbury Plain and invited aircraft to compete for a £5,000 prize.

Cody required a new, more powerful engine for these trials and it was for this reason that The Gyroscopic Syndicate visited him in May 1912. and Joseph Stansfield flew with Cody in "The Cathedral" over Laffans Plain. After further negotiations Charles arranged for a second-hand modified Austro-Daimler car engine to be supplied to Cody. The engine was fitted into "The Cathedral" and Cody went on to win the £5,000 prize. He was then also able to sell "The Cathedral" to the British Army, (Plate 3-14). Cody built a successor to "The Cathedral", a huge float biplane, and it was in this that he was killed when it broke up over Laffans Plain in 1913.

Plate 3-14 Cody's "Cathedral"

A cowboy in every sense of the word, Cody used to test the thrust of his engines by tethering his aircraft's tail to a tree at the end of the Farnborough runway using a rope and a spring balance. This tree was kept for many years as a tribute to Cody, but was finally removed when it decayed to the point where it became a hazard. However Cody's memory is still retained at Farnborough because a replica of the tree now stands at the entrance gate to Qinetiq, formerly the Royal Aircraft Factory. (Plate 3-15).

Plate 3-15 Cody's Tree

Chapter 4
Reactionless and Radial

With the First World looming, Charles Redrup turned his attention urgently to the war effort and reviewed the needs for engines for wartime aircraft, which were substantially different from those for light aircraft. The main difference was the need for much more power, and for engines which were reliable enough for the pilot to be able to concentrate on attack and defence, rather than on keeping the engine running.

Early in 1913 Charles left the Gyroscopic Syndicate to form a business partnership with some financiers from Yorkshire. The new company was called the Hart Engine Company and Charles set up a works in Hunslett, Leeds. He moved the family from Barry to Methley Drive in Chapeltown, Leeds to be close to the works. They kept the house in Barry and Charles' brother Harry junior took over the Gladstone Road works where he set up a factory manufacturing copper products such as canopies for fireplaces, boilers, cylinders and combination tanks. Harry junior had set up a laundry at 2a, Jewel Street in Barry Dock, next door to his father's hairdressing saloon. Harry was a competent engineer and as the workload grew over the next few years he found that the water heating system for the laundry was less than adequate and he developed water heating cylinders to solve the problem. The Gladstone Road works enabled him to concentrate on copper products for a living. He soon expanded to manufacture a much wider range of copper products.

Many years later, in the 1930's, Harry designed a geyser to provide hot water on demand and, with Charles' help, patented it and found a market for the equipment. It was a very clever device and used a shallow dish in which water was heated by a gas burner thus enabling almost instant hot water. The Redrup's Copper Works were in existence for many years and Harry's six sons all went into the business. After Harry retired they ran the works for many years but as they retired or died the remaining son Edward found he could not sustain the business on his own and reluctantly closed it down. The works were eventually demolished and flats built on the site.

In Leeds the Hart Engine Company, which consisted of Charles, his brother Alfred, John Boyle from the Gyroscopic Syndicate and his son

Plate 4-1 Nine-Cylinder 150 Horse-Power
"Reactionless" Aero Engine

Walter together with another financier Major Arthur Bray, was created with intention of developing the Reactionless engine to commercial production. Charles had re-designed the engine to have only nine cylinders as this made the firing order better balanced. The prototype engine was run on a test bed in 1913 in the works in Hunslett, which was a very large railway engine manufacturing complex (Plate 4-1). This engine demonstrated the principle of the "Reactionless" concept but also showed the difficulties of fuelling such a large engine when both crankshaft and crank-case were rotating in opposite directions, as the diameter of the hollow crankshaft effectively restricted the mixture flow.

Plate 4-2 Gnome 100 Horse-Power Monosoupape Rotary Engine

Thus, at a time when rotary engines were in their heyday as the First World War got under way, Charles too began to query their effectiveness. The whole intention of the rotating cylinder block was to improve cooling, but in practice, especially as ratings increased, they were not very efficiently cooled as the cylinders, whirling around in the slipstream, shadowed each other, causing much turbulence but poor heat transfer. They also caused high drag which detracted from overall aircraft performance. When parked or taxiing, the engines were even less effectively cooled. The engines were also difficult to fuel and to control. Most designs were fuelled by a fuel-air mixture from a crude carburettor via a flap valve and fed along the hollow fixed crankshaft.

The mixture was injected into the crank-case and fed to the cylinders via inertia valves fitted in the piston heads or ports which were uncovered by the pistons as they moved down the bore. The fuel was ignited by a spark plug in the cylinder head which had to be fed from a distributor coupled between the rotating cylinder block and the mounting shaft, using a commutator or slipring arrangement. In most designs the cylinders each had a single exhaust valve in the head, opened by a push-rod operating off a fixed cam ring. (Plate 4-2). The mixture could not therefore be throttled easily, and power was controlled in the air by running at full throttle and blipping the ignition on and off, so accurate flying was very difficult.

For ground running the flap valve was either open or closed, and this made taxiing tricky to say the least. The rotary engine cooling assumptions had led engineers to neglect the actual efficiency of the cooling process. Most rotary engine cylinders had a few cooling fins which were whirled around in the slipstream but the very high windage losses of the whirling cylinder block and its auxiliaries sapped up to a quarter of the engine power. Furthermore, as engines increased in size and power output, the length of the intake tube restricted breathing and set a limit to the maximum size of the rotary engine. Engineers, Charles Redrup in particular, were starting to realise this and looking at other air-cooled engine arrangements, such as the fixed radial engine.

The radial engine was very similar to the rotary engine, consisting of a number of cylinders arranged radially around a crankshaft. However, with the cylinder block firmly attached to the aircraft framework, the crankshaft protruded from the front to drive the propeller. With this arrangement more conventional and convenient means could be used for air intake, carburettor and ignition. The cylinders were fitted with cooling fins and relied on the motion through the air to cool them, or, when stationary, the slipstream from the propeller. However contemporary radial-engined aircraft, like those fitted with rotary engines, could not stay stationary for long, as the propeller slipstream alone was insufficient for adequate cooling.

Charles realised that very little was known about how cooling fins worked, and carried out experiments to see how effective different types of cooling fins were. He soon found that conventional wisdom was wrong. The current thinking at the time was that only a few fins could be used, as a lot of space was required around them for air to flow. Charles found that in general, the more fins there were the better, as the fin cooling area was more important than the space for air. Provided the

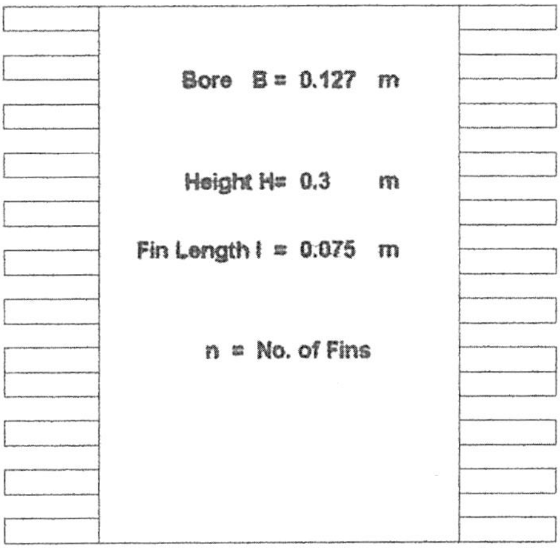

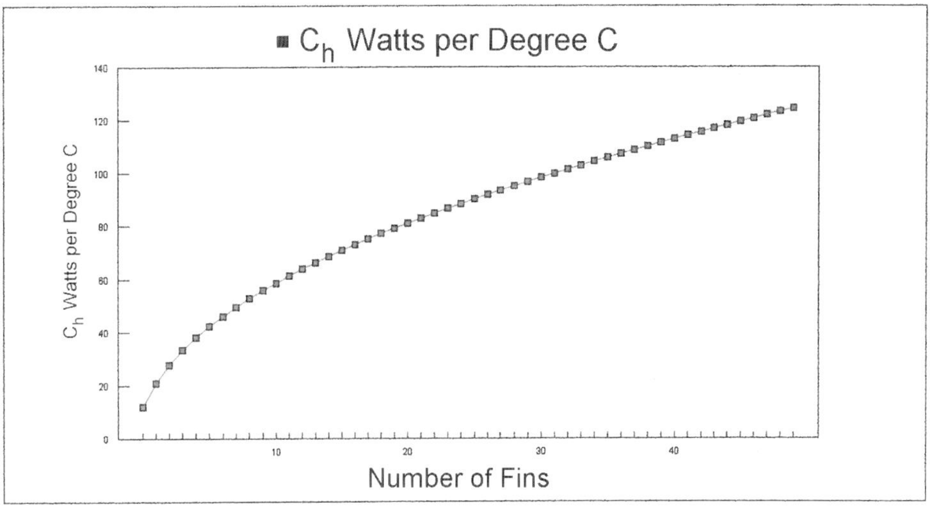

HART ENGINE COOLING

150HP 9 Cylinders

C_h = 224*n*(B+l)/F * Tanh(3.9*l*F)

Where F = Square root of (2*n-1)/H

Heat Transfer Coefficient C_h

300 Deg.C Cyl. Head Temp. 25% Thermal Efficiency

Power = 150X746 Watts = 111,900 Watts

Heat Loss = 3X 111,900/9 Watts Per Cylinder = 37,300 Watts

Required Coefficient = 37,300/30000 = 124 Watts per Deg. C

Hence 50 Fins are required

Plate 4-3 Cooling of a Close-Finned Cylinder

air space was wider than a certain minimum, cooling remained effective even with very closely spaced fins. The minimum spacing we now know to be the space occupied by the boundary layer, where air clings to the surface and does not flow very fast. The diagram, Plate 4-3, shows the effect of varying the number of fins on a Redrup cylinder of five inches bore, six inches stroke and twelve inches length. The final design is limited more by the cost of machining many fins than anything else.

Charles made a seventeen horse-power single-cylinder engine to such a design, of five inches bore and six inches stroke, with very close finning based on his studies, and incorporating the features of many of his earlier patents. On one test, consisting of running at full throttle for sixty hours in hot summer weather, the cylinder performed well without any overheating problems despite only the propeller slipstream for cooling. Accordingly he took the close-finned cylinder design and used it for a nine-cylinder 17 litre radial aircraft engine which he patented on behalf of the Hart Engine Company. He also patented the 35 horse-power radial engine at the same time.

Plate 4-4 The Hart 150 Horse-Power Engine on Test at Hunslett

The larger engine was financed for development by the Company and it was named the Hart engine. Charles made this engine mainly in the Hunslett works with very limited machine tools. He was an expert

Plate 4-5 The Parts of Hart Engine

machinist, welder and pattern-maker and so could make engineering components with very little outside assistance. His brother Alf was a regular visitor to the home in Leeds and helped Charles with his engineering development. During one of the test runs on the Hart engine Alf lost two fingers whilst starting the propeller by hand. Eventually Alf moved to Leeds and met a Leeds girl, Florence May and their first daughter Mary was born in Leeds. (See colour plate C10).

The Hart engine, when tested, (Plate 4-4), produced 158 brake horse-power (118kw) at 1400 rpm and had a dry weight of 300 pounds (136kg), giving a power to weight ratio of 1.9lb per horse-power (10.64kg per kw), a very creditable performance for any contemporary engine, especially air-cooled. The parts for the engine are shown in Plate 4-5.

During 1913 The Royal Aircraft Factory offered a prize of £5,000 in an aero engine competition to be held in April 1914. The excellent provision for engine testing and accurate performance measurement at the RAE was testified to by *Flight* magazine in its 7th May issue of 1914. It was into this competition, The Military Aero-Engine Trials, that Charles Redrup entered the nine-cylinder 150 horse-power Hart engine. The engine was subjected to the Air Board type test and, rated at 150 horse-power it passed at the first attempt. This was unheard of in the early days of engine design, as many teething problems usually arose and had to be solved on new engines. There were a total of twenty-eight entries and no reports survive of the comparative performances, but the prize was eventually awarded to a 100 horse-power six-cylinder in-line Green engine.

The Royal Aircraft Factory had roots going back to long before heavier-than-air flight was possible. During the American Civil War balloons had been used for aerial observation. In 1863 the Royal Engineers made experimental flights in a gas balloon provided by a famous showman Henry Coxwell. However the government did not consider the cost worthwhile in "times of profound peace". It was not until 1878 that the War Office permitted further development and authorised Captain H P Lee, based at Woolwich Arsenal, to spend up to £150 on designing and testing a balloon for use by the Army. Current "Air Estimates" run at a somewhat higher level!

The balloon was duly built and tested, making its first ascent under the command of Captain James Templar of the 2nd Middlesex Militia, who subsequently used it for training. His unit became known as the School of Ballooning, the very first fore-runner of what was to become the Royal Air Force. Templar was given an allowance of ten shillings a day for his instructional work, probably the first example of Flight Pay.

In 1879 a Balloon Equipment store was established at Woolwich and over the next two or three years manoeuvres at Aldershot convinced the War Office of the value of balloons for air observation. Consequently in 1882 the School of Ballooning and the Balloon Equipment Store were moved to the School of Military Engineering at Chatham. Over the next few years activity increased and following manoeuvres at Aldershot in 1890 it was decided to move the activities to Aldershot to improve communications with Army life.

Work in America on man-lifting kites was closely followed in the United Kingdom. Such kites became effective at the wind speeds where tethered balloons start to become unstable, and so the two technologies were seen to be complementary. Consequently in 1894 a Kite Section was added to the School. In 1897 the facility was re-named the Balloon Factory and Templar, by now a Lieutenant Colonel was appointed superintendent. The unit saw its first active service during the Boer War in 1899. By 1904 the Factory had outgrown its site at Aldershot and it was moved over the next two years to a 22 acre site at South Farnborough. The existing balloon sheds were re-located to Farnborough and a much larger new one built.

It was around the time that the Balloon Factory re-located to Farnborough that Samuel Cody started to work with them and that the Factory started to take an interest in manned gliders and eventually powered flight. In 1908 the Factory was bestowed the title of His Majesty's Balloon Factory, in honour of its achievements. Over the next few years the Factory expanded immensely, constructing and testing engines and aircraft to its own designs and to the designs of private individuals and companies. However critics remained unimpressed. In particular, C G Grey, editor of the journal *The Aero*, started a sustained campaign against what he saw as "War Office folly".

In recognition of the wider scope of work with both balloons and aircraft the factory was appropriately re-named His Majesty's Aircraft Factory in April 1911 whilst the Balloon School was re-named The Air Battalion. Grey took this as another opportunity for criticism. He was by now editor of *The Aeroplane*, and continued, through what was to be a long and distinguished but controversial career, to attack those running the factory for "straining every nerve and using every means in their power to justify their existence".

In December of that year the first official competition for aero engines took place, competing for a £1,000 prize. The engines were tested in a brand new test house fitted out with two dynamometers. Two ensure energy efficiency even in that day and age, the dynamometers used electricity generators to absorb the power and this electricity was used in turn to produce hydrogen for the balloons by electrolysing water. The other by-product of electrolysis, oxygen, was bottled and sold to local industry.

In 1912, following a government white paper reviewing naval and military aviation, the Air Battalion was replaced by the Royal Flying Corps which encompassed naval and army aviation together with a joint flying school. The War Office continued to direct what had now become the Royal Aircraft Factory which was to continue with its development work on aircraft and engines of both British and foreign design. The factory continued in this role right up to and beyond the end of the First World War but in April 1918 the Royal Flying Corps was merged with the Royal Naval Air Service to form the Royal Air Force. Thus the Army lost control of its aviation provision.

During the First World War the Factory became the subject of further political attack. What was probably the most successful, albeit less than perfect, product of co-operation between the Factory and private industry, the B.E.2C aircraft, was attacked by Grey as being a "grotesque" concept as, despite the fact that B E stood for Bleriot Experimental, it was being mass-produced. The use of the word "Bleriot" did not imply that the aircraft was of foreign design or manufacture. The standardised terminology by the Factory for aircraft categorised them on their layout and "B" stood for the tractor monoplane concept as developed so successfully by Bleriot and used on his cross-Channel flight. However Grey and his fellow critics were not averse to using subtle xenophobia in pursuing their objectives.

In March 1916 a newly-elected Member of Parliament used his maiden speech to attack the War Office, but in reality his criticism was aimed at the Factory. Noel Pemberton Billing had resigned his commission as Flight Sub-Lieutenant in the Royal Naval Air Service to fight a by-election. He referred to the aircrew of the B.E.2C as "Focker Fodder" (not an unknown expression even in the RFC), and accused the Factory of building outclassed machines powered by unproved and untested engines. The fact that this latter claim was totally untrue did not prevent him demanding an inquiry into the whole affair. In a subsequent debate he accused the Factory of being overstaffed and inefficient. His friend C G Grey was not slow in backing him up in print.

However the outcome was of unexpected and welcome news to the Factory. With commendable speed the Army Council appointed a committee under Sir Richard Burbidge to examine whether the resources available and the management of the Factory were adequate. Within six weeks the Committee had drafted its report. It found that the production, although not entirely of experimental aircraft, was appropriate to meet urgent war needs and that staffing levels were not inappropriate. However it did criticise the proportion of staff devoted to administration rather than production, and recommended that the balance be redressed. It concluded that such an establishment was necessary and that efficiency standards were met. It also concluded that salaries were not adequate compared to the private sector! Publication of the report was delayed for a few weeks whilst the War Office considered it and meanwhile Billing continued his attacks, especially on the B.E.2C.

By June 1916 the Factory's latest aircraft, the R.E.8, had entered the testing phase and proved a splendid, highly manoeuvrable flying machine. When the Burbidge Committee Report was published in July it was highly supportive of the Factory but made recommendations for a total managerial re-organisation. The recommendations on the role, scope, technical responsibilities and manning levels of the Factory were accepted, but the Air Board did not accept the organisational recommendations. Instead they instituted their own changes which they considered to be more appropriate to the joint civil-military nature of the Factory. This was not an outcome expected or desired by the critics but it set the tone for the Factory for the rest of the war and for many years afterwards.

In June 1918 the factory was re-named the Royal Aircraft Establishment to avoid confusion with the newly-formed RAF. It retained that title right up until 1988 when, in recognition of its widening role, it kept the same initials but was re-titled the Royal Aerospace Establishment. In 1995 in a major re-organisation of defence research organisations it was merged with other establishments to become the Defence Research Authority (DERA), During the mania for public-private partnerships DERA was retitled Qinetiq in 2001 and partly privatised, with the Ministry of Defence retaining a 56 percent share. It was launched on the Stock Market to institutional investors in 2006 with a capitalisation of £1.1bn. The government retained a "Golden Share" to ensure that British military interests were not compromised.

Following the 1914 trials of the Hart engine the Air Board took steps to introduce the Hart Engine Company to The Vickers Aircraft Company Limited of Crayford in Kent. The engine, whilst having a very creditable performance, did not meet Air Board requirements in terms of ease of manufacture for mass-production, or provision for reliability. Prior to the War the ignition for aircraft engines came almost exclusively from magnetos made by Bosch, the German company. Supplies of these magnetos understandably dried up immediately the war started and British manufacturers scrambled to design and make their own magnetos. These attempts were not highly successful and the resulting equipment was not very reliable. . The Air Board therefore introduced regulations that stipulated that all engines should be fitted with two sparking plugs per cylinder and duel magnetos. They believed that Vickers, with its experience of aircraft requirements, would quickly turn the Hart engine into a production job. Vickers immediately took an interest in the engine and in September 1914 started negotiations with the Hart Engine Company concerning a contract to finance its development further. In October the Hart engine was transferred to the Crayford Works and subjected to a thorough test by Charles with Vickers' staff observing and it passed all tests required of it by Vickers.

The Vickers Company can trace its antecedents as far back to 1828 and its prime products were military. The aircraft division was created in 1908 and started out by constructing airships. Fixed-wing aircraft manufacture commenced in 1911. The company started with a factory in Kent and with a Flying School at Brooklands in Surrey, and later expanded to Weybridge from 1915. Among the earliest designs of Vickers was the Experimental Fighting Biplane of 1913, which led to many more army contracts, including the F.B.5 fighter and an improved and faster version, the F.B.9. A total of 241 F.B.5s, nicknamed the Gunbus, were supplied to the Royal Flying Corps for frontline service and were joined in the summer of 1916 by 95 F.B.9s. Smaller quantities were produced of the F.B.14 reconnaissance biplane and the F.B.19 single-seat fighter.

During wartime the Vickers factories at Brooklands, Weybridge, Surrey and at Crayford, Bexley Heath and Erith on the south-eastern outskirts of London were also kept busy building large numbers of other manufacturers' aircraft, B.E.2s, S.E.5a's and Sopwith 1 1/2 Strutters, as well as several designs of Vickers' own. A requirement for a strategic bomber produced the twin-engined F.B.27 which flew for the first time on 30th November 1917. This huge biplane with twin fins and rudders, later renamed the Vimy, came too late for operational service in the war but is remembered for its pioneering long-distance flights in peacetime, such as the first trans-Atlantic flight and the first flights to Australia and to South Africa. These flights have recently been re-enacted by a Vimy replica which is now based at Dunsfold airfield and makes regular flights from Brooklands.

Plate 4-6 The Vickers F.B.5 "Gunbus" Pusher-Type Fighter

In the early days of the war the interrupter gear to enable the pilot to shoot through the propeller arc of a conventional "tractor" aircraft had not been developed. The Gunbus was a "pusher" type of aircraft with a fuselage shaped rather like a bathtub. (Plate 4-6 and colour plate C9). The pilot sat at the back of the tub with the engine just behind him, whilst the gunner sat in the front with an uninterrupted view. His gun was mounted on rails so it could be moved in all directions without being obstructed by the airframe. The tail unit of the aircraft was joined to the wings and fuselage by widely-spaced struts which had to span the propeller arc. These created a large amount of drag. Starting the aircraft by hand was precarious as the unfortunate ground crewman had to stand within this framework behind the engine to flick over the propeller.

After the Vickers tests on the Hart engine in October 1914 The Hart Engine Company was advised by Major Wood of Vickers that they wished to proceed with the development, not only of the Hart engine, but also of 300 and 500 horse-power versions. The Hart company therefore proceeded with all haste to set up the necessary development. In June 1915 Major Wood wrote to the Hart Engine Company stating that he had been given full powers by the Vickers directors to negotiate on their behalf and requested the Hart company to manufacture engines of 150 and 300 horse-power. He requested options on the patents and experience of the company to last for one month following completion of acceptable engine tests, and sole manufacturing and selling rights to be conducted in the Vickers name.

Chapter 5
The Hart Saga

During August and September 1915 the Hart Engine Company and Sir Trevor Dawson and Mr Savage of Vickers made arrangements for the assets and business of the Hart Engine Company to be transferred to Vickers and it was agreed that Vickers would use all reasonable endeavours to promote the manufacture and sale of the engines. In January 1916 most of the machinery and staff of the Hart company were transferred to the Vickers works at Bexley Heath and in March all of the assets were transferred to the Crayford Works. All this did cause delay and disruption and meanwhile the Hart company had not received a penny for their work. Charles was given a workshop in which to conduct his development work whilst Vickers used the Hart company equipment for manufacture of the production version of the engine and submitting it for the Air Board type-tests at Farnborough. Charles and the family moved to Kent. Charles bought a house, "Selkirk", in Freta Road Bexley Heath as he had to travel frequently to Joyce Green Aerodrome to witness flight testing.

Joyce Green, an airfield on the Dartford Marshes at Long Reach was established by Vickers prior to the First World War for the testing of their prototype aircraft. At the outbreak of war in 1914 it was decided that the aerodrome should also house two F.B.5 Gunbuses as part of the defence of London. Later, work was put in hand to extend the aerodrome facilities at Joyce Green in order to house a permanent Royal Flying Corps unit under the auspices of No.6 Wing which was responsible for training potential pilots. The construction of hangars, workshops and ground staff quarters took place out at the northern end of the airfield alongside the Long Reach Tavern. Early in 1915, the construction of the Royal Flying Corps base at Joyce Green was completed and No.10 Reserve Squadron moved in. Equipped with Henry Farman, Vickers F.B.5 and F.B.9, D.H.2 and F.E.8 aeroplanes, the squadron's main function was to receive pupils from preliminary training schools for final training and qualifications for their wings.

During the first half of 1916 Charles worked hard with Vickers on developing the Hart engine but found progress agonisingly slow. He found the Vickers staff unfamiliar with engine design yet unwilling to allow him to get involved in production matters. Charles had made the prototype engine from VNCA steel and machined the crank-case from solid. Vickers wanted to cheapen the engine by using a lighter, stamped casing but Charles was concerned that this would not give adequate bearing support. The creditors of the Hart Engine Company were pressing for payment and threatening liquidation. By June 1916 Vickers had the engine ready for test and on July 10th 1916 the Vickers solicitors wrote to the Hart company stating that the engine had met its test requirements and claimed the exercise of the option to purchase the rights to the engine. However this was too late for the Hart Engine Company for on 10th June 1916 the company was wound up in the High Court and a Receiver appointed to dispose of the assets. This was to prove more difficult than expected however, as these assets had now been absorbed into Vickers' works, and in view of the imminent exercise of the Option Agreement the Receiver agreed to hold his fire.

The Hart engine was type-tested at Farnborough in late July 1916, where it achieved an output of 150 horse-power at 1350 rpm, but despite meeting the performance requirements, Vickers had still not fitted it with dual ignition, and the Air Board declined to give it a type rating. Vickers returned it to the works and put in hand the necessary modifications. In October 1916 Vickers and Boyle and Redrup signed an agreement for Vickers to purchase the assets of the Hart Engine Company for £20,000 on successful completion of the Air Board type test, and at the Hart Company's insistence, Charles Redrup was given verbal authority by Vickers directors to see these tests through to completion.

In anticipation of successful acceptance of the Hart engine by the Air Board Vickers prepared to flight-test it in one of their new prototype aircraft, the Vickers F.B.12 Scout. This was a single-seater wartime development of the Gunbus. In this aircraft fixed guns in the nose were directed by the pilot aiming the aircraft at the target, the technique used subsequently by most fighter aircraft, especially after interrupter gear had been invented to enable guns to be fired through the arc of the propeller.

The Vickers Chief Test Pilot was Harold Barnwell. (Plate 5-1). He and his brother Frank from Stirling in Scotland were the first to design, construct and fly a Scottish-built aircraft. Frank joined his brother in a motor business in Stirlingshire, which they ran to support their greater interest, flying. From their garage they produced three aircraft between 1908 and 1910, gaining confidence and skill with each, flying them over a half-mile course. Wishing to progress, the brothers headed south to join the new aviation enterprises that were beginning to spring up and build aeroplanes. Harold took up a position with Vickers, but after rising to become their Chief Test Pilot he was killed in a flying accident in the prototype F.B.26 single-seater pusher aircraft, the Vickers "Vampire" in August 1917. Frank meanwhile had been offered a post with A.V.Roe when Sir George White of Bristol made him a much more exciting offer. He joined Filton in March 1911, a place he would remain at for most of his life, until he too died in an aircraft accident in 1938.

Plate 5-1 Harold Barnwell

The prototype of the F.B.12 Scout was manufactured in June 1916 at the Vickers works in Crayford Essex and was powered by an 80 horse-power Le Rhone engine, as the Hart engine was still on test at Farnborough. The aircraft was a compact two-bay biplane with wings of unequal span and chord and rounded tips. The nacelle was of roughly circular cross-section made of steel tubing. (Plate 5-2). Despite being seriously underpowered it gave a creditable top-speed of 95 mph, against the design specification requirement of 100 mph.

Following trials the wing was re-designed to give greater span and straight raked tips. The undercarriage was also re-designed to be braced directly onto the nacelle. The prototype aircraft was then fitted with a Gnome Monosoupape engine and sent to France for evaluation on

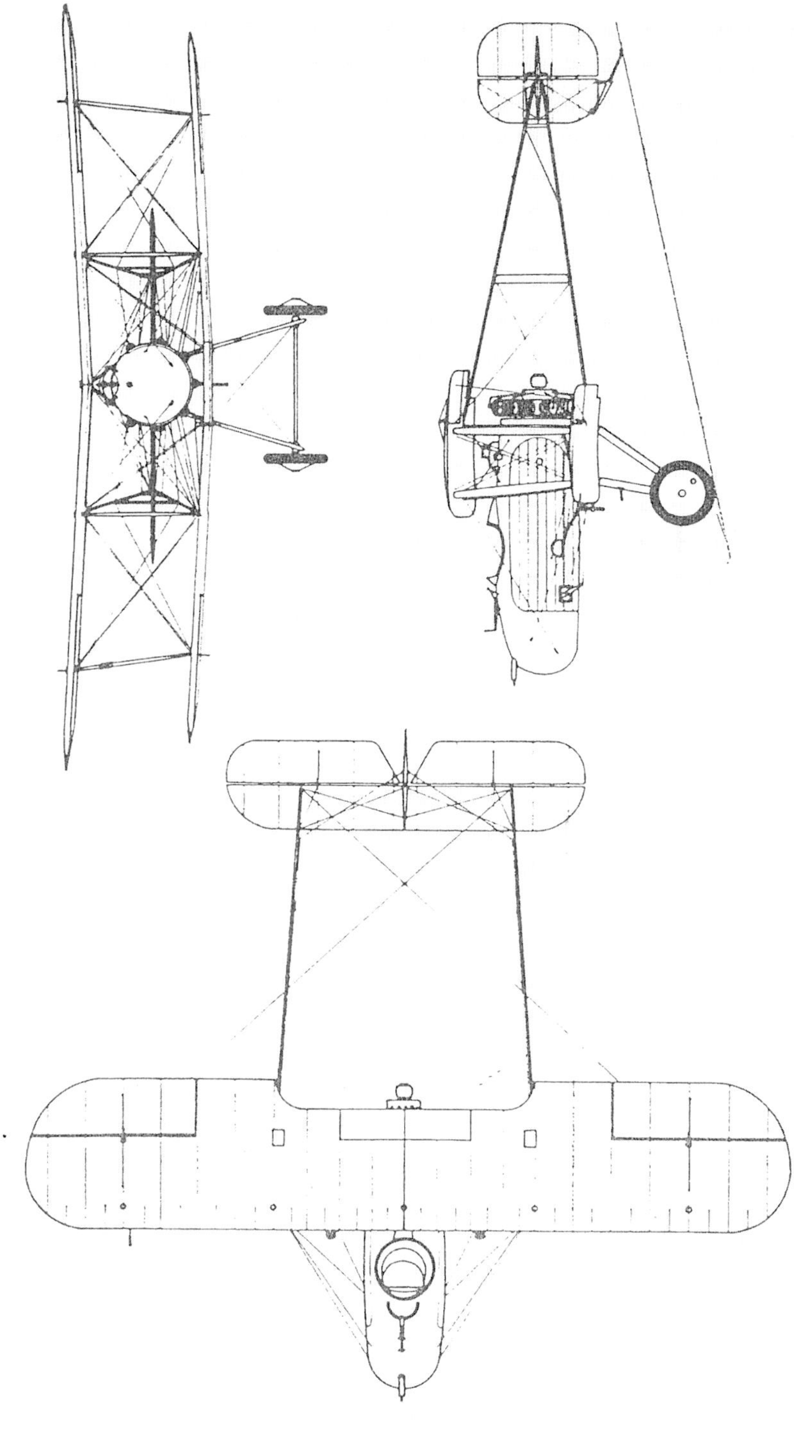

Plate 5-2 Vickers F.B.12 Scout

Christmas Eve 1916. This aircraft type was rejected by the RFC owing to the poor visibility over the sides due to the rounded nacelle.

There was also concern about the integrity of the tail booms according to Air Ministry records. In addition the RFC were dissatisfied with the Monosoupape engine owing to the risk of fire in the air and this aircraft was returned to the UK in January 1917, with the suggestion that it be modified and fitted with a Hart engine. However Air Ministry records also show that at this stage of the war they no longer regarded Vickers as a serious aircraft or engine supplier. They preferred to give orders to the more successful manufacturers such as Sopwith, de Havilland, The Bristol Aeroplane Company, the Royal Aircraft Factory with their very successful S.E. 5A, Rolls Royce with their Eagle and Falcon engines, and Beardmore. At this time the Hart company also had under development the 300 Horse-power two-row 18-cylinder version of the Hart engine but Air Ministry documents released under the sixty-year rule revealed that by late 1916 they had no intention of proceeding with it.

Meanwhile a Hart-engined version of the wider-span aircraft, designated F.B.12B was ordered from the Wells Aviation Company under sub-contract for delivery early in 1917 to be sent to Martlesham Heath for evaluation and then to France for combat experience.

Charles was concerned that the engine would be tested on an aircraft which was itself under development. During the war many aircraft manufacturers were unable to meet government production orders directly and had to sub-contract manufacture to other companies, often ones with no previous aircraft manufacturing experience. The Wells Aviation Company of Chelsea, a pre-war furniture manufacturer was one such company. Whilst it soon was able to turn out mass-produced models of established designs, it was not well suited to prototype development.

John Boyle had confidence in the Hart engine and Charles Redrup, and persuaded the Receivers to write to Brigadier-General Pitcher of the Air Board in September 1916. This letter expressed concern at the experimental nature of the test aircraft and requested that Vickers be required to give the engine a fair trial. On October 4th 1916 Vickers received an order from the Air Ministry for fifty Hart-engined F.B.12 Pusher Scout aircraft to be delivered to Farnborough at the price of eight hundred pounds each, including engine. The aircraft were to have a top speed of one hundred and ten miles per hour (176 kph) and an endurance of three hours at full load and equipment.

However the Ministry order for production aircraft was for a new nacelle design of rectangular cross-section made of wood, no doubt to meet RFC criticisms on downward visibility and for economy and ease of construction by unskilled labour. A new fin and rudder with greater area was also fitted to this version which was designated the F.B.12C.

Thus it was that the Receivers held their fire, but despite the representations it was the F.B.12B prototype aircraft that was used by Vickers for the Hart engine acceptance trial. (Plate 5-3). Furthermore, having been built by the Wells Aviation Company and despite a specific instruction from the Chief Inspector of Aeronautics that it should be subjected to Air Ministry Aircraft Inspection Department type testing, it was not.

Plate 5-3 Hart-Engined Vickers F.B.12B Prototype

This time another member of the Hart Engine Company, Major Arthur Bray, wrote to the Air Board complaining that the Vickers Company were not pursuing the engine development as expeditiously as they should. He expressed concern on two fronts. Firstly, that as the Receivers were still needing to account for the company's assets his share of those assets should be identified. Secondly, he stated that as long as the War continued, he had no interest in pecuniary return but was anxious that the country should benefit from the engine. With the contract for fifty aircraft the Air Board now had a direct interest and immediately took steps to review the situation. After a meeting with Major Bray early in January 1917 Lieutenant-Colonel Bagnall-Wild, the Director of Inspection in the Aeronautical Inspection Department sent a Chief Examiner, Lieutenant C.V. Brearey into the Vickers works and instructed him to send fortnightly reports back to the Deputy Inspector Captain Verney.

Brearey set about his task with vigour and very quickly uncovered a sorry tale of mis-management. He found that Vickers had several Marks of the Hart engine under manufacture, incorporating different stages of modification but that no clear record had been kept of the changes. Charles Redrup had been prevented from effective involvement in the re-design and was on bad terms with the Vickers staff. Brearey also found that a ship carrying jigs and fixtures ordered from a company in the United States had been sunk by a German U-boat in the Atlantic.

He set about cataloguing the different engines and found, to his dismay, that no real progress had been made in implementing the Air Board requirements. The changes to the crank-case had resulted in cracked shafts owing to poorly-supported bearings and the solution adopted was to thicken the crank-shaft. Owing to a drawing office error exhaust valves had been made too thin and had failed. Vickers had then made valves with much thicker bases which had proved too massive for the springs which had also failed. Valves had been made with no root radius resulting in stress-concentration and further failure. Brearey put in hand a reversion to the Redrup design of valves. To enable the various materials and modifications to be tested Charles was asked to loan his single-cylinder development engine to Vickers.

Over the next few weeks Brearey put in hand the production process that should have been implemented two years previously. The engine had been re-designated A.E.8 by Vickers and about five variants were in existence. The Mark I was the original engine used on the July 1916 Farnborough test and had been given a number of poorly-recorded modifications for re-submission to the fifty-hour endurance test required by the Air Board but when run late in January 1917 failed due to the valve failures already mentioned. After these had been replaced a satisfactory run was obtained and the engine fitted to an F.B16 tractor aircraft for air tests. It was found that whilst the engine ran well in level flight it miss-fired when banking. This was attributed to excessive oiling of the lower cylinders and an oil-thrower ring modification was instigated. The tests also showed that the aircraft itself suffered from poor handling and visibility problems and considerable modifications were put in hand.

A Mark II engine was also put on test in January 1917 and ran well once leaking holes in the inlet pipework had been spotted by Charles and sealed. A six-hour run was completed without incident. The main problem had been poor vibration owing to the changes of so many components and this was cured by reducing the weight of the pistons. During March 1917, owing to material shortages and lack of tooling facilities in the United Kingdom, Vickers re-ordered the jigs and fixtures for the engine from the United States of America. This was a busy month as a Mark III engine was also erected on the test stand to prepare for a fifty-hour test. Also in March the Mark II engine was fitted into the F.B 12B Scout for flight testing and Charles went to Joyce Green to witness the first flight test.

If this test proved satisfactory the intention was to then fly it to the Royal Flying Corps Test Squadron at Martlesham Heath. On first starting the engine one of the aluminium fuselage frames attached to the tail boom behind the engine fractured and struck the propeller which was broken. The machine was severely shaken before the engine could be shut down. When the fuselage had been repaired and a new propeller fitted a few days later, Vickers test pilot Harold Barnwell took it up for a short test flight. Flight test reports indicate that the elevator control was very course and on landing he struck the ground heavily. The tail of the machine was severely damaged and all the bracing wires slackened. With the aircraft repaired once again, a few days later Barnwell started it up but the engine ran very roughly.

Charles Redrup was called to attend and checking over the engine first of all thought that the carburettor might need adjusting. He changed the jets, but eventually found that with the previous crash impact the distributor had moved thus mis-timing the ignition. On re-adjusting and re-starting the engine it was found on ground test that whilst operation at full power was very good, the engine gradually lost power at medium outputs, due to the different jets which had been fitted. Charles wanted to reset the carburettor jets but as it was getting late, Barnwell took it up for a short test flight and recorded that it attained one hundred and five miles per hour (168 kph) at three thousand feet with a rate of climb of twelve hundred feet per minute. (366 metres/min.) Instead of remaining in the local area however, Barnwell flew it direct to Martlesham Heath. Due to the incorrect jets the engine gradually lost power during the journey. On inspection after arrival the RFC found that several of the internal fuselage ribs were broken from the earlier accident. Barnwell was lucky to have made the flight successfully and the RFC evaluation could not go ahead. The engine was partly dismantled to explain its workings to the officer in charge at Martlesham but the whole aircraft was then loaded onto a lorry and returned to Bexley Heath.

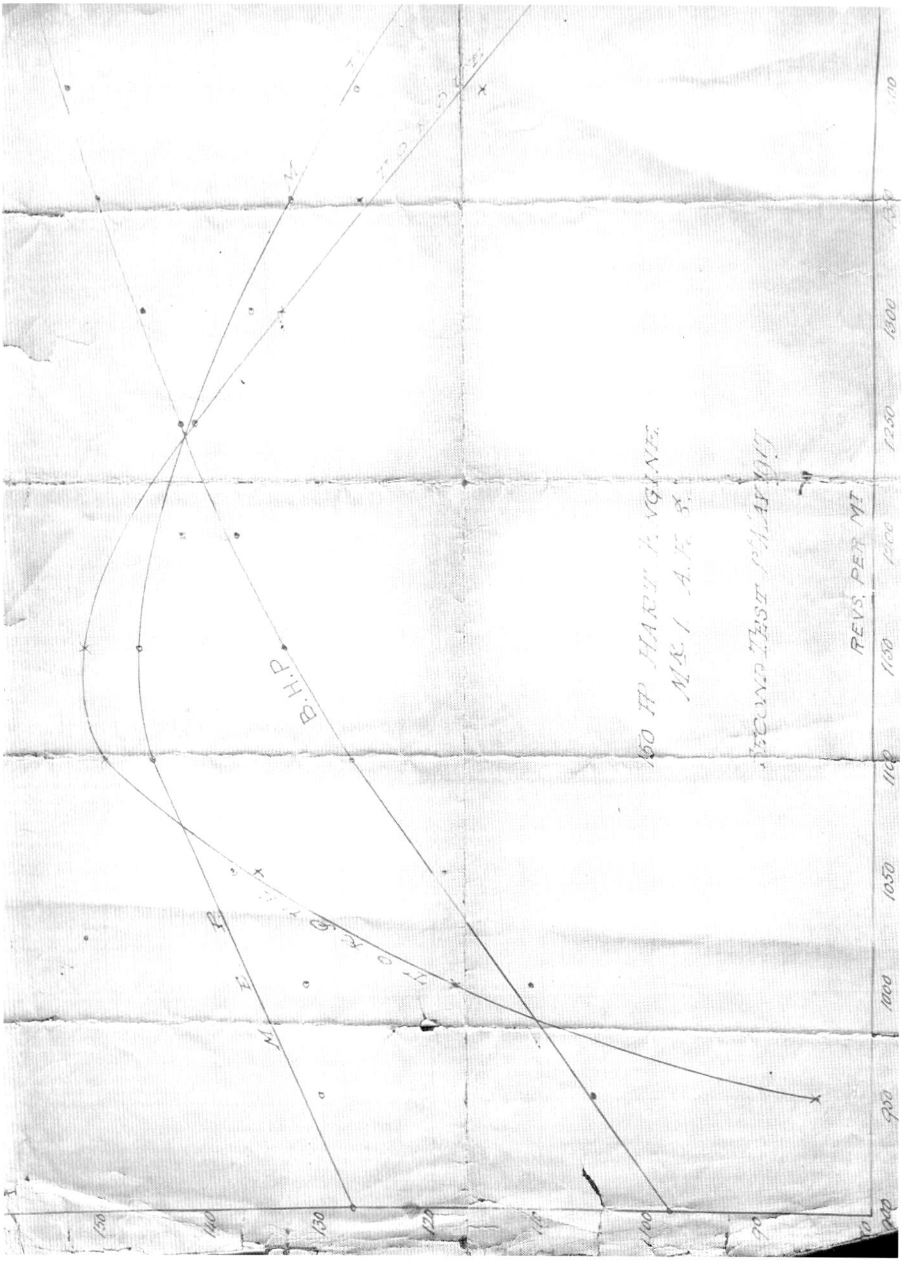

Plate 5-4 Performance Curve of Hart A.E.8 150 Horse-Power Engine

At this point a marked change occurred in the attitude of Vickers. In the middle of March 1917 they had received an order for three hundred A.R.1 150 HP Bentley engines. Thereafter very little work was done on the A.E.8 engine and the U.S. orders for jigs and fixtures were cancelled. By the end of April 1917 the efforts at Vickers were all going into the production of the A.R.1 engine. They intended to complete the four Hart engines that they had in erection but were not intending to go into production. Brearey reported that he was having to superintend all the work on the Hart engines, which would not have progressed without his intervention. At this time Charles Redrup left Vickers as his workshop facilities had been closed down and all the staff re-allocated to work on the A.R.1 engine.

In May 1917 the heavily-modified Mark 1 A.E.8 original Hart engine was tested and gave an output of 150 horse-power (112kw) at 1350 rpm. (Plate 5-4). It had maximum torque at 70% power and 1150 rpm with a specific fuel consumption of 0.59 pints per BHP per hour (0.45 litres per kw per hour), a very economical performance.

During May, June and July 1917 Brearey, virtually single-handed, pushed forward the work on the various Hart engines still in the works. The main objective was to get the Mark V engine through its fifty-hour test, but it was dogged by frustrating failures. Some of the pistons, which had been shaved down to lighten them, burnt out, and casing studs failed which turned out to have been made of inferior material instead of the VNCA which Charles Redrup had originally specified.

Plate 5-5 Hart-Engined Vickers F.B.16, 1916

As mentioned earlier the Hart Mark II engine was fitted to another Vickers aircraft the F.B.16. It was becoming clear that because of the drag of the tail struts, pusher aircraft could never compete with tractor designs, and once interrupter gear for forward-firing guns became common, the only advantage of pusher aircraft disappeared. Aircraft such as the S.E.5a and the Sopwith Camel were starting to run rings around the German aircraft and so Vickers developed their own tractor biplane around the Hart engine, the F.B.16, designed by Rex Pierson. It was built at the Bexley Heath works in the summer of 1916. It was remarkably modern in appearance, comparable to aircraft of a decade later. It had a partially-cowled engine and fuselage of elliptic cross-section throughout. The top wing was level with the pilot's head and the turtle-deck was also high behind the pilot. (Plate 5-5). The top speed was 130 mph, it was fully aerobatic and on test in a dive to its limiting speed it was recovered successful with a smooth application of power.

Plate 5-6 Vickers Wellesley Bombers
Fitted with Townend Ring Cowling

Although Charles' testing of the Hart engine in the open air had demonstrated the effectiveness of close-finning there were problems with overheating of the engine when installed in an aircraft. In the pusher configuration, as in the F.B 12B, where the nacelle screened the engine, and in the partially-cowled arrangement on the F.B.16, the blanking of the engine caused problems. It was not until 1928 that experiments at the National Physical Laboratory by Dr H C H Townend demonstrated the effectiveness of a fully-cowled engine. He discovered that if a radial engine were enclosed in a cowling ring of aerofoil section, not only did this streamline the airflow and improve cooling dramatically, but that the "Townend Ring" as it became called, actually produced forward thrust and thereby reduced engine drag considerably. The first Vickers aircraft to use the Townend Ring was the Wellesley bomber in 1934. (Plate 5-6). Reductions of engine drag of up to 60 percent were demonstrated. None of this was known in 1916 and the partial cowling of the F.B.16 gave the worst of all possible worlds.

Plate 5-7 Modified F.B.16 with narrow Fuselage and Uncowled Hart Engine

With the F.B 16 as with the F.B.12A, the pilot's view over the sides was very bad, and lateral control was poor and so the next model the F.B.16B, again with a Hart engine, had a cut-down fuselage and the engine was uncowled. (Plate 5-7). A new fin and rudder were fitted and a four-bladed airscrew fitted. Although the close-finning design gave much improved cooling at high power outputs, the partial cowling of the original model had caused overheating problems.

Another version of the aircraft, the F.B.16D, fitted with a 150 horsepower Hispano-Suiza engine flown by Captain H. R. Deighton Simpson undertaking terminal-speed aerobatic exercises crashed, killing the pilot. A thorough investigation showed that the design of the leading edge of the wing was defective. Although the wing was re-designed and a very much modified aircraft sent to Martlesham Heath with a Hispano-Suiza engine, the reports were still unfavourable. It appeared that the improved streamlining had led to reduced access for engine maintenance, and controllability was still a major problem despite the much enlarged fin and rudder. The F.B.16 never went into production because at this late stage of the war records show that the Air Ministry requested Vickers to concentrate on the production of other manufacturers' designs, such as the S.E.5a and the Sopwith Camel which were proving very successful in Northern France.

Plate 5-8 Hart-Engined F.B.12C with Charles Redrup at the Wing Trailing-edge

Charles was still in creative mode throughout all these tribulations and patented a design for improving air mass flow and scavenging through the engine by opening of the exhaust valve towards the end of the induction stroke, and by boosting the carburettor fuel rate to augment the increased air flow. (British Patent No. 118,390).

In May 1917 the Hart-engined F.B.12C (Plates 5-8 and 5-9) aircraft was eventually manufactured and sent to France for evaluation but the aircraft

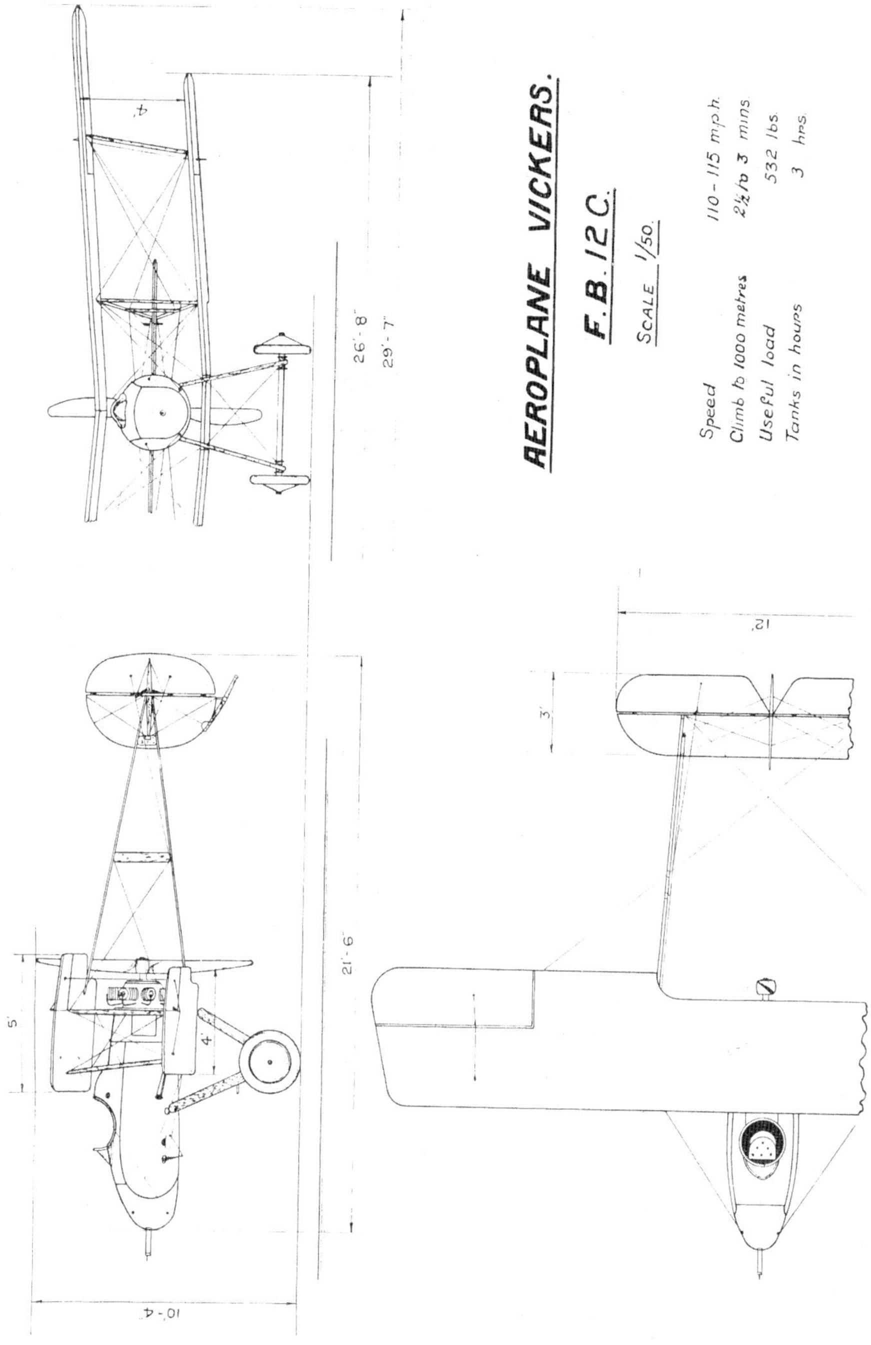

Plate 5-9 *Plans for F.B.12C*

crashed shortly afterwards and was destroyed. The examination of the wreck showed that the tail-boom attachment had failed and subsequent Air Board correspondence shows that this was an on-going concern.

After this Vickers lost interest and abandoned further development of the engine and never submitted it for Air Board type-testing. Only eighteen of the original order of fifty F.B.12s were completed by the Wells Aviation Company and these were fitted with different engines. At this stage the Receivers moved in again. Vickers did however offer Charles Redrup a ten year contract to design aircraft engines at an annual salary of £1,500. It is clear from Vickers production drawings for the 150 horse-power engine (Plate 5-10) that they had fully expected it to go into mass production and for Charles to join them.

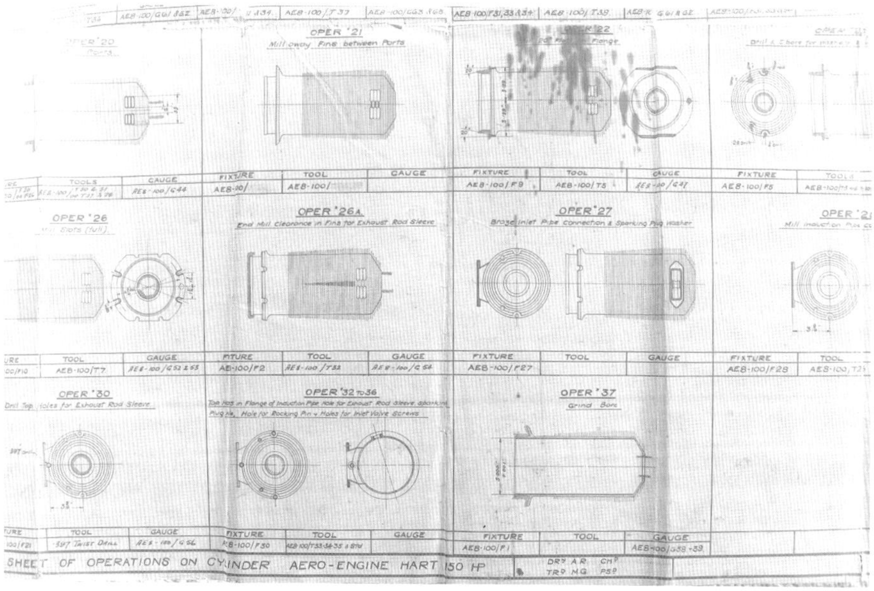

Plate 5-10 Vickers Production Drawing for Hart Engine Cylinders

The collapse of the Hart Engine Company led to a legal dispute between the partners and Vickers which were unable to reach a financial settlement. The partners requested that Lieutenant Brearey should be allowed to testify on their behalf as he had witnessed first-hand the fiasco at Vickers and his written reports were sympathetic towards the Hart Engine Company. After many months deliberation between the Solicitor-General and the Air Board it was agreed that Brearey should be allowed to testify, but that his written reports should not be made available as evidence and his testimony should be vetted by the Ministry of Munitions. The former partners of the Hart Engine Company issued a writ against Vickers on 12th March 1918 alleging failure to perform the contract to develop the Hart engine and seeking recompense for the contract value of £20,000 and/or the return of their assets.

By this time Lieutenant Brearey had been posted to Paris but a week after the War ended, in November 1918 he sent a draft affidavit to Major Bulman, the Controller of Inspection at the Ministry. This confirmed much of the incompetence which had taken place during the critical months of development, but also stated that a significant reason for the delay was the loss at sea of the manufacturing jigs and fixtures. In the light of this statement the solicitors for the former Hart Engine Company partners advised that the writ was unlikely to succeed and so they settled for a much smaller sum, amounting to the cost of just one engine. Vickers were still keen to engage Charles as an engine designer but he was not prepared to agree to this without an acceptable settlement for his former partners and so the matter rested.

Chapter 6
Motor-Cycles and Marine

As well as persevering with his rotary and radial engine designs, Charles had, in 1911 turned his fertile mind to other possible engine geometries. Realising that rotary engines were likely to become a dead-end, but favouring the axial engine arrangement, he designed a static axial engine in which the cylinders were stationary but drove the parallel main shaft through a wobble-plate. He invented at this time the “Z” shaft configuration which was to feature in many of his later engines. Throughout the First World War he refined this design and patented it in 1917, (UK Patent No. 115,656, Plate 6-1), but left implementation in abeyance until peacetime.

Following the collapse of the Hart Engine Company and the end of the First World War Charles thought that a smaller version of the Hart engine would be of value for the emerging light aircraft market. He designed and built a five-cylinder engine based on the Hart engine but incorporating the exhaust valve modification for which he had been granted a patent in 1917. This was a means of improving the power output by opening the exhaust valve near the end of the induction stroke to increase the breathing capability of the engine. He built and tested the engine in the Leeds works in 1918 but could get no interest from aircraft manufacturers.

John Boyle from the Hart Engine Company had retained his confidence in Charles despite the difficulties with Vickers. Later in 1918 Charles, his brother Alf, Boyle and Boyle’s son Walter set up a company, Boyle and Redrup Limited in St Stephens Road, Burmantofts Leeds to further develop and market a three-cylinder radial industrial engine. Consolidating his base, Charles moved his family to a new house, Heather View, Lawnswood in Leeds and it was here that their fifth daughter Jessica Winifred was born in September 1919. Working with John Boyle and using the knowledge he had gleaned from designing motor-cycle engines and aero engines with close finning, Charles set about designing a compact radial engine for multi-purpose use. This was a somewhat unconventional static radial engine of 309 ccs, and could be mounted with its axis horizontal or vertical. (Plate 6-2). His brother Alf was in charge of the manufacturing side.

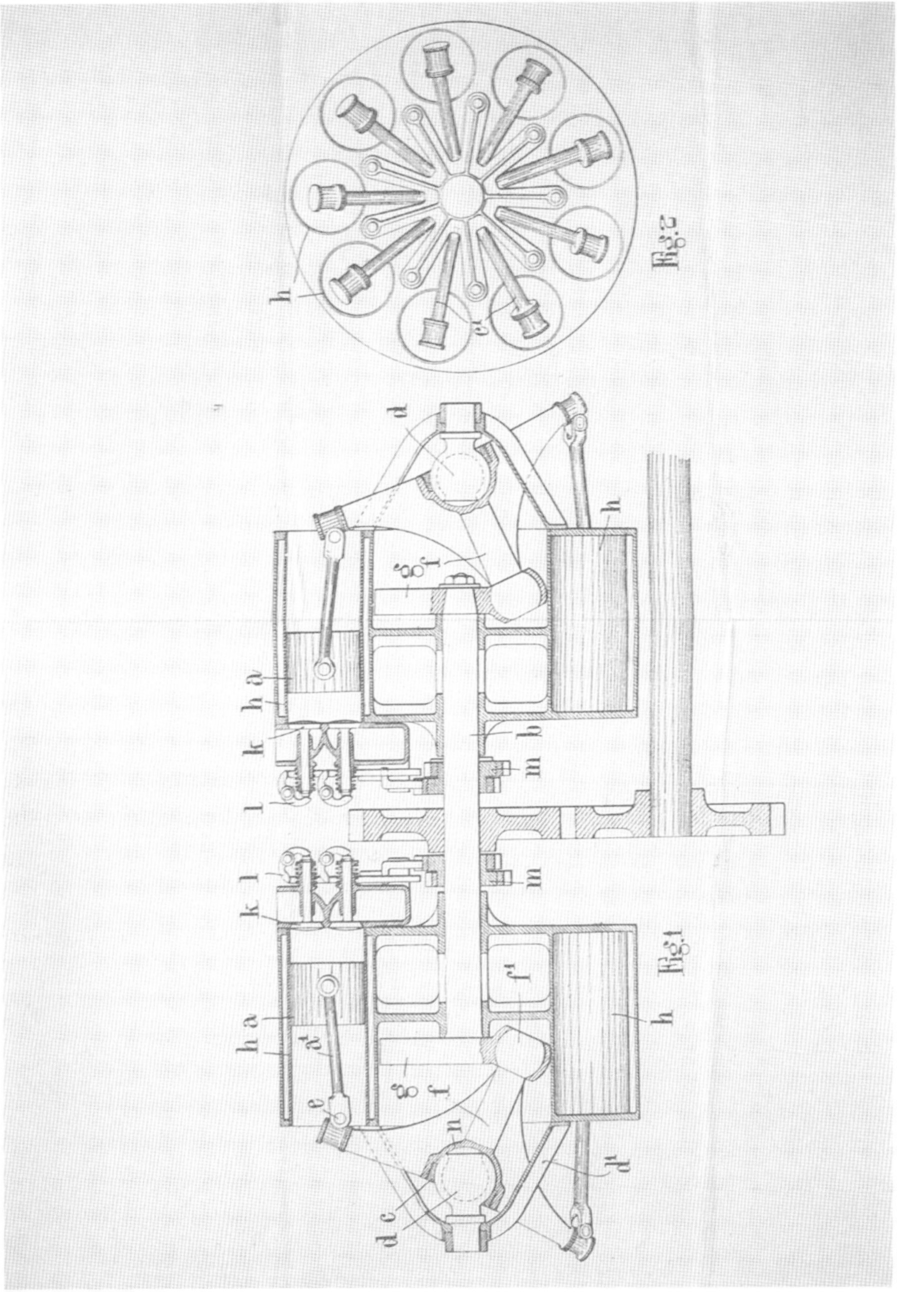

Plate 6-1 The 1917 Patent for Double-Ended Wobble-Plate Engine

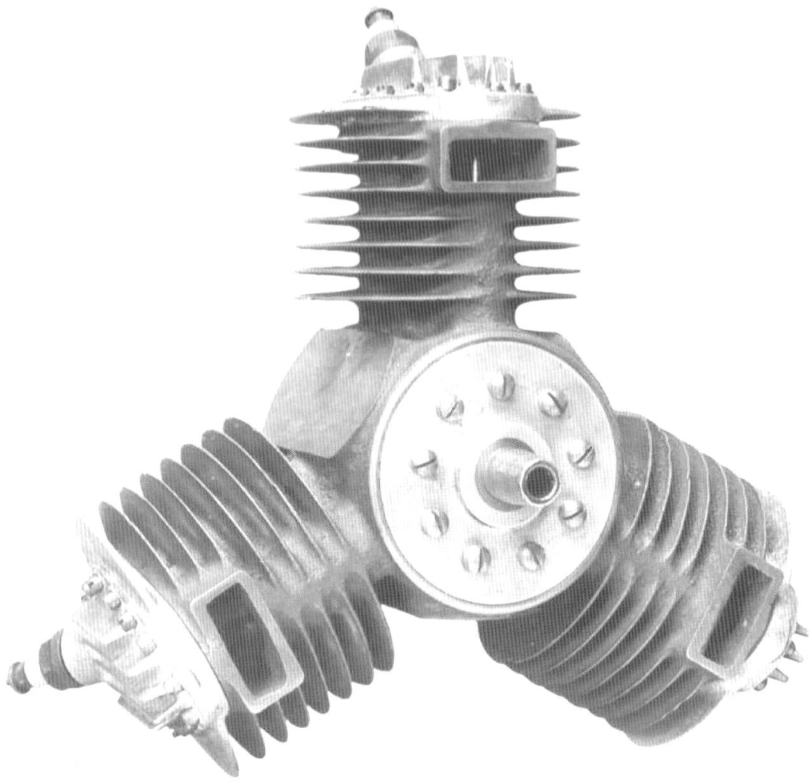

Plate 6-2 Boyle and Redrup general Purpose Radial Engine

During 1919 and 1920 Boyle and Redrup Limited manufactured several hundred of these engines for industrial use where they were used to drive generators, pumps, blowers, lighting installations and a variety of other applications. One of the engines was described by *The Motor Cycle* magazine in its February 5th 1920 edition and Charles Redrup set about installing this engine in a motor-cycle frame for his own use. The engine was mounted vertically with one cylinder upright and the other two in a fore and aft configuration. A large cooling fan was attached to one side of the drive shaft and the other side drove a Burman two-speed gearbox with clutch and kick-start via a chain, and the drive from the gearbox was by another chain to a large pulley on the rear wheel. The large cooling fan was necessary because the rear cylinder in particular was shielded from the slipstream, and so uniform cooling of all cylinders was provided, as well as giving a desirable flywheel action. The machine had Saxon pressed- steel forks which was very innovative for the time.

John Boyle was of the opinion that the company should steer clear of manufacturing anything but engines. Although Charles completed the

Plate 6-3 Redrup Radial Motor-Cycle Engine

motor-cycle, the company did not set up a motor-cycle line but sold engines to a number of motor-cycle companies for installation into frames of their own.

One of the first to construct a Redrup powered-motor cycle was H.C.M. (Monty) Beaumont of Beaumont Motors (Leeds) Ltd who had a factory at the Cleopatra Works, Harehills Leeds and had been building 269cc two-strokes with Wall-Liberty and Blackburne engines. (Monty Beaumont would again be "involved" with the Redrup design many years later). Beaumont built a further three machines using the 309cc engines, and two of these were entered for the 1920 ACU Six- Days Trial. *(Auto Cycle Union)*. (Plate 6-3). These carried the "Redrup Radial" name on the tank. One of the machines, U 4676 was ridden by Charles Redrup himself, and the other, U 5524, by N A. Woolley (Plate 6-4), a well-known motor-cycle racer of the time. Unfortunately the machine ridden by Charles came adrift at Park Rash on the first day's run, and the next day Woolley also had to retire.

Plate 6-4 N.A. Woolley on the Redrup Radial Before the ACU Six-Day Trial.

The Redrup Radial was a two and three-quarter horse-power fan-cooled three-cylinder side-valve engine with cylinders set at an angle of 120 degrees to each other. The bore and stroke were each 50.8mm. (2 inches). Charles aimed to ensure economy of construction and made his engines symmetrical about the central axis. Thus the side valves were arranged on the T-head principle, (Plate 6-5) with the inlet valves on the output shaft side and the exhaust valves located next to the fan. Collector pipes joined into a common integral manifold to which the short stub exhaust was fitted. The inlet valves had guides with an X-shaped cross-section, thus allowing the inlet air to pass freely around the valve shaft. Keyed onto the shaft was a cam of somewhat complicated profile which drove the valve tappets.

The cylinders were of cast iron with aluminium heads and the pistons were also of aluminium, and of remarkably modern appearance. The carburettor, which was designed specifically for the engine by Charles, was mounted directly onto the crank-case below the driving sprocket and the whole carburettor and throttle assembly was kept warm to prevent icing as they were surrounded by the hot oil sump. As can be seen from the exploded diagram of the engine, (Plate 6-6), the crankshaft and big-ends were of a clever design. The connecting-rod for each piston was different, one with a central driving bush and the other

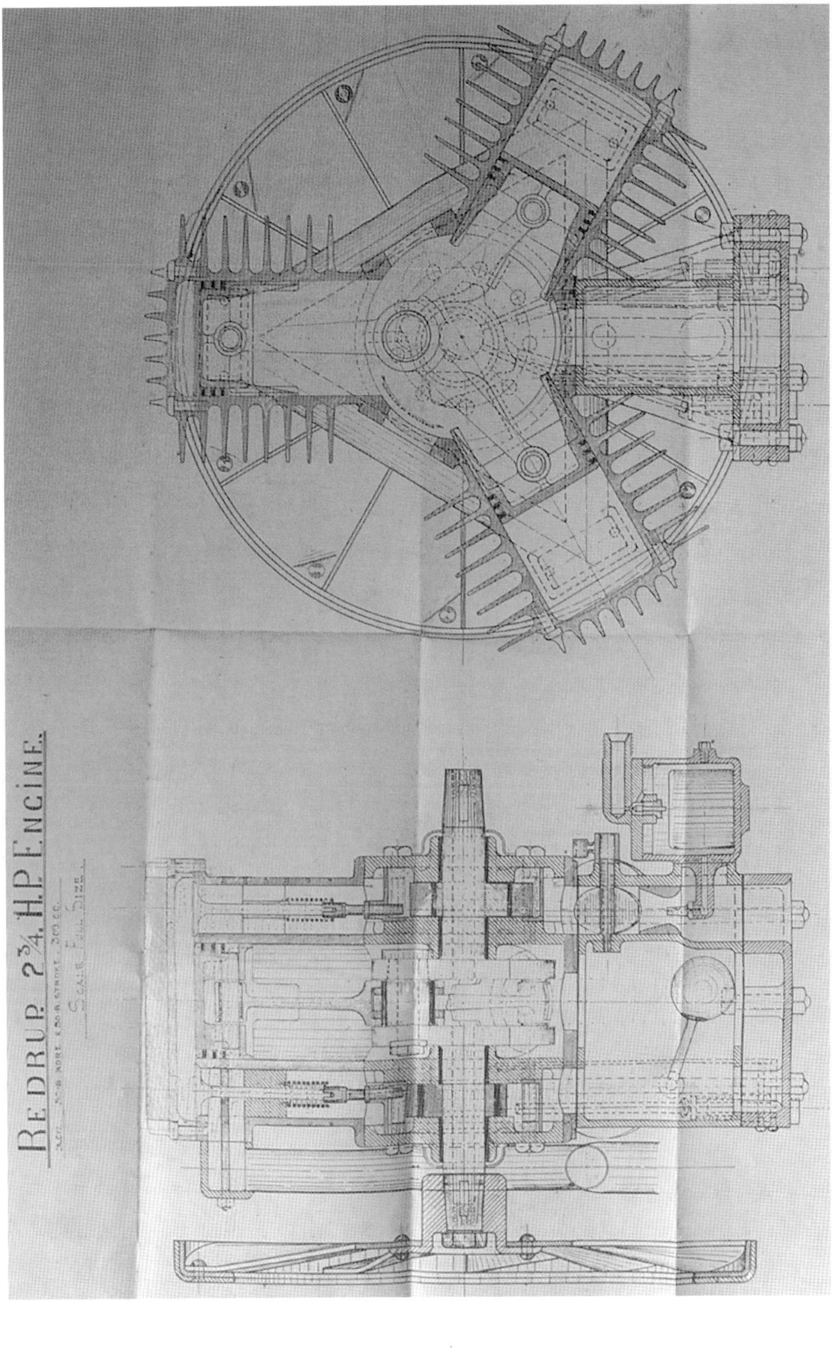

Plate 6-5 Section of the Boyle and Redrup Radial Engine Showing the "T"-Head Construction

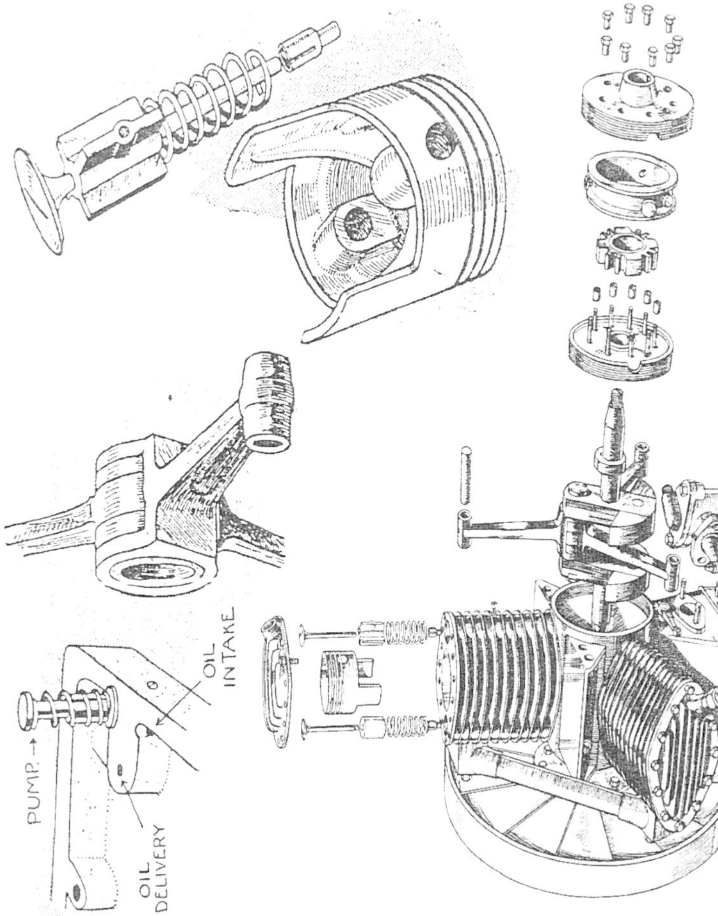

Plate 6-6 Assembly of the Boyle and Redrup Radial Engine

two each with two symmetrical bushes of different spans. Thus the three rods fitted snugly onto the crank throw which was in itself a removable bush connecting two half-cranks with balance-weights, so the whole could be easily assembled. This arrangement gave excellent balance and did away with the split bushes and big-end clamp bolts of conventional radial engines, as well as the master-rod, slave-rod configuration. It had a further advantage in that the crank-case was symmetrical and the cylinders were all aligned, unlike many other radials where the cylinders are offset to accommodate the side-by-side connecting-rods. Although the different connecting-rods would have increased cost marginally the half-crankshafts were almost identical using the same forging, and would have been cheaper to forge and machine on a production basis than a conventional whole crankshaft.

The engine used a Thompson-Bennett magneto mounted behind the vertical cylinder and had two sets of points. It was geared to run at three-quarters engine-speed so gave three impulses for every two revolutions. This is just what a four-stroke three-cylinder radial engine requires and so an epicyclic distributor was geared to ensure that each cylinder received an impulse every second revolution. This distributor technology was taken directly from Charles' three-cylinder aero-engine of 1911. Oiling was by means of a Best and Lloyd lubricator feeding the big-end and crank-shaft bearings and from tiny mechanical pumps driven with the timing-gear on each side of the engine to feed all other moving parts.

Charles used his own motor-cycle for general use and strait after a 500-mile round trip to visit his family in South Wales, without any adjustments, he handed it over to *The Motor Cycle* magazine test team for evaluation. They were very impressed by what they found. After standing overnight in a wet, cold, exposed place the engine fired on the first kick. It took a few minutes to warm up but it then ticked over very slowly yet responded to full throttle without hesitation. They observed that full power was not generated until

operating temperature had been achieved. The team took the machine on a round trip from Leeds to Coventry and back and with a passenger on board the total load was 21 stone, (134kg). The very first road took them up an incline of one in seven which the machine took in low gear of 11 to 1 without difficulty. They likened the ride to travelling on a free-wheeling pedal-cycle because the radial configuration and enclosed engine gave such noiseless and vibration-free performance. The main source of noise appeared to be a ringing resonance from the fan blades at certain speeds.

The round trip was 130 miles and timing was carried out over given stretches of road. On the level forty to forty-five miles per hour was attained easily, and thirty miles per hour could be sustained indefinitely. Timed over a ten mile stretch of the Great North Road, thirty-one point six miles per hour was achieved, a very considerable performance for an engine of only 309 ccs. Immediately afterwards it was run over a mile distance in low gear at twenty miles per hour which is harsh treatment for a small engine. It recovered into high gear without demur. Despite running with a somewhat rich mixture the machine achieved one hundred miles per gallon (thirty-nine kilometres per litre). The rider commented that a smaller jet would have improved consumption.

Plate 6-7 Charles and Jessie circa 1916 with Daughters Florence, Violet and (foreground) Twins Marjorie and Dorothy

The Motor Cycle team concluded that there should be a great future for radial engines for motor-cycles, especially in larger sizes. They commented that they were particularly impressed by the low noise, lack of vibration and smooth torque. This latter feature in particular should give reduced tyre wear and indefinite chain and transmission life as snatching was completely eliminated.

The Redrups and John Boyle eventually parted company, primarily because Charles was passionately interested in motor-cycles and was also designing aero engines in his spare time. He set up his own company, The British Radial Co. Ltd, who had an office in Kings Road, Chelsea, and which employed motor-cycle frames built for them by Chater-Lea. He eventually bought out the rights to the 309 cc engine from John Boyle. It is from this British Radial Company that we have the only solid news of production, for *Motor Cycle Index* lists them as having built a total of 30 machines, using engines numbered from 82 to 112. One of these engines, Number 107 was retrieved many years later by Ken Blake who overhauled and rebuilt the motor-cycle - of which more later. (See colur plate C11).

Plate 6-8 Redrup radial Six

In 1922, after so far raising an all-girl family, (Plate 6-7), Charles and Jessie had a son, John Arnold, who would in due course follow his father's passion for engineering. John would be instrumental in reviving, with his father, the Redrup Radial motor-cycle in the 1940s. Family life at this time was very busy as the girls entered their teenage years. They all learnt to play the piano and at evening family concerts would sing and play music together, with Charles playing the harmonium. They were regular churchgoers and Marjorie in particular spent a lot of time working for the local parish church.

Alf Redrup also spent time experimenting with the motor-cycles. In 1922 he had castings made for an engine with a double crank-case, and produced the "Redrup Six" which was a 618 cc capacity engine consisting basically of two Redrup Radials side by side, U-8879. The motor-cycle was reported to have a very smooth and quiet operation, with strong pulling power. His nephew remembered that it had tremendous acceleration. (Plates 6-8 and 6-9).

Plate 6-9 Close-up of the Radial Six

Charles had another brother Sidney Arthur who joined the Barry lifeboat crew as a mechanic. Eventually he was promoted to a more senior role and used to travel around the coast visiting lifeboat stations and supervising engineering matters. He ended up at a station in northern Scotland. He used to tell Charles about the lifeboat service and, of course, the engineering aspects. A major problem was that self-righting boats needed high buoyancy and low weight as well as ample cabin space for rescued survivors. Current internal combustion engines were bulky and took up much of the cabin space. They were also heavy and had high fuel consumption. The restricted space for fuel tanks meant that the range of the craft was limited. Charles conceived the idea that a wobble-plate engine would be ideal for marine applications. It would be much more compact, could be buried below decks and would have a very economical fuel consumption because of its higher efficiency.

He had not given up on his aero engine designs and tried hard to re-ignite interest in the Hart engine. However by the end of the War there were a great number of surplus engines available and moreover the large engine manufacturers were competing fiercely for what little new requirement existed. Charles had designs for a "Double Hart" of eighteen cylinders and nominally rated at 300 horse-power, and also for a compact thirty-five horse-power five-cylinder version of the engine for use in the growing market for light recreational aircraft, but try as he could, no orders were forthcoming.

Plate 6-10 Six-Cylinder Two-Stroke Axial Marine Engine 1922

Not to be beaten, he dug out his designs for axial engines and turned away for the time being from the highly-competitive aviation field to the marine environment. Having looked at the options for axial designs

Charles felt that the swash-plate arrangement was too complicated, relying on too many rotating parts and sliding surfaces. The swash-plate engine dated back to the late nineteenth century and later patents and consists of an angled plate attached to the drive shaft with a thrust-bearing joined to it, carrying the drives from the pistons. Thus one revolution of the shaft corresponds to one complete cycle of the pistons backwards and forwards. The thrust bearing could be a flat or tilting-pad bearing, as patented by Michell, or with ball-bearings as shown earlier in Plate 3-11.

As already alluded to Charles was not enamoured of the swash-plate design but preferred his 1917 patented wobble-plate type of design. This used a Z-shaped drive shaft and a star-shaped member mounted on the centre, angled section of shaft. The extremities of the arms of the star were linked to the pistons via a ball and pin arrangement. It was the latter arrangement that he developed for a six-cylinder six-combustion-chamber two-stroke engine which he had running by 1922. (Plates 6-10 and 6-11).

Plate 6-11 Arrangement of Pistons and Inertia Valves in Crown

This engine was a double-ended machine with two star members of three arms each in the centre and three combustion chambers at each end. It also had pumping pistons for inlet air with inertia-operated inlet valves in the crowns, a feature of which Charles seems to have been very fond as it dated back to some of his Barry engines. This type of engine has a complicated motion of the ends of the star-members, which ideally all follow a figure-of-eight pattern. However unless restrained, the star-members have a tendency to rotate with the shaft. For this engine Charles designed one arm of each star-member to be constrained to move only axially, whilst the other two arms followed figure-of-eight paths. The two star-members had diametrically opposite arms constrained thereby ensuring dynamic as well as static balance.

Plate 6-12 shows the crankshaft with two offset "Z" sections. Ball-ended spider arms fitted into similar sockets in the piston. Based on test results with this engine he constructed his two-stroke six-cylinder marine engine which he had completed late in 1924, which was single-ended. (Plate 6-13).

Plate 6-12 "Z" - Shaft and twin Ball-ended Spiders

In this engine he catered for the circumferential movement of the star-member arms by hinging them onto the central spider and fitting the ends into sliding trunnions in the pistons. The design resulted in a very compact layout with the cylinders lying parallel to the shaft and arranged concentrically around it. The pistons were double-ended but only one end fitted into a combustion chamber. They were fitted with a single piston-ring of a double form, patented by Charles (British Patent 219,054). The other end fitted into another cylinder which acted as the air-pump or turbo-charger. The cylinders were surrounded by water-cooling jackets and had sparking plugs in the centre of the domed cylinder heads.

The air induction system was very novel and rather complicated. Being a two-stroke engine without valve gear and only inlet and exhaust

Plate 6-13 Six-Cylinder Two-Stroke Axial Marine Engine 1924

Plate 6-14 Carburettor and Inlet Pipework

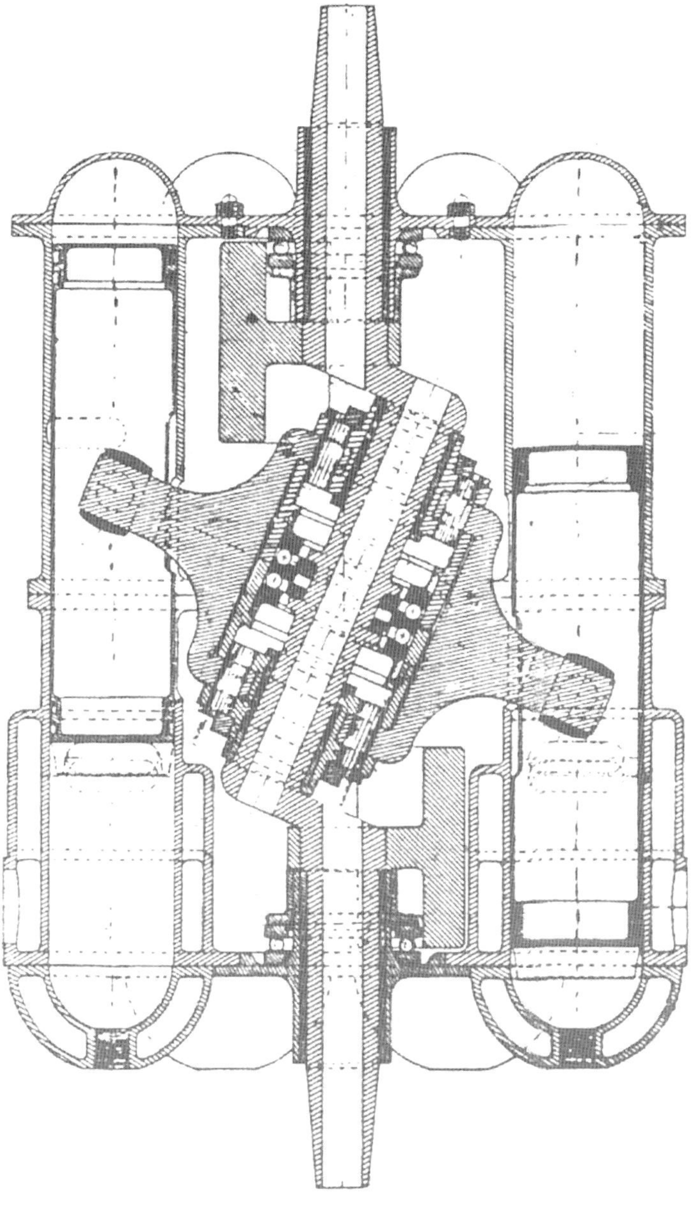

Plate 6-15 Cross-Section of Six-Cylinder Axial Marine Engine 1924

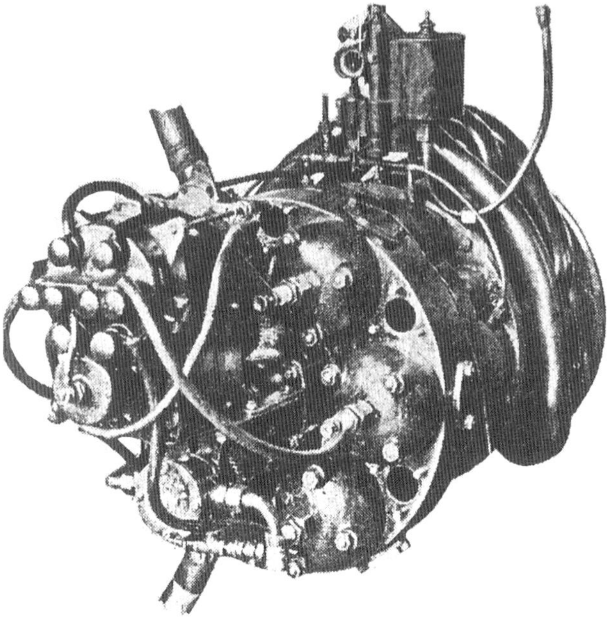

Plate 6-16 Cylinder Heads

ports along the power cylinders, it had no natural induction suction and relied on the piston pumps to breathe. Air was drawn into the Solex carburettor and the fuel-air mixture was sucked through a manifold into the pumping cylinders via six long snaking tubes connecting to ports in the side of the pumping cylinders. (Plate 6-14).

The pistons then pumped the mixture with a positive pressure through ducts off the hemispherical heads of the pumping cylinders back into bores in the casing along to the inlet ports of the power cylinders. (Plate 6-15). The pistons then compressed the mixture and the plugs fired. (Plate 6-16). The use of six cylinders meant that the manifold pressure was almost constant, and torque output very steady. A flywheel was unnecessary. At the end of the firing strokes the exhaust ports opened and the gases escaped to an exhaust manifold and then to a common exhaust pipe. Again, the common exhaust manifold resulted in reduced pressure pulses and less noise. (Plate 6-17).

The cylinders had a bore and stroke of 2.5 inches (63.5mm) and 4 inches (102mm) respectively, giving a cubic capacity of 118 cubic inches (1.94 litres). The power output, driving a large-area three-bladed propeller of 18 inches (0.46m) diameter was 5 horse-power (3.7kw) at 300 rpm, 11.8 horse-power (8.8kw) at 700 rpm and 16.72 horse-power (12.5kw) at 1000 rpm. The two-stroke engine, because of its complete

Plate 6-17 Exhaust Manifold and Starting Handle

symmetry could be made to run in either direction. Charles patented this design, and a double-ended four-stroke version with valve-gear at each end and twelve cylinders. (British Patent 236,696).

Lubrication was from a rotary pump driven from the shaft by means of a gearwheel. Oil was pumped into one end journal bearing and along the hollow shaft to the other end. Oil also bled from this shaft to the bearings in the "Z" shaft and along the arms of the spider to the ball-ends inside the pistons.

The spider was mounted on the angled section of the "Z" shaft by means of double-ball bearings at the centre and stabilising journal bearings at each end. This angled section of shaft was connected to the two straight sections by bolted joints and substantial balance weights were mounted on each of the end shafts to counteract the masses of the angled shaft and spider. The arms of the spider ended in cylindrical sections which slid in cylindrical slots in trunnions in the pistons. Thus there was a generous bearing area between the spider arms and the pistons. The reason for this arrangement is due to the fact that the motion of the ends of the spider arms was quite complicated being three dimensional.

Plate 6-18 The "Redrup 1" Motor Cruiser Fitted with the Redrup Axial Marine Engine

The complete engine was very compact, only 13 inches (0.33m) in diameter and 17 inches (0.43m) long, without the pipework for intake and exhaust. The central bearing for the "Z" shaft was just over 7 inches (0.18m) long and bearing loads were therefore low. Charles purchased an old ship's lifeboat which had been converted to a cabin cruiser and named it *Redrup 1*. It was a double-ended steel boat, 25 feet (7.6m) long and had a beam of 7 feet 6 inches (2.3m) . (Plate 6-18). Because of its compact size the engine could be mounted low in the hull giving a great saving in space. It was very much an experimental arrangement, but in commercial applications the installation would be entirely below the deck enabling an increase in passenger or cargo capacity. Its low noise and vibration level made it ideal for leisure craft where engine noise often spoils the pleasure of cruising.

For a demonstration of the engine Charles overcame his aversion to water, and can be seen in the photograph of him proudly standing in the prow of the cruiser. The motor launch was demonstrated to *The Motor Boat* magazine in May 1925 who were highly impressed by the performance. They considered that a more compact form of power unit could hardly be conceived. The concept could be applied to marine or aero engines of much larger ratings and because of the simplicity of construction could be manufactured without difficulty. They were very impressed by the low noise and vibration levels.

It is believed that the engine did suffer some resonance problems, and although nothing is recorded, they probably stemmed from the instability of the spider and piston combination, as in later versions of the axial engine Charles made several changes to these connections. The work however was interrupted by an unexpected development.

Charles had written to several aero and car manufacturers to try to interest them in his engine designs. One such manufacturer was Crossley Motors with whom Charles had worked previously and they responded by commissioning him to design a five-cylinder axial engine for the company based on the marine engine.

Francis (Frank) and William (later Sir William) Crossley were two brothers who had served apprenticeships at two great Newcastle engineering companies, Robert Stephenson and Armstrongs, and in 1867 they set up in partnership as Crossley Brothers. Frank had bought the engineering business of John M Dunlop at Great Marlborough Street in Manchester with financial assistance from his uncle. Dunlop manufactured pumps, presses and small steam engines but of course went on to become famous as the inventor of the pneumatic tyre.

The Crossley brothers were strictly teetotal refusing to supply their products to any company such as breweries which conflicted with their beliefs. They adopted the early Christian Coptic Cross as the badge for their road vehicles. In 1881 Crossley Brothers became a limited company and in 1882 as their business grew, they moved to larger premises in Pottery Lane, Openshaw, in east Manchester. In 1869 they purchased the worldwide patent rights of Nicolaus Otto and Eugen Langden of Cologne for the new gas fuelled atmospheric internal combustion engine and in 1876 these rights were extended to the famous Otto four stroke cycle engine. Considering that Otto had only patented his engine in 1861 this was a remarkably prescient move, but the inventors did retain their rights in Germany. The change over to four stroke engines was remarkably rapid as the first one was built in 1876, and the last atmospheric engines were made in 1877!

Whilst the introduction of the carburettor allowed much more volatile hydrocarbons to be used with hot tube or spark ignition, the Crossley brothers concentrated on developing the heavy oil engine with the first one being demonstrated in 1891 and in 1896 they obtained rights to the Diesel system which did not require spark ignition. After Frank died in 1897, the company did produce petrol engines and in the early 1900s supplied these for Leyland buses.

The brothers saw the growing market for cars, and their first one was produced in 1904. The company realised that a separate business was required to build cars and so Crossley Motors Ltd was registered in 1906 as the vehicle manufacturing arm of Crossley Brothers. It was initially based in the main factory but soon moved to a nearby site they owned in Napier Street, Gorton. In later years as the company's fame grew, the street was renamed Crossley Street.

Crossleys were among the first to introduce a continuous production line, with its huge advantages in production efficiency and Henry Ford visited the company at Pottery Lane around 1900 and he was probably heavily influenced by what he saw. Despite the move of vehicle production the limits of the Pottery Lane site were again soon reached and in 1914 a further 48 acre site was bought in Heaton Chapel, Stockport which became the Errwood Park Works. The new factory was rapidly given over to war work and the western half the site became the Crossley Motors-managed National Aircraft Factory No 2 which was built in 1917. After the end of the First World War this factory was bought from the government in 1919. The eastern side became the final home of Crossley Motors. In 1919 Crossley Brothers bought Premier Gas Engines of

Plate 6-19 Redrup Marine Engine Fitted to a Crossley Chassis

Sandiacre, Nottingham who built very large engines. Over the years more than 100,000 Crossley engines have been built and it is a testament to their quality that many of these are still in use to this day.

At the outbreak of hostilities in August 1914 Crossley Motors moved almost totally to war production. The only model made was the 20/25 chassis which was supplied to the forces in huge numbers with production running at up to 45 a week. The first had been supplied to the Royal Flying Corps (RFC) in 1913 and at the outbreak of war they had

56. By the time of the armistice this had risen to over 6000. The 20/25 became one of the standard staff cars but most of the chassis were used to carry ambulances, mobile workshops, light trucks and, most importantly, the RFC Light Tenders. Every squadron in the RFC was supposed to be equipped with nine Tenders and one Staff Touring Car but it seems likely that most never had the full complement.

At the war's end all government orders were cancelled. Some 20/25's went straight into store and many others returned from France. Some of these were rebuilt to the new 25/30 specification and stayed with the RAF. The remainder were gradually sold off by the War Office. Many of these were bought back by Crossley and refurbished

The Manchester-based A.V.Roe aircraft company was in financial difficulties at the end of the war because the orders for aircraft had dried up and civil aviation was struggling to re-establish itself. Crossley on the other hand had more work than it could handle. In 1920 Crossleys bought sixty percent of the A.V.Roe shares, thereby securing the future of the aviation company, but as a result, Alliott Verdon Roe lost control of his company. Fortunately the managements of the two companies got on well together and this worked to their mutual benefit for the next few years.

Crossleys fulfilled their military contracts by refurbishing the vehicles in a newly bought A.V.Roe factory and sold them as Avro RFC's, mainly as bare chassis or with van bodies. Sales continued until 1924 and A.V.Roe were fully occupied building bodies for Crossley and refurbishing the thousands of 20/25's released by the RAF. After the war in an attempt at diversification A.V.Roe had announced its intention of entering the light car business predicting sales of 100 Avrocars per week. This was post -war optimism, and A.V.Roe production ceased when Crossleys bought the controlling interest in 1920 and only about 100 Avrocars were made.

Because of the slump in aircraft orders A.V.Roe produced motor vehicle bodies for Crossleys during the 1920s. A V Roe came to hear of Charles Redrup's work in 1925 following the demonstration of the marine engine which Charles had transferred to one of the Crossley chassis. (Plate 6-19). A.V.Roe proved particularly interested in the thirty-five horse-power five-cylinder radial aero engine prototype designed in 1918 which was sitting in Charles' workshop and after a demonstration in the middle of 1925 he was invited to work for A.V.Roe as an engine designer. With their agreement he continued his work on the axial car engine for Crossleys and the five-cylinder axial motor designed by Charles was installed in one of their cars in 1927.

Chapter 7
Avro and Alpha

In June 1925 Charles and Jessie's last child, Raymond George Redrup was born in Leeds. Just after he was born the family moved to a new home close to the Crossley Motors factory at Heaton Chapel, Stockport. Charles transferred his family and workshop to this new home at 7, Milwain Drive, Heaton Chapel. At the age of sixteen his daughter Violet, who had shown great promise at school, was found a place with A.V.Roe as a trainee tracer and soon became an accomplished draughtswoman. Florence, the eldest daughter had trained as a schoolteacher but obtained a post as Chief Records Clerk with the Manchester royal Infirmary. Later she taught briefly in a school in Heaton Chapel. However, in 1928, although only twenty-three, she set up her own junior school, Stamford School in Fairfield near Manchester and both John and Jessica were educated at that school by their own sister. (Plate 7-1). The twin sisters Dorothy and Marjorie led different lives. Dorothy had aspirations to become a nurse but this did not materialize until the outbreak of the Second World War as she stayed at home and helped Jesse with the other children instead. Marjorie became a secretary in Manchester. She was the most religious of the family and worked hard with the local church.

When Charles and Alf closed down the Leeds works Alf returned to Barry with his family and took over the Guthrie Street premises which Charles had retained. Alf set up a business manufacturing copper products, much like his brother Harry. There was a large copper-mining industry in South Wales and many such industries sprang up to exploit the mineral. The two brothers were not in competition and used to work together on many occasions. Alf died at a the relatively young age of forty-six in 1934 and his son Dudley Anthony (Tony) took over the Guthrie Street premises and set up a car repair business. This grew in size and moved to larger premises in Barry and became well known as Redrup Motors Limited. When Tony retired his son Simon took over the business. Simon himself has now retired but leases out the premises to a car sales company and still uses an office in the building on a regular basis. Alf also had two further sons, Frank who had a career in the Navy, and Arthur who was in the Royal Engineers and killed by a land-mine in Holland in 1944. Alf's eldest daughter Mary had a younger sister Joan

Plate 7-1 Florence (Centre) with Jessica on her left and John Middle Row fourth from Left

who married an engineer Elwyn Williams. In 1979 Elwyn became Mayor of Barry Town and Joan his Mayoress. Most recently, Elwyn became Mayor of the Vale of Glamorgan County Borough Council in 2004 with Joan again acting as Mayoress. (Plate 7-2).

Plate 7-2 Elwyn and Joan Williams,
Mayor and Mayoress of Barry Town, 1979

A.V.Roe, the company Charles had joined, was one of the foremost aircraft manufacturing organizations in the country, and had the distinction of having produced the most prolific and widely-used British aircraft of the First World War, the Avro 504K. Although this was a training machine A.V.Roe had also produced fighting aircraft many of which were variants of the 504, and a bomber, the Avro 529.

Alliott Verdon Roe (Plate 7-3), was born in 1877 in Manchester to Doctor Edwin Roe and his wife whose maiden name was Sofia Verdon. Alliott was the youngest of four sons and he together with his brother Humphrey to whom he was always very close went to St Paul's School where his interests seemed to be more sporting than academic. Despite his father's ambition that he should enter the medical profession Alliott soon made it clear that engineering was his chosen career, and as soon as he could at fourteen he went, through a friend of his father, to Canada to work in civil engineering. This did not prove a success as the country was entering a depression and so he returned to England and took an engineering training in the dockyard at Portsmouth. He also studied marine engineering at Kings College before going to sea as a junior engineer. Whilst on a voyage from England to Capetown he was attracted to the idea of flight from watching the endless soaring of the albatrosses which followed the ships. About this time news of the Wright Brothers flights started to circulate and Roe decided that this was the future. He built several model gliders based on the shape of albatross wings. Although these were not successful several later models were.

Plate 7-3 Alliott Verdon Roe

After a number of unsuccessful attempts to build flying machines on his own or with others he became Secretary to the *Aero Club of Great Britain*, having been interviewed by the Hon. C S Rolls, later of Rolls-Royce fame. He continued with his model studies, building ever larger craft, and also producing designs for a full-sized aircraft, which he patented. Curiously, although he had never flown in a man-carrying aircraft, in 1906 he patented a control system which replaced the two control levers used up to that time with one control column, which was very similar to the control column and wheel arrangement used to the present day. This patent was challenged some years later by a Frenchman who claimed a million pounds damages, but the action was successfully fought off.

Lord Northcliffe of the *Daily Mail*, who was to sponsor aviation for many years to come, offered a prize of £150 for a model capable of sustained flight. Alliott took the prize but because the judges were not impressed overall by the performance, he was only awarded the second

Plate 7-4 Humphrey Verdon Roe

prize of £75. Using the prize money, which was quite a lot in those days, he proceeded o build his own aircraft which he had designed. Another brother, Spencer, provided facilities in his coach-house in Putney, and Alliott negotiated the use of the Brooklands motor-racing track near Weybridge for trial flights. On the 8th June, 1908, A.V. Roe actually flew for the first time, but his short flights were not registered officially by *The Royal Aero Club*. The management at Brooklands were not very sympathetic to aviation and Alliott was eventually evicted, moving first to Hackney Marshes, and then to Wembley Park where he continued development of the biplane.

Alliott Verdon Roe's brother Humphrey (Plate 7-4) had by now become a successful business man and made a fortune from the manufacture of braces through his business Everard and Company, which he had purchased in a run-down state from his aunts. The name 'Everard' was a traditional Roe family name and Alliott had another brother named Everard who worked with him from time to time and who eventually went into the Church. Humphrey decided to back Alliott and the new venture A.V. Roe and Company became the first company ever to be registered as an airplane manufacturer.

Humphrey Roe was very generous towards his brother. He put up all the money and Alliott paid him one pound in consideration of the deal. Profits would be divided fifty-fifty but if the company failed, Humphrey would shoulder all financial responsibility. He took on finance, administration and management, leaving Alliott to get on with invention and design co-ordination. The manufacturing company was moved to the Everard factory in Manchester as an economy measure, and an A.V.Roe flying school was set up at Brooklands where a new, enlightened management had taken over. However work proceeded at such a pace that they outgrew Brooklands and the Flying School moved to Shoreham near Brighton, to establish the country's first airport. There development took place of a variety of triplanes and biplanes.

Alliott had decided to concentrate on design and manufacture and let his flying qualifications lapse. Instead he recruited a skilful test pilot, F.P.Raynham and two design engineers, R.J.Parrott and Roy Chadwick. Chadwick later became the Chief Designer for all A.V.Roe aircraft. R.H.Dobson also joined the company in 1914 as a works superintendent, and a young energetic manager from Everards, John Lord was brought in, who was also to become a director of A.V.Roe. With the coming of the First World War, A.V.Roe and Co. had a first rate training aircraft for the forces in the Avro 504J fitted with the Monosoupape rotary engine.

The quality of flying training in the early stages of the First World War was such that more injuries arose from pilot error rather than enemy action. The Commanding Officer of No. 60 Squadron, Major Robert Smith-Barry was so concerned about this that in 1916 he wrote to the General Officer in Command of the RFC explaining the problem and proposing a training school for instructors. The response was surprising and immediate and Smith-Barry suddenly found himself in command of No. 1 Reserve Flying School, based at Gosport in Hampshire with the

Plate 7-5 The Avro 504K

express role of training instructors. He was not only an expert flyer but proved also to be a natural instructor and evolved the training technique soon to become famous as the "Gosport" method. The School expanded to several more squadrons with Smith-Barry now a Colonel. He chose to standardise on the Avro 504J as the training aircraft because of its safe yet typically sensitive characteristics. He realised that an aircraft that was too easy to fly would not inculcate the necessary qualities required when flying more demanding aircraft.

It was a good basic design and A.V.Roe were told at one stage to expect to receive orders for up to 1200 aircraft a month. This was quite beyond the means of A.V.Roe alone and so sub-contracts were placed with a number of other companies. There was also another, more immediate problem. The 504J was designed around the Gnome Monosoupape engine and these had become in short supply. Engine manufacture took longer than airframes and it became obvious that this would be a bottleneck. So A.V.Roe re-designed the engine mounts to make it suitable for a wide variety of engines and proceeded to purchase all that they could lay their hands on. This "Universal" aircraft was designated the 504K, and so good was it that it became a standard trainer after the war and was developed into many versions. (Plate 7-5). In total, although production did not start in earnest until near the end of 1917, over eight thousand 504Ks were produced during the war, nearly half of these by A.V.Roe themselves. More 504K aircraft were produced during the war than any other aircraft. Smith-Barry worked closely with A.V.Roe to ensure that the aircraft was suited to his training needs. He arranged for a communication tube to be fitted between pupil and instructor, and this "Gosport Tube" as it became known was used widely in many aircraft until electrical intercoms became widespread.

During the war A.V.Roe had to move several times into larger premises to keep up with war production, finally ending up at Newton Heath, Manchester. In 1916 Alliott decided to build a water-side factory at Hamble on Southampton Water with a view to building seaplanes. Materials shortages put a constraint on production at Hamble and in the end only a few 504s were produced, but after the war Alliott moved the design and development teams to Hamble. His brother Everard managed this works at one time as well as being the vicar of the Hamble parish church.

In 1917 Humphrey Roe sold his interests in the Everard and A.V.Roe companies and joined the Royal Flying Corps. He really wanted to fly but being in his forties was considered too old. He persevered and was finally trained to fly as an observer and posted to the recently formed Royal Air Force. He was seriously injured in a night landing accident in the last months of hostilities but rejoined A.V.Roe after the war. In 1918 he married an extra-ordinary woman, Marie Stopes who had annulled her first marriage on the grounds of non-consummation because of her husband's impotence. Realising her ignorance on sexual matters she had researched the subject and had written a book, *"Married Love"* with advice for young brides. She used to comment wryly on the fact that the very first marriage guidance book was written by a virgin! The book was still in draft form when she married Humphrey but he arranged to have it published. Marie Stopes went on to set up marriage guidance and birth-control clinics and was the foundation of the enlightenment which led to women's suffrage and the liberation movement.

Following the war, production collapsed and A.V.Roe were reduced at times to manufacturing billiard tables and perambulators as well as re-furbishing and building small batches of 504s for the RFC. A.V.Roe did however attempt to produce a small aircraft based around the 35 horse-power Green engine. This aircraft, quickly named the "Baby" had a measure of success and several were manufactured at Hamble. Alliott Roe also designed a 12 horse-power sliding-head saloon car and plans were made to concentrate aircraft production at Hamble and use the Manchester factory for car production. The car was fitted with an epicyclic gearbox for which Alliott had purchased patent rights and production was well under way when the take-over of a controlling interest by Crossley Motors put a stop to it by mutual agreement. Alliott and John Lord were to stay on the Board and the MP Henry Fieldes was appointed Chairman. William Letts of Crossleys became Managing Director. This helped revive the fortunes of A.V.Roe with the production of Crossley motor bodies, but it was not until the mid-twenties that aircraft production started to make an upturn. In 1924 A.V.Roe's lease on their Manchester aerodrome at Alexander Park ran out and they purchased farmland near the village of Woodford, which became the A.V.Roe base from henceforth.

In 1920 A.V.Roe decided to produce a modernised version of the 504K with up to date engines and re-designed undercarriage. The 504 was best-suited to radial engines and a range of engines from 100 horse-power to 200 horse-power, but mainly Armstrong-Siddeley, were fitted to the new type, designated Avro 504N.

Up until this time the 504s had a skid-type undercarriage with rubber shock absorbers. The weight of an undercarriage was a serious penalty to

Plate 7-6 Redrup 1918 Five-cylinder Radial Engine on test in Avro Works

aircraft performance and so the design was kept as light as possible for the duty. Only if a customer specified arduous operating conditions would a strengthened undercarriage be fitted. In the A.V.Roe design office was a nineteen year old engineer, George Dowty who was interested in hydraulics. He designed a hydraulically-damped undercarriage for the Avro Aldershot bomber and pioneered the use of damped undercarriage and a hydraulically operated tail hook for deck landing trials of the incredibly ugly Avro Bison. He designed the undercarriage arrangement whereby the first movement of the axle would be taken up by an oleo-type damper leg with oil forced through a dashpot, before the rubber compression blocks became effective. This enabled less rubber weight to be carried and provided a much more robust performance. The same concept was used for the new 504N aircraft. The long nose skid was still retained for the prototype 504N but this was discarded in most production versions, when the oleo type of undercarriage had been further developed by 1923. Many hundreds of these aircraft were built before production ceased in 1927, and used by air forces and navies all around the world for the robust design was well suited to landing on carriers.

George Dowty left A.V.Roe in 1924 to go and work for the Bristol Aeroplane Company and then went on to set up his own company manufacturing undercarriages and propellers. In later years he extended his expertise in hydraulics to also manufacture powered pit-props for the mining industry, and he was to re-appear as a colleague in Charles Redrup's later career.

As the aircraft industry revived in 1925, Alliott Roe wanted a lighter, simpler aircraft to meet the growing leisure aviation market and as a replacement for the 504K trainer. This aircraft was the only really profitable business at that time and was being challenged by the new de Havilland Moths. As a short-term measure he set his designers the task of taking the best of the 504 series of aircraft and modifying it to meet the perceived need. He also put in hand the design of a new lightweight aircraft, destined to become the Avian. Meanwhile his designers took the 504J design and devised a lightweight mount for the 100 horse-power Gnome Monosoupape engine. They reworked and cost-engineered every part of the airframe and reduced the weight from 1,830 pounds (832 kg) to 1,690 pounds (768 kg). The ailerons were redesigned with taper to create an aircraft with the delightful yet docile handling characteristics of the 504J. For economy the skid-type undercarriage was retained.

But Alliott also had another agenda. He invited Charles Redrup to test his 1918 five-cylinder radial engine (Plate 7-6) in the A.V.Roe works in Manchester, which Charles did with evident satisfaction to Roe. Roe wanted to fit an engine of A.V.Roe manufacture to the new aircraft and thus it was that in 1925 he recruited Charles to design a 100 horse-power engine based on the 1918 radial. The new aircraft was designated the Avro 504R Gosport in honour of the Flying School at their base in Hampshire. It first flew with the Gnome Monosoupape engine in June 1926, but Alliott did not consider this engine, with all the idiosyncrasies of a rotary, to be suitable for private fliers and so the engine mount was designed from the start to also take the Redrup engine as soon as it became available.

Charles was based at the A.V.Roe Newton Heath factory but spent a lot of time visiting nearby Crossley Motors where production engines would be made. He also spent a lot of time travelling to the A.V.Roe development department at Hamble. Within six months of his arrival at the Company

Plate 7-7 The Australian Flying Ace H.J. (Bert) Hinkler

the first engine incorporating his close-finning design much like the Hart engine had been hand-made. When it was put on test it achieved its designed output of 100 horse-power straight away. It was designated the Avro Alpha I. A smaller three-cylinder version, the seventy horse-power Beta was planned, and a single cylinder for this rated at 24 horse-power was put into manufacture for test in the A.V.Roe works. Charles also designed a newer version of the Alpha, the Alpha II which incorporated modified valvegear but would not be ready for test until April 1927. Eventually A.V.Roe contracted with Crossley Motors to build a further six Alphas on a production basis, with even more orders anticipated. In addition Charles was also working on the five-cylinder axial car engine for Crossley Motors and had become drawn into developing bomb-carrying crates for some of the A.V.Roe military aircraft projects.

The first two Gosports G-EBNE and G-EBNF with Gnome engines were built at Hamble and were fitted with the 504J type of undercarriage with nose skid and rubber blocks. The first one was used for development work. In 1926 the Lancashire Aero Club was founded and based at Woodford and the A.V.Roe managing Director Sir William Letts donated the second Gosport G-EBNF to the Club in April of that year. It was loaned back to A.V.Roe almost immediately however and was used by test pilot Bert Hinkler for a demonstration to foreign government representatives at Croydon Airport a few days later. The third Gosport, G-EBOX, the first to be built at Woodford, was also demonstrated by Hinkler in July 1926 at a meeting of the Yorkshire Aero Club with immediate success. The aircraft was sold on the spot to the Argentinean Government and several overseas orders were received.

Herbert John Hinkler, (Plate 7-7), was born in Bundaberg, Queensland in December 1892. He was the son of a mill worker and was fascinated by the idea of flying. From 1911 to 1913 at Mon Repos Beach near Bundaberg he flew manned gliders and later in 1913 Bert moved to England and worked for a while for the Sopwith Company. He served during the First World War and was awarded the Distinguished Service Medal. In 1919 he joined A.V.Roe in Southampton and was their Chief Test Pilot from 1921 to1926, testing many new types and setting records.

In January 1920 Roy Chadwick who had recently gained his pilot's licence took the second prototype Avro Baby up for a cross-country flight from Hamble. He had not flown more than a short distance when a downdraft blew him into treetops and he crashed into the garden of Everard Roe's vicarage! Chadwick was seriously injured and it was many months before he could walk unaided, but this did not stop him directing operations from his sickbed. The aircraft was virtually written off but was re-built using some of the components and the engine. From his brief flight experience Chadwick proposed some modifications which were incorporated into the re-build. Bert Hinkler came to an arrangement with Alliott Roe and purchased the aircraft for a nominal amount as he was planning a spectacular inter-continental flight. (Plate 7-8).

Plate 7-8 The Avro "Baby"

In May 1921 he took off from Croydon and on only twenty gallons of fuel, he flew non-stop to Turin. The trip took nine and a half hours for the 650 mile flight and he then flew on to Rome. His intention was to fly home to Australia but engine trouble put a stop to that objective and he returned to Hamble in short hops. His original objective was not widely known and he received wide acclaim for his feat, being awarded the Britannia Trophy for the year's most outstanding flight. From then on Bert Hinkler became a household name. Between 1920 and 1931 he made many record flights both in Great Britain and internationally. Hinkler's Baby was exhibited at the Olympia Aero Show in July 1920 and drew large crowds. Afterwards Hinkler flew it to second place in the Aerial Derby Handicap race.

Sadly, in 1933 whilst attempting another record flying solo from England to Australia in a de Havilland Leopard Moth, Bert Hinkler was killed in a mountain-top crash in Italy. Before this however he added further achievements to his record.

The second prototype Gosport G-EBNF owned by the Lancashire Aero Club suffered several problems with the Monosoupape engine and did not fly much until the following year. By summer of 1926 the 100 horse-power Alpha I engine was ready for flight trials and it was installed in the fourth Gosport, G-EBPH which was also built at the Woodford works and had its maiden flight in September. This aircraft had a streamlined nose to accommodate the compact Alpha engine, and was the first to use steel interplane struts of a narrow chord section. It also used tapered ailerons which gave much lighter control forces. (Plate 7-9). The aircraft and engine combination was very successful and many flights were made over the next three months.

The Lancashire Aero Club, like a number of flying clubs established about the same time, arose from an Air Ministry decision in November 1924 to sponsor the formation of such clubs. Ramsay MacDonald formed the first Labour Government in January 1924 and immediately took steps to boost employment. Amongst other things he appointed Lord Thompson and Air Vice-Marshal Sir Sefton Brancker to set up an Air Ministry and to raise the profile of civil aviation and give assistance to the aircraft manufacturers who were still suffering from the aftermath of the war cancellations. By giving subsidies to clubs rather than industry the Ministry avoided accusations of favouritism, yet club purchases boosted aircraft sales and development. The Lancashire Aero Club purchased two De Havilland 60 Moths plus a spare engine under the scheme, one of which, G-EBLV is still in immaculate flying condition today. The donation by A.V.Roe of the Gosport G-EBNF was also intended to boost interest in aviation and to publicise A.V.Roe

Plate 7-9 Alpha-Engined Gosport G-EBPH with 504K-Type Nose-Skid

aircraft. The erratic behaviour of the Gnome Monosoupape engine was therefore something of an embarrassment.

The Ministry was keen to further aviation in a number of ways and John Leeming of the Lancashire Aero Club considered that whilst Woodford was fine for aircraft manufacture and development, it was not well-suited for enlargement to meet his vision of an expanding civil aviation industry. He therefore started petitioning for Manchester to have an airport of its own.

John Leeming went to school in Birkdale, near Southport, and it was his observation of the pioneering efforts to fly aircraft from nearby Freshfield Sands that inspired him to start a flying career. He made his first monoplane glider of twenty foot wingspan in 1910 out of bamboo and piano wire and took it on to the sand dunes nearby, but he was too heavy for the craft, causing the wings to bend alarmingly upwards. He and his assistant Alan Goodfellow made three more gliders without real success but their efforts taught them many valuable lessons.

In 1922 Leeming started to design his fifth glider as a cheap way to get into the air. He knew that A.V.Roe had made over eight thousand Avro 504K trainers, and many were then stored but unwanted. Clement Wood of the A.V.Roe Sales staff became a firm friend and together with Tom Prince an A.V.Roe foreman they built a glider, the LPW which showed clear resemblances to the Avro 504K. LPW stood for Leeming,

Prince and Wood. The gliding group grew to be ten strong, and flew initially from Alexander Park airfield. When this closed they moved to Woodford to form the Lancashire Aero Club.

Leeming stalled and crashed the LPW at Alexander Park and it was re-built with an engine. Although it was too heavy to fly it was used for taxiing practice. When the embryo aero club got the De Havilland 60 Cirrus-powered Moths in 1925, they were able to start flying in earnest. Leeming created the stunt flying routine in which he pretended to be a novice flyer accidentally taking off without his instructor and getting into all sorts of scrapes. Such flying actually requires exceptional skill and Leeming invented flour bombing and picking up a handkerchief from the ground using a spike on the wingtip.

In March 1925 our old friend C G Grey published a picture of Mount Snowdon in *The Aeroplane* and his editorial remarked that, until an aeroplane could land on a mountain and take off again, aviation would still not have come of age. This appears to have stuck in the mind of Sir Sefton Brancker, for at a private dinner the following summer, Brancker, who was now Director of Civil Aviation, jokingly suggested to John Leeming that he should show Grey what he could do! They agreed that such a feat would do wonders for civil aviation, and if a suitable mountain could be found, would help their campaign for an airport for Manchester.

At the Lancashire Aero Club's second meeting, the Aero Pageant on September the 25th 1926, Flying Officer H D Waghorn had carried out a display flight with the Redrup Alpha-powered Gosport G-EBPH and then gone on to win the Open Handicap race in the same aircraft. This race was round a twenty-eight mile course with turning points at Marple and Knutsford and the performance was described by the correspondent of *The Aeroplane* as being miraculous for such a new engine and aeroplane and he remarked that ownership of such a combination would be "a very pleasing property." Waghorn went on to win the Schneider Trophy Race in 1929 flying the Supermarine S6, which was the predecessor to the Spitfire.

Leeming, who was now Chairman of the Club, approached Brancker who was present, with a firm proposal to land an aircraft on top of Snowdon. Brancker was very supportive and so Leeming then approached the A.V.Roe Board for support, but one of the A.V.Roe directors lived close to Snowdon and knew it intimately. He told the Board that such a landing was impossible and so A.V.Roe rejected the proposal. Leeming then did further research and found that there was a flat area on Helvellyn near to the summit. He put this option to A.V.Roe

Plate 7-10 Alpha-Powered Gosport G-EBPH
Fitted with Dowty Undercarriage

and this time they were very supportive, seeing it as a way to promote A.V.Roe aircraft. With the new Redrup Alpha engine now performing so well in the Gosport, they also saw it as a means to promote the A.V.Roe-manufactured aero engine. The aircraft was prepared for the flight and in particular the skid-type undercarriage was replaced by the Dowty-designed oleo undercarriage from the 504N. It was also further strengthened to suit a hard landing on an uneven surface. The Gosport was re-designated Avro 585 in this form. (Plate 7-10).

The plan was for Leeming to land on the 3,118 foot high Helvellyn peak in the Lake District, which was just a short flying time away. He would leave a letter to the manager of the Thirlmere Waterworks on the cairn at the summit to prove that he had actually landed.

Leeming had been told that there was a flat area, as smooth as a billiard table near the top. He had climbed the mountain to survey it, and had indeed found that there was a flat area at the top with clear approaches from most directions, but not only was it as smooth as a billiard table, it was also only about the same size! Bert Hinkler would accompany him in another aircraft and would be accompanied by a correspondent of *The Manchester Guardian*, Walter Doughty who would report the event and as the newspaper's first official photographer, take photographs.

On 15th December 1926 the two aircraft took off from Woodford and headed for the Lake District. Unfortunately the hail and snow was of such severity that the attempt had to be abandoned and they returned to

Plate 7-11 Alpha-Powered Gosport over a Storm at Lancaster

Woodford. Plate 7-11 shows Walter Doughty's photograph of the Gosport flying over a storm at Lancaster. It was not for another six days that they were able to make a second attempt.

On 21st December conditions were suitable and the Gosport was started up. However the Armstrong-Siddeley engine in Hinkler's aircraft would not produce full power. After some discussion and with much reluctance they decided that Hinkler would travel as passenger with Leeming and that Walter Doughty would have to be left behind. As a poor substitute Leeming took with him his little Box Brownie. They knew from their previous flights that the Gosport could easily lift their combined weight up to the necessary altitude. John suspected that Bert's engine had failed to run properly because he had "inadvertently" forgotten to turn on one of the magnetos! From Leeming's memoirs it appears he was very relieved to have had Bert Hinkler with him!

All went well up to Lancaster where they landed to re-fuel. After take-off visibility was excellent and they arrived within striking distance of the 3,118 foot high Helvellyn. (See colour plate C12). The wind was so strong however that to attempt to land would court disaster. They flew around for about an hour and a half hoping conditions would improve but then had to return to Lancaster to re-fuel. For the return to Woodford Bert Hinkler was in command as he wanted to get the aircraft away from the windy coast to hanger the aircraft. However on take-off the engine mis-fired and he put his skills to good use by turning the aircraft around to make a tricky cross-wind landing. On examination it was found that the carburettor and filters were blocked with sediment. By then it was too late to fly and so Bert and John protected the Gosport as best they could by parking it in a hedge and then tramped into Lancaster.

After staying overnight in a local hotel, to their horror they found that they only had four shillings and sixpence (22 1/2 New Pence) between them! The hotel proprietor was most unhelpful but they telephoned the proprietor of Atkinson's Garage, who as well as promising them assistance with cleaning the engine filters, loaned them sufficient funds for the overnight stay.

Chapter 8
To Helvellyn and Back

The next day, 22nd December had better weather. Visibility was good but, more importantly, the wind had dropped. The garage proprietor helped them to professionally clean the filters and plugs and after some debate they decided to make another attempt on the mountain. Its engine purring smoothly, the Avro Gosport made slow time to the mountains. The air was very turbulent and made flying uncomfortable. Bert Hinkler was lifted right out of his seat and the cushion flew out of the cockpit. John Leeming who was holding the letter to the Water-Works manager was also thrown upwards only to see the letter whisked out of his hand and carried away in the slipstream. Only their safety belts stopped them also being thrown out. At one point the aircraft hit a huge downdraft which dropped them by five hundred feet in a few seconds.

As they approached the Lake District they saw Helvellyn rearing out of the clouds. Banking steeply and turning into the wind the aircraft buffeted and reared in the turbulence rolling off the mountain. The co-pilot Bert Hinkler craned his neck out of the cockpit looking for the cleared area a few hundred feet below the summit. This was their third attempt to land on the mountain, and weather conditions today were very much better, albeit not perfect.

Hinkler shouted over the noise of the slipstream, guiding Leeming westwards towards the cleared area for an initial flyby. Reducing power, the aircraft nosed towards the ground but Leeming noticed that despite reducing his airspeed the speed over the ground was increasing. At this altitude, because of the strange wind patterns around the mountain the wind was actually behind him, from the north-east.

Climbing away again from the area, whilst Leeming piloted, Hinkler looked back to assess the situation. He realised that they could not turn to land into the wind because the cleared strip, on a rocky ledge, had an obstructed approach from that direction. He saw on the peak of the mountain a speck-like figure, sheltering behind a cairn and watching mesmerised as they circled once again. They knew from their previous climb that there was a small flat but narrow area at the very peak, but it was not aligned with the prevailing wind. However, with the current wind conditions it was just possible to approach it into wind. Hinkler shouted his suggestion to Leeming who swooped down once again over the peak to assess the new landing area.

As they passed the black-clad figure on the top of the mountain Hinkler could clearly make out his walking gear and cane. The head wind was so strong that the aircraft seemed virtually stationary as they sailed past almost at walking pace. Bert could see the surface of the mountain top, and was relieved to see it clear of stones. He remembered as a child climbing the mountain, and throwing small stones over the edge. Generations of children and walkers must have scoured the surface clean. Bert shouted to John through the Gosport tube that he thought a landing on the peak was possible, and John gave a thumbs-up sign in agreement.

Swooping back up John circled the area into an approach pattern. He gradually reduced power and the aircraft slowed and reared up into its landing attitude. As the speed washed off the controls became more sluggish and John needed to correct with large inputs to the rudder. At these speeds use of aileron was not only ineffective but dangerous as a stall could result. The aircraft started to sink rapidly as the drag increased and John corrected with a boost in power. The engine responded superbly and the Gosport inched forward against the wind, buffeted by the gusts around the mountain peak, but staying on track for the small flat area. As the aircraft touched the ground it bounced and lurched but John cut the throttle and thankfully the sturdy Gosport stopped in a very short distance, but still disturbingly close to the sheer Striding Edge of the mountain.

Whilst John held the machine from sliding backwards with the engine throttle, clambering out of the aircraft, Bert immediately used stones to secure the wheels against the gusting wind and the sloping ground. As he did so he was approached by an incredulous man, who congratulated them on their feat. He was the walker they had seen on the mountain from the air. By immense good fortune he turned out to be E. R. Dodds, Professor of Greek at Birmingham University, on a lone walking tour of the peaks. John locked the throttle to a setting that held the aircraft against the wind and with the wheels securely chocked he climbed out of the aircraft.

Bert took some photographs and they then set about trying to improvise a certificate for the professor to sign. Neither Leeming nor Hinkler could find a scrap of paper but Professor Dodds found an old hotel bill in one of his pockets and John drafted out a statement :-

"I hereby certify that an aeroplane, G-EBPH, pilots Bert Hinkler and John Leeming, has landed on the summit of Helvellyn on Dec. 22nd 1926."

Professor Dodds was 33 and a more prestigious and suitable witness to their feat could not be imagined. In due course Dodds went on in 1936 to become Regius Professor of Greek at Oxford where he remained until his retirement in 1960. He signed the certificate and John Leeming took photographs of the event with his Box Brownie (Plate 8-1)

Plate 8-1 Professor Dodds (Left) and Bert Hinkler on the Summit of Helvellyn

Soon it was time to leave, and they manoeuvred the Gosport to point into the wind. With the professor steadying one wing they climbed aboard. Leeming pushed the throttle wide open and the aircraft surged forward. The Gosport reached the sheer cliff of the mountain barely achieving flying speed, and dived over Striding Edge. As the wings bit the air, the aircraft steadied, then soared upwards over Red Tarn, famous for its small, sweet trout, under the smooth power of the Redrup Alpha engine.

After Leeming and Hinkler made their precarious take-off from the summit of Helvellyn they descended to land in a field at Windermere to re-fuel. They then returned in triumph to Woodford. The publicity following the flight outclassed anyone's expectations and made a lasting impression about aviation on the public. A memorial was erected on the summit of Helvellyn at about the point where the landing took place but not untypically, neither the Alpha engine nor Charles Redrup got a mention. Throughout his career Charles seemed to have the credit for his work taken

Plate 8-2 John Leeming with the Gosport on the Summit of Helvellyn

by others. In 1988 however the memorial stone was found to be severely damaged by weather and replaced. The replacement stone does credit the Avro Gosport but the Alpha engine is not mentioned. (See colour plate C13).

Walter Doughty got his scoop for *The Manchester Guardian*, even if it was with John Leeming's Box Brownie photographs! (Plate 8-2).

Leeming and Brancker were successful in their campaign to get an airport for Manchester, and Barton Airport was opened on 2nd April 1929. It was superseded in 1938 by a larger airport at Ringway, which became a military base during the Second World War and is now a major international airport. Leeming demonstrated his confidence in the new industry by founding an air taxi and cargo airline to give the new Barton airport some initial purpose. Sadly Sir Sefton Brancker was killed in the R101 crash at Beauvais in October 1930. The Air Ministry received much criticism for the accident and it was alleged that the design, construction and putting into service had been too hastily implemented to enable Lord Thompson to make a prestigious visit to India. John Leeming's clear recollection in his memoirs however, was that Brancker, although a hard driver to achieve, was also very fair and being ex-RAF himself, safety conscious, open to constructive criticism and would not have embarked on the journey if he believed it to be in any way unsafe to do so.

Bert Hinkler continued with A.V.Roe for a little longer and was instrumental in popularising their next venture, the Avro Avian. When he left A.V.Roe to pursue his other aviation interests, his post as Chief Test Pilot was taken over by Sam Brown. A painting of the scene of the Alpha-engined Gosport at the summit of Helvellyn was made by an accomplished amateur artist Peter Nield of the A.V.Roe Structural Test Department, (Frontispiece) and owned for many years by Roy Chadwick. This now hangs in the Hinkler Museum in Bundaberg Australia along with many other artefacts, including the Avian in which he flew from England to Australia in 1927.

The success of the Alpha I engine was very welcome to A.V.Roe and they eagerly awaited the tests on the new Alpha II model, which started in April 1927. At the same time tests on the single-cylinder prototype for the Beta engine got underway. We are fortunate in having Charles Redrup's detailed notebook for this period and the following is based on his notes.

On Wednesday 20th April 1927 the 24 horse-power single cylinder test bed model of the 70 horse-power engine was started up at four thirty and developed its 24 horse-power straight away at 1800 rpm, and then 26 horse-power at 2000 rpm. It had a five to one compression ratio but even at this modest compression it was apparent that the ignition was set too far in advance and the engine had to be run with the ignition fully retarded on the magneto to stop pre-ignition. There were also distinct signs of the airflow being too small to keep the cylinder properly cooled. Charles pointed this out to John Hubble the General Manager and to Roy Dobson the Works Manager.

John Hubble had come to A.V.Roe from Crossley Motors, where he was still a director. Charles knew him well and had a great respect for him, but he was less enamoured of Roy Dobson who he considered impatient and technically ignorant. Dobson told him to continue running, and so the engine had to carry on under these very adverse conditions. There was only a three horse-power fan to cool the engine.

Meanwhile Dobson stopped all work on the full 70 horse-power Beta engine until the problem could be resolved.

Charles worked overnight and devised an improved cooling arrangement for the single cylinder and when it was started at 7.30 a.m. the next day it ran until 6.00 p.m. and was found to be much cooler and in good order. The valve guides and valves were examined and showed no undue wear. The engine ran again the next day from 7.30 a.m. until 5.00 p.m. perfectly satisfactorily, so on Saturday 23rd April Dobson ordered work to start again on the 70 horse-power engine. Manufacture of the exhaust valve cages and other parts were put in hand. Meanwhile the single cylinder engine was running satisfactorily having done 25 hours without trouble.

On Monday 25th April the single cylinder engine was running satisfactorily and Mr Walker the Works Manager came in at about 11.00 a.m. with Roy Dobson whilst the engine was running. With Charles' agreement they decided to stop the engine and examine the exhaust valve and its guide. The valve and guide were examined and found to be in excellent condition. They appeared to have run very cool but with some carbon formed around the stem of valve on the lower part of guide. The clearance for the valve in its guide was always critical for if it was too tight, when the valve-stem heated up it could seize in the guide causing a stuck valve. If the fit was too loose excessive oil could seep along the guide and carbonise with the heat, eventually causing friction and again, a stuck valve. The examination showed that much less clearance could be given for the stem in the guide. It was agreed to assemble the engine again and run on indefinitely. The engine ran again all next day and Charles put in hand the valve guide modifications on the full-size Beta engine.

A month later on Tuesday 23rd May the Alpha II engine had completed preliminary bench testing and in the light of this was being modified. Work was carried out to fit new exhaust cages and to re-metal the big end bearings. A new back cover was fitted with a drain from a rib back into the casing to do away with an external drain pipe from the back of the engine. A new magneto and pump housing with modifications to mount new magnetos was also installed. The engine was finished and re-mounted in the test bed and started running-in ready to do a preliminary test on the next day.

On Wednesday 24th May at about 4.00 pm. the Alpha II engine was run at ninety percent full power and held 81 brake horse-power where it was quite steady. For the last five minutes it was opened up to 101 horse-power at 1800 rpm, but the oil temperature was too high. Charles made some changes to the oil cooler pipework and readied the engine for a sustained power run. For these tests the engine was suspended in a cradle and the casing was attached to a long arm which carried a balance weight. As the engine power was increased the balance weight was changed to counteract the torque. This form of dynamometer gives an accurate measure of brake horse-power by multiplying the torque figure by the engine speed. A test run was carried out next day to check out the revised oil cooling which proved satisfactory. The engine was run for a two-hour test at 80.75 horse-power and 1700 rpm with a weight on the brake of 57 pounds (26.0 kg). The oil consumption was 2 pints (1.1 litres) per hour and the oil temperature a very acceptable 75° C.

The next day, 26th May, Charles took a power curve:-

90 horse-power 5 cylinder radial engine 4” 5 /8 bore x 5” stroke. (117 mm x 127 mm).

Rpm	Dyno-Weight, pounds	Brake Horse-power
1000	64	53.25
1100	59	54
1200	64	64
1300	66	71.4
1400	67	78
1500	68	85.7
1600	69	92
1700	68.5	96.5
1800	66	98.5
1900	64	101
2000	64	106.5

After this very successful power run Charles examined the engine and prepared it for a fifty-hour acceptance test. It was necessary to fit a new piston and a new gear plate owing to faulty material. The run was started on Friday 3rd of June and ran satisfactorily for ten hours. The test was repeated for ten hours the following day again at ninety horse-power and it was then taken to an outside test stand for a run using a propeller as load.

On Monday 6th and Tuesday 7th of June the engine was run at ninety horse-power using the propeller and it was opened up for five minutes at the end of the second test to 1975 rpm but the power output fell off badly almost immediately. It was concluded by the works staff that the engine was over heated especially as the air speed was not more than 50 mph past the cylinder heads. However Charles was not convinced that it was due to overheating and during the test next day when the engine ran for another ten hours at ninety horse-power he discussed his thoughts with Roy Dobson and the works staff Mr Bolsover and Mr Walker.

The latter was concerned about the seriousness of the engine over-heating and being incapable of opening up to full rpm for the last five minutes as this was an essential part of the acceptance test, to simulate an engine's capacity to sustain a short-term overload. Charles told them all that in his opinion the engine was not over-heating and that the trouble was due to faulty carburettion. He made the point that the engine did not overheat on the dynamometer and that it was because much more heat was supplied to the carburettor on the dynamometer than on the propeller test. There was an exhaust heated muff on the induction pipe just above the carburettor and this was a heated 3/4" bore pipe (19 mm) when the engine was on the dynamometer. This was completely shielded from the cooling fan, being behind the engine mounting frame. In the case of the engine on the propeller test the exhaust gas for heating the muff was through a pipe about 3' long (0.9 metres), and was exposed mainly to the slipstream from the propeller. This arrangement had the effect of supplying very much less heat to the carburettor through the heating muff with the consequence being that the engine would run well at part throttle but would not maintain sufficient heat to hold full throttle.

Before opening the engine up to full throttle for the last five minutes it was agreed to shield the pipe from the air stream. This was done with a piece of jointing sheet, a strip of which was clipped over the part of the pipe carrying the heat from the exhaust pipe of one of the cylinders to the induction muff. This shielding of the pipe was a rather dangerous procedure to carry out while the engine was running. However, it appeared that the shielding was better fixed than was realised as Charles observed that the end of the strip of shielding acted as a scoop and carried a great deal of hot exhaust gas around the outside of the heating pipe as well as shielding a great deal of it from the propeller blast. This had the good effect of enabling the carburettion to be more effective. The engine was opened up to 1975 rpm and maintained this for five minutes without showing any signs of overheating.

The tests continued on Tuesday 14th of June when the engine registered 108.5 horse-power and the next day it ran for a further ten hours at ninety horse-power to complete the fifty-hour test. It was opened up for the last hour to full power and for the last 5 minutes to full throttle at 97 horse-power and 1700 rpm. John Hubble and Roy Dobson were present for the last five minutes. Further tests were carried out two days later and for a full throttle test at maximum speed, 101.5 horse-power was achieved at 1860 rpm.

Over the next few days the engine was dismantled and examined for general condition and to measure wear. All parts were found to be in good order with no undue wear. One piston ring had broken and one had stuck in its piston groove and Charles attributed this to the engine being over heated on the propeller stand when there was not enough heat on the carburettor. The engine was re-assembled and re-tested for half an hour. It did not show good power as there was not enough heat on the carburettor with the pipe too far away to collect sufficient carburettor heating. As a result of this the carburettor heating muff was nearly cold. Major Buliman from the Air Ministry was present during the half hour and felt the carburettor muff with his hand and remarked how cold it was.

John Hubble asked Charles to go to Roy Dobson's office and to take the general arrangement drawings of engine. When Charles went in, Dobson said that he had decided to make six more engines, one engine to be the of the same materials as the present engine and rated at maximum power of one hundred horse-power and two more of the same materials at the present power of ninety horse-power. He also wanted to build three engines of cheaper materials in which the forgings and high-tensile steels would be replaced by castings and ordinary steels. One of these would be rated at one hundred horse-power and two others of ninety horse-power. Charles' memory flitted back to the arguments with Alban Richards and Vickers over cheap materials for the "Barry" and "Hart" engines but on this occasion he held his counsel.

Dobson also asked Charles to sign two Patent Specifications concerning some of the engine parts, in the joint names of A V Roe Limited and Charles Redrup. He told Charles that the test engine was to be fitted into a Gosport machine, (Probably G-EBNE) for a trial flight, and then it was intended to be fitted into an Avian to enter for the King's Cup Race at the end of July.

These notes enable us to see into the heart of Charles Redrup, and to understand some of the tedium, frustration and joys experienced in the test shop when developing a new engine. In particular it highlights the misunderstandings which can arise when management lacking technical knowledge tries to get involved in the process!

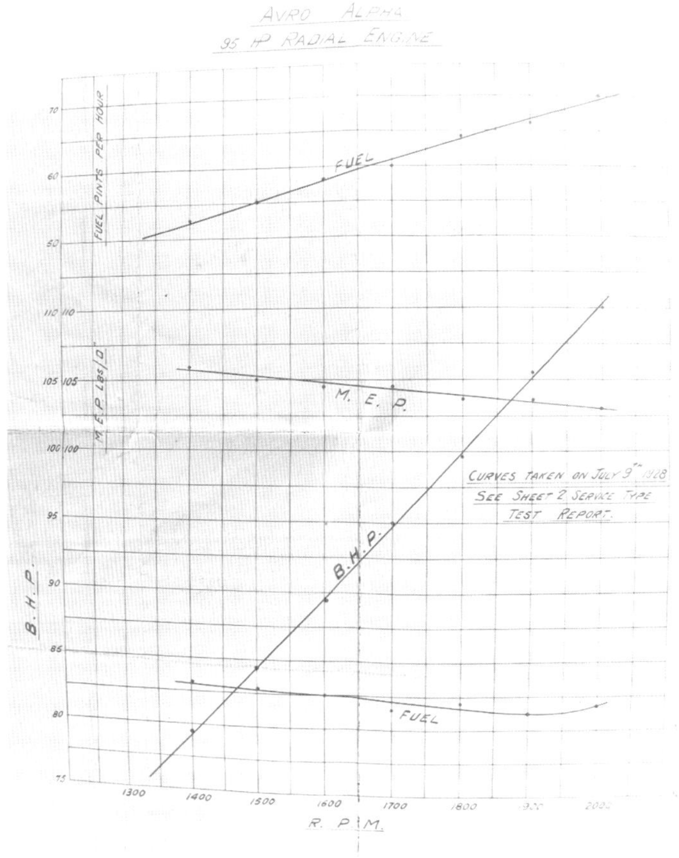

Plate 8-3 Test Results for an Alpha II Engine

The Alpha engine was a five-cylinder radial engine which incorporated Charles Redrup's close-finning design. It had a bore of 4 5/8 inches (117 mm) and a stroke of five inches (127 mm) giving an engine capacity of 6.83 litres. It also incorporated his push-rod design in which double rods ensured that there was no transverse force on the valve stem, making for smooth operation and low wear. The nominal power of the Alpha was 100 horse-power but for certification purposes it was declared at 90 horse-power. The results of a test on another engine on 9th July 1928 is shown in Plate 8-3 where it is seen that 110 horse-power was readily achieved but that best fuel economy in terms of fuel consumption per horse-power was achieved at 100 horse-power.

During 1927 Charles' design for the Crossley axial car engine became reality and the engine (Plate 8-4) was fitted into a Crossley Motors Limited car. This engine was based on the earlier six-cylinder two-stroke marine engine but had five cylinders as an odd number was better-suited to a four-stroke engine. The car was extensively tested by Crossleys who drove it backwards and forwards over the Snake pass between Manchester and Sheffield.

Plate 8-4 Redrup-Crossley Five-Cylinder Axial Motor Car Engine

The Redrup story continues with the Gosport machine, but attention at Avros was now turning to their new light aircraft, the Avian.

Juan de Cierva the Spanish inventor had experimented with giroplane designs in 1920 and in 1924 built his first successful autogiro, the Cierva C.6A using an old Avro 504K fuselage fitted with out-rigger ailerons from a Bristol Fighter. He also purchased from A.V.Roe the 504N undercarriage. The machine was constructed in Madrid and after progressive testing, was flown under perfect control to 650 feet and then landed gently almost vertically with a forward speed of only fifteen miles per hour. Alliott Roe made several visits to Madrid to advise on the 504 structure and became a personal friend of Cierva. Several historic flights were made with successive aircraft and Cierva was invited to demonstrate his craft at Farnborough in 1925.

Plate 8-5 Don Juan de la Cierva

Don Juan de la Cierva, (Plate 8-5), was born in Murcia in Spain in September 1895. Whilst he was interested in flight as a teenager and experimented at the age of fifteen with gliders with his friends, he took a civil engineering degree. He soon turned to aviation again and in 1918 he built his first aircraft, a tri-motor. It stalled and crashed in 1919 and he became convinced that the future of aviation lay in stall-proof aircraft that could make steep takeoffs and landings at slow speeds. He knew that the only way to do that was either to have sufficient engine thrust to overcome the weight of the aircraft, or to have rotating wings. At that time engine power was far too low to overcome gravity directly and it is only in the last thirty years that this has been routinely used in aircraft such as the Harrier. Cierva analysed the subject of helicopter-type lift but concluded that the current state of the art precluded this. He began experimenting with rotating-wing aircraft in 1920 and developed the autogiro as a more stable form of aircraft. His first attempt, the Cierva C.1 with a rigid rotor attached to a converted 1911 Deperdussin monoplane fuselage failed to lift off. Next he built models C.2 and C.3

with different fuselages and fixed rotor blades but these were similarly unsuccessful in that whilst they would lift off, they were uncontrollable. In such an arrangement the rotor blades have a fixed angle of attack and lift can only be controlled by varying rotor speed. As soon as the aircraft starts to move forward the lift on the forward blade increase and that on the retreating blade reduces, causing the craft to keel over. In practice even the slightest drift in any direction results in instability.

Cierva then applied the idea of mounting the blades to the hub of the rotor on hinges so they could flap up and down. By angling the axis of the hinge-line the blades can be made to flap such that the advancing blade has reduced lift and the retreating blade has increased lift, thus compensating for the altered relative airspeed over the blade when the craft is in forward flight. His first successful flight with the C.4 machine took place on January 9 1923. The craft was equipped with a conventional propeller for forward flight and a rotor with hinged blades that could be adjusted to balance lift. It was this automatic compensating property that gave the autogiro its name. By pre-spinning the rotor blades by hand or by a rope wrapped around the shaft the aircraft could move forward under the power of the forward thrust and the blades then continue to rotate automatically because the forward-moving blades have less drag than the retreating blades. Sufficient lift is generated to enable the aircraft to take off at very low forward speeds. Thus Cierva realised his dream of an aircraft that cannot stall and can manoeuvre at low speeds whilst having a reasonable high-speed capability. After the success with the C.4 he was able to get Spanish Government funding for his next research aircraft which was the one using Avro 504 parts.

The autogiro at this stage had to be steered using ailerons on stub wings with a conventional rudder. His major achievement in which the rotor hub was mounted on a moveable head which was attached to a control stick was made whilst Cierva was working with A.V.Roe. The pilot could thereby direct the rotor in the direction of desired travel. Eventually the design progressed to the point where the stub wings could be dispensed with entirely. Cierva went on to work with a number of manufacturers and his work on articulated rotor blades made possible the eventual solution to the helicopter problem. Ironically he died in a conventional aircraft crash on the outskirts of London in 1936, the year of the first successful true helicopter flight by Igor Sikorski.

Prior to this however, in 1925 further tests on the C.6A autogiro led to an order by the Air Ministry for two autogiros to be built under licence by A.V.Roe. The first, the Avro 574 was flown at Hamble in June 1926

Plate 8-6 Two-Seat Avro 587 Autogiro

but it crashed at Worthy Down in January 1927 due to fatigue of a blade root. This accident convinced Cierva that as well as flapping up and down, the blades of the rotor should be able to flex fore and aft to absorb tangential stresses, and he developed a hinge joint that enabled this without allowing complete freedom. The second fuselage, (Plate 8-6), the Avro 587 was the first two-seat autogiro and Cierva, piloted by the German pilot Ernst Udet, became the first passenger to fly in an autogiro in July 1926. Several other variants were built and Bert Hinkler was deeply involved in the test flying. He carried out the type-conversion of Cierva to autogiro flying after Cierva had obtained his fixed-wing licence at the Hampshire Aero Club in 1927. In September 1928 Cierva flew the editor of the French journal L'Aeronautique from Croydon to Le Bourget, making the first rotating-wing aircraft flight across the Channel.

Late in 1926 A.V.Roe received an Air Ministry contract for two further autogiros. This order resulted in an entirely new fuselage design not derived from the Avro 504K. The first model had a slim plywood-covered square section fuselage with fabric-covered turtledeck. The autogiro, labelled the Avro 576, or C.9 in Cierva notation was first flown by Bert Hinkler in September 1927.

The second fuselage was fitted with two seats and the opportunity was taken to complete it as a conventional biplane so as to be able to compete in the Daily Mail light aircraft trials for two-seaters. The trials were aimed at encouraging the club and private owner market and so there was an engine weight limit of 170 pounds. (77 kg). This aircraft, G-EBOV was designated the Avro 581 Avian and had a very light overall weight. In the trials Hinkler flew over 1,000 miles in three days and was placed second in three of the six events. Hinkler eventually purchased

Plate 8-7 Avro 581 Avian

the aircraft much modified, to take a Cirrus II engine and re-designated Avro 581A. (Plate 8-7). He went on to win a number of competitions in April 1927 and after further modifications with a wide-track undercarriage and folding wings to make it suitable for long distance flight over rough terrain set off for Australia in February 1928.

Fifteen days later he arrived in Darwin, having covered over eleven thousand miles in a flying time of one hundred and twenty-eight hours, an average flying speed of eighty-six miles per hour. He then carried out tours of Australia and Tasmania and eventually the Avian was placed in honourable retirement with over thirty thousand miles on the clock in the Brisbane (Bundeberg) Museum where it still displays its British registration G-EBOV.

Encouraged by the success of the Avian, A.V.Roe put it into production as the Avro 581B Avian. Only two of these were made however as A.V.Roe decided to adopt Hinkler's' Cirrus II and undercarriage modifications and other changes to reduce drag resulting in a new designation, the Avro 594 Avian II. The first of these, G-EBRC created an altitude record of 12,750 feet in September 1927 but ran out of fuel on the return journey from Copenhagen and sank off Ventnor on the Isle of Wight. Notable also was the third Avian II G-EBRS owned by Mrs S C Elliott-Lynn. An almost fanatical aviatrix, she was so enamoured of the Avian that she flew over three thousand miles around Great Britain and Europe to publicise it.

The runaway success of the Alpha engine in the Helvellyn Gosport aircraft resulted in the prototype Alpha II engine, whose tests have already been so graphically described by Charles Redrup, being installed in the next Avian in anticipation of the aircraft being entered as a “dark horse” in the Kings Cup Race at Hucknall on July 30th 1927.

However, before this on Tuesday 28th of June Major Scott flew the Alpha II engine in a Gosport machine and although prior to the flight he had been of the opinion that the engine would not be powerful enough for the machine he was quite taken by surprise and stated when he landed that there was ample power and remarked strongly upon the smoothness of the running at all speeds. The next day Bert Hinkler flew in this machine and was surprised to find the engine so powerful. He stated that there was very little difference in power between the Alpha engine and the Genet and that it was smoother than the Genet at full throttle.

By Tuesday 12th of July the Alpha II engine had been fitted into a specially modified Avro Avian fitted with a four foot (1.2 metre) wider wingspan and a different wing section. This aircraft, G-EBSD was flown by Bert Hinkler, who remarked that the speed of 116 miles per hour was not as good as expected but that the machine took off and climbed and acted generally satisfactorily. There appeared to be some undue drag. Three different pitch and diameter propellers were tried and all gave the same speed. The pitches were 4’3”, 5’ and 5’6” (1.3, 1.5 and 1.68 metres respectively), and the engine rpm were 2100, 1960 and 1900 respectively. Charles recorded that these results were obtained with 1/2“ (13 mm) lift on the valves, a large choke in the carburettor and an exhaust-heated induction pipe. The engine was very smooth but Bert Hinkler remarked that the engine was labouring very hard with the 5’6” propeller. The 4’3” propeller was the one used to fly the Gosport machine previously with a speed 88 miles per hour.

Charles made some modifications to provide oil heating to the carburettor and Bert Hinkler flew the Avian again on Wednesday 20th of July when he tested it in the air for forty minutes. He reported that the machine was flying very well but that the engine rpm was down by fifty owing to carburettion. A new muff was made to improve heating and Hinkler seemed quite pleased with the engine. At about six pm he flew off to Hamble which was two hundred and fifty miles away. As this took over two hours it demonstrated his confidence in the aircraft.

Plate C1 Robin Loder with the Prototype Stephens Car at Clevedon

Plate C2 Charles Benjamin Redrup at the age of Nineteen

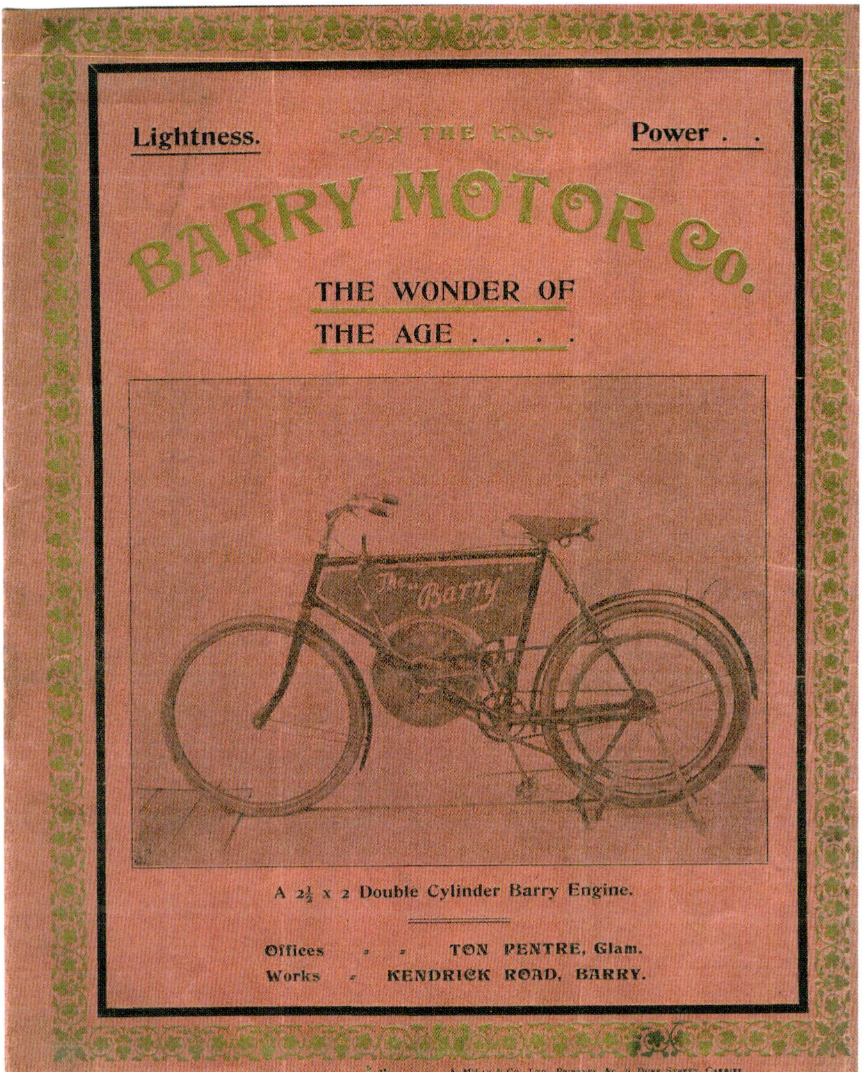

Plate C3 The Brochure from the Burners Hall Exhibition in 1904

Plate C4 The Stepney Spare Wheel

Plate C5 The 50 Horse-power "Barry" Car Engine form 1910

Plate C6 The Crossley-mounted Hucks Starter

Plate C7 Jessie Redrup

Plate C8 1912 "Reactionless" Contra-rotating Aero Engine

Plate C9 Vickers F.B.5 "Gunbus"

Plate C10 Alfred Leeson Redrup

Plate C11 1922 "Redrup Radial" Motor Cycle

Plate C12 The Flat Surface on the Peak of Helvellyn

Plate C13 The Commemorative Plaque on the Top of Helvellyn

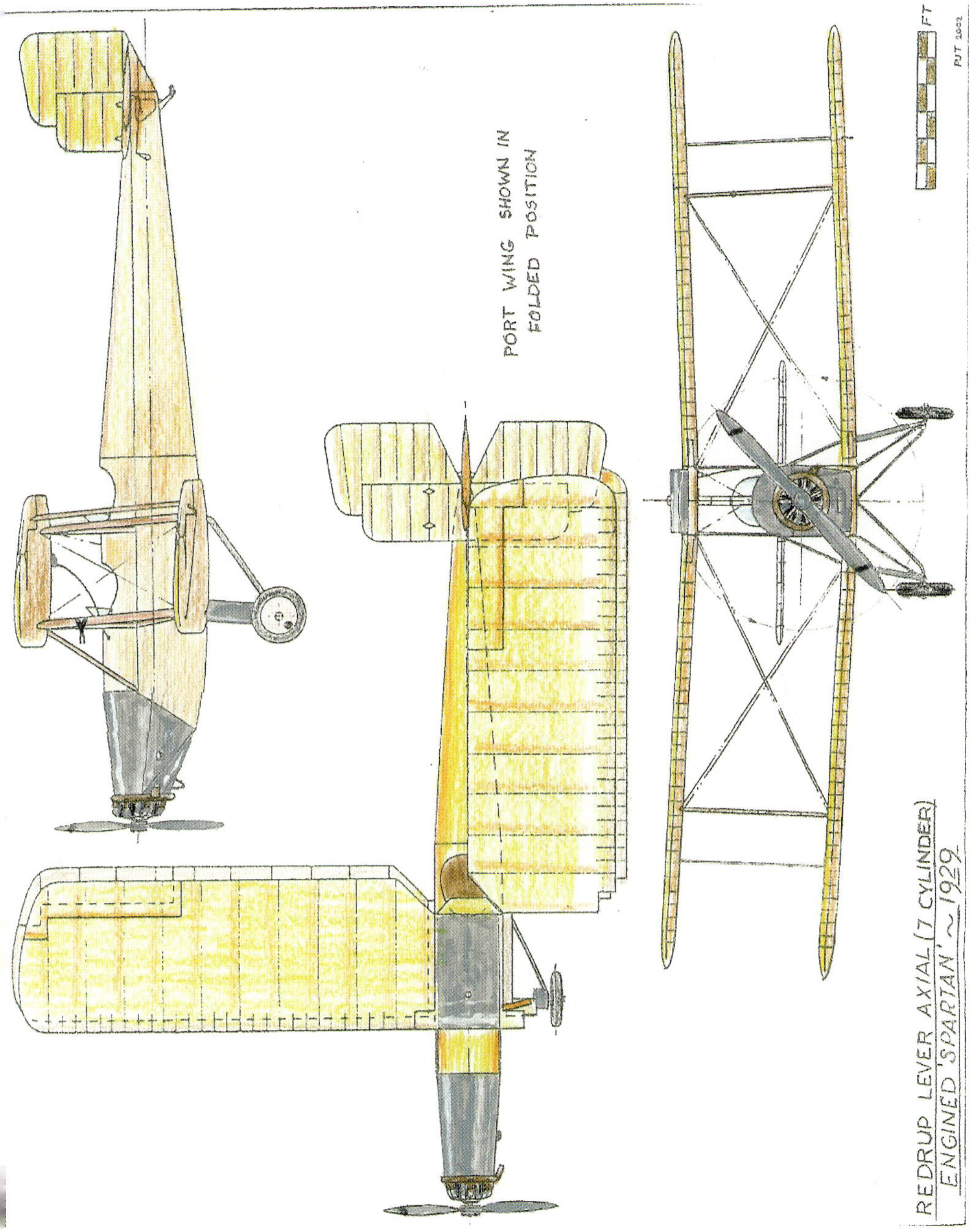

Plate C14 Simmonds Spartan Aircraft with Redrup "Fury I" Engine

Plate C15 Painting by Alan Jones of the Spartan Aircraft in Flight

Plate C16 Bristol Tramways Redrup RR4/1 Axial Wobble-plate Engine

Plate C17 Bristol Tramways "G" Type Bus

Plate C18 Bristol Bus in "Royal Blue" Livery

Plate C19 A.V.Roe Lancaster

Plate C20 Charles Redrup in Contemplative Mood

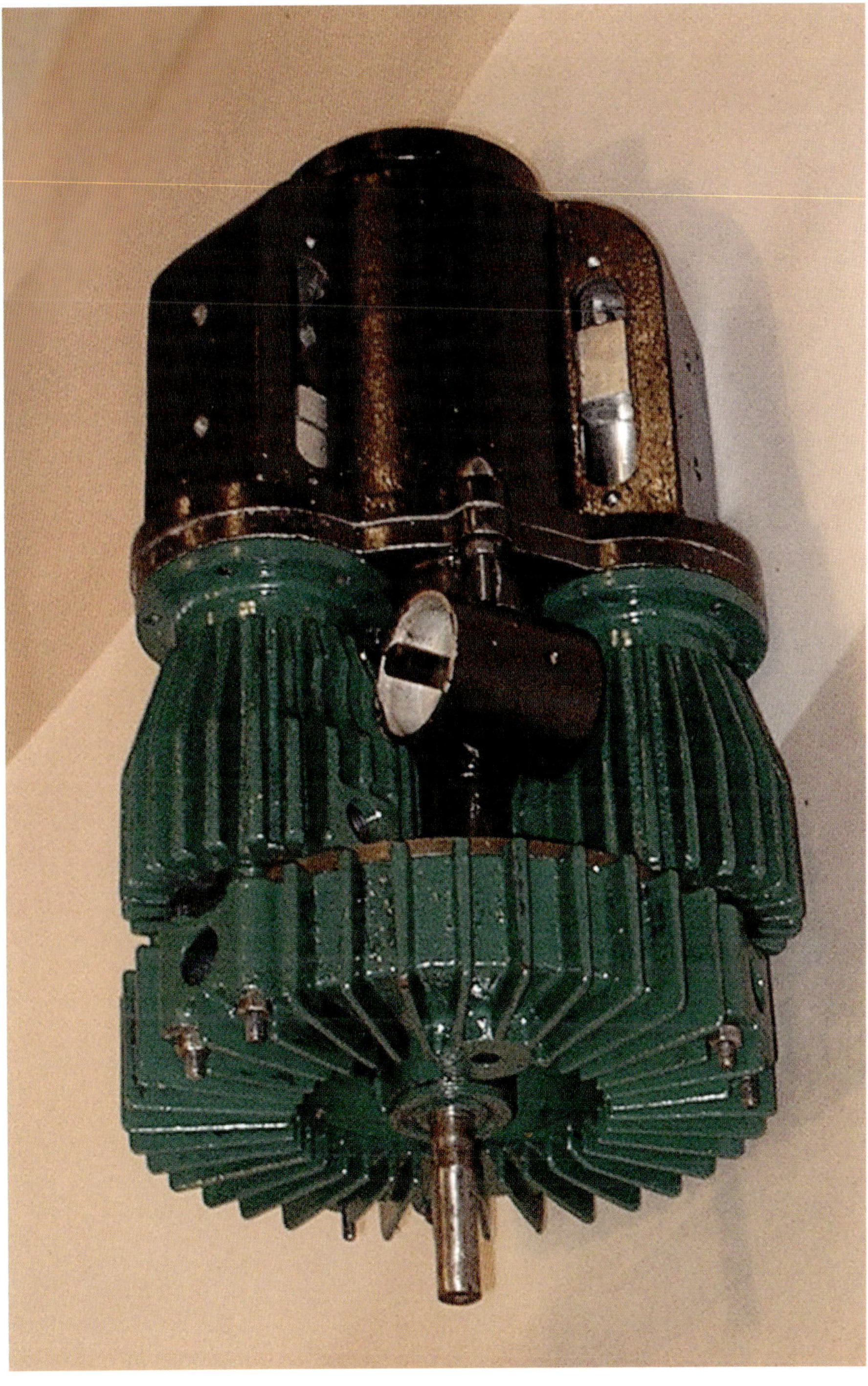

Plate C21 Axial Rotary-valve Motor Cycle Engine

Plate C22 1946 Axial Wobble-plate
Three-Cylinder Rotary-valve Motor Cycle Engine

Plate C23 1946 Three-Cylinder 248cc Overhead-valve Radial Engine

Plate C24 1,000 Horse-power Cam-drive Eight-cylinder Axial Engine

Plate C25 1946 Redrup Radial Overhead-valve Engined Motor Cycle

Plate C26 John Redrup and his
Redrup Radial at the Sammy Miller Museum

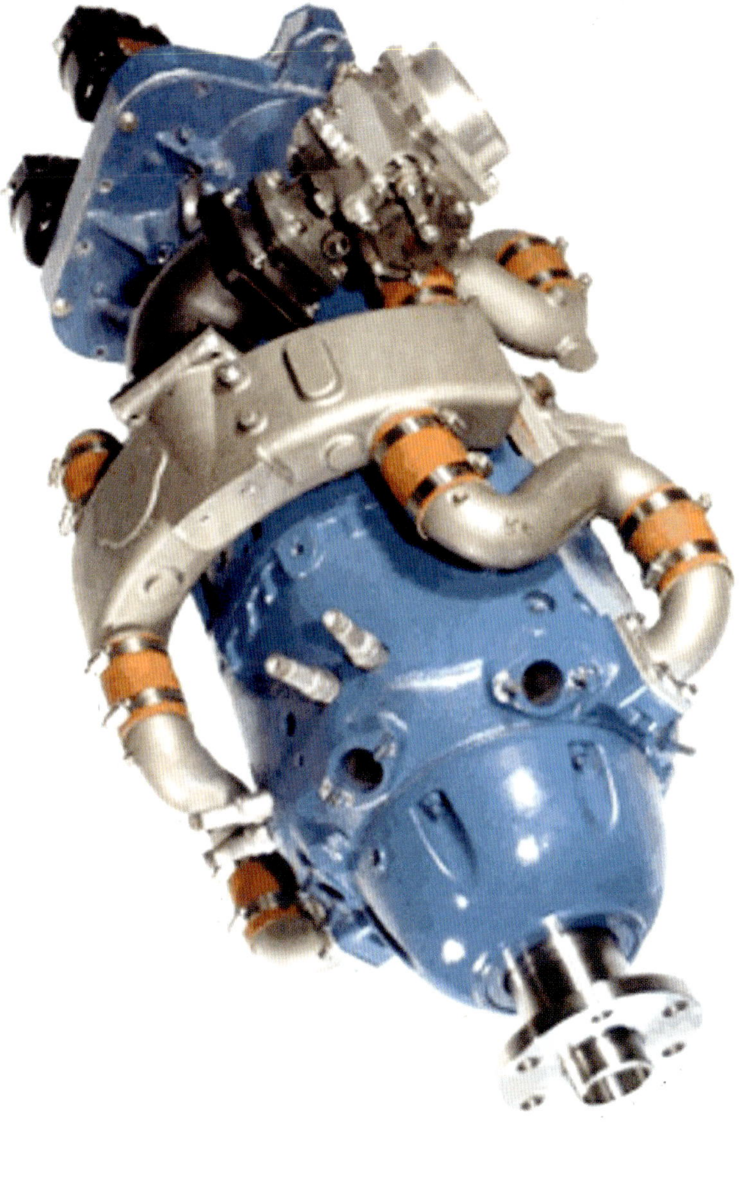

Plate C27 The Twelve-cylinder Dynacam Engine

Plate C28 The Opposed-Piston Two-stroke FairDiesel Cam Engine

Chapter 9
Fired and the Fury

Charles Redrup was present at Hucknall Air Races on July 30th 1927. The Avian was flown in from Hamble by Bert Hinkler the day before. Charles was told by an A.V.Roe technician Mr Bolsover that Hinkler had complained of the heavy fuel consumption, but that Bolsover himself did not think it was nearly so much fuel as stated. As a result work was started on the machine almost as soon as it had arrived. The carburettor was taken off and the jets changed. The engine was started up at intervals and the jets changed again. This went on repeatedly right up to the running of the race and the carburettion was in such a state of confusion when the time for the race arrived that the engine could not be started and had to be withdrawn from the starting line. Charles was very frustrated at the way the engine had been treated and it transpired that the bottom of the carburettor had been cracked by all the tightening and re-tightening without the use of a torque spanner. Charles sent for a spare carburettor from the Works in Manchester and it was fitted the next day. When he had carried out the necessary tuning the engine ran extremely well.

Just before the Grosvenor Cup Race the Avian was air-tested by Bert Hinkler whilst Captain Waghorn flew the Alpha I powered Gosport for some air-to-air photography. In the Grosvenor Cup Race, piloted by Hinkler, the Avian came a very close third in its heat. There was some comment by A.V.Roe staff on the long handicap it had been given. The engine had not been given full throttle early enough in the race and it appeared that if the engine had been opened out earlier it would have won its heat. Plate 9-1 shows the line-up of A.V.Roe staff in front of the Avian after the Grosvenor Cup Race, with Bert Hinkler on the left, Captain Waghorn in the centre in flying helmet and Roy Dobson and John Lord on the right. Charles Redrup, the engine designer is noticeable by his absence.

Plate 9-2 shows Mrs Elliot Lynne at the same pageant with Captain Broad, winner of the Kings Cup. Later in the day Squadron Leader Noakes took the Avian into the air and gave a stunt display and when he landed was greeted with applause from the crowd. Charles took particular note when he stated that the engine ran very smoothly, except

Plate 9-1 Avro Staff Line-up After the 1927 Grosvenor Cup Race

at very low rpm. Noakes also emphasised the wide range of smooth running. Since he was a very experienced pilot Charles took it that he meant compared to other engines he had flown. While the machine was at Hucknall very favourable comment was expressed regarding the clean appearance and engine design and a very positive report appeared in the September 30th edition of *Flight*.

During August the Avian engine was fitted with a Claudel carburettor from a Genet and an oil-heated induction pipe, developing 85 horse-power at 1760 rpm and 95 horse-power at 1800 rpm. The carburettor had to be choked to start the engine and took rather a long time to get going properly. Once started it ran well but Charles put in hand a further modification to improve the starting characteristics.

Plate 9-2 Mrs Elliot Lynne with Captain Broad, King's Cup Winner

In November Charles flew with the A.V.Roe Chief Test Pilot Sam Brown, who had taken over when Hinkler left, in a Gosport fitted with an Armstrong Siddeley Mongoose engine for a trial flight. This aircraft, G-EBUY had been ordered by the RAF for testing at Martlesham Heath but was tested first in civil form. The engine behaved well and the machine flew very satisfactorily.

Charles noted that the engine vibration could be distinctly felt when the throttle was at all open. After the flight he got into the Gosport with the Alpha Mk I engine and went up again for a comparative test. He found it gave much smoother running with a cruise speed of eighty-eight miles per hour. He remarked that the machine climbed with engine all out at 1450 rpm but that the propeller was a bit too heavy. Improved performance would be obtained by lightening. At a later date when this had been done the machine handled exceptionally well and was particularly easy to control.

G-EBSD was used by Mrs Elliott Lynn, now titled Lady Heath, on another publicity flight, to create a new altitude record. The Avian, fitted temporarily with new wings of RAF 28 section having rounded tips, was re-designated the Avro 594C in this form. (Plate 9-3). On October 8th 1927 she took a passenger up to an altitude of 19,200 feet, a new light aircraft record. She stated that the Alpha II engine ran at full throttle for two hours whilst climbing. On the return journey there was fog over Woodford and so she had to land in a field at Frodsham in Cheshire. The high-performance wings were taken from this aircraft and fitted to G-EBOV which Bert Hinkler flew to Australia in April 1928, where the aircraft now hangs in the Bundeberg Museum along with other Hinkler artefacts.

The original wings were re-fitted and G-EBSD was sold to Somerset Taxiplanes Limited and used for joyriding in 1928 before passing into private ownership. It crashed in 1932 and was sent to the breakers in 1933 but what became of the engine is unknown.

Although Charles was very occupied with the works tests of the Alpha he also had to spend considerable time at the design and development department at Hamble. He would invariably take Jessie on these trips. The fact was that Charles was very introspective and totally immersed in his work. It was Jessie who kept his feet on the ground and made all domestic and financial arrangements. She ensured that patent renewals were kept up to date and that the family always had enough to live on. It was typical of how close the family were that Dorothy was still prepared to look after the younger children at home and this gave the family great flexibility.

Plate 9-3 Avro Avian Fitted with Wide-Span Wings for Attempt on Altitude Record by Lady Heath

After the spectacular successes of the Gosport and the Avian fitted with the Alpha engines, A.V.Roe put in hand an order with Crossley Motors for a further fifty Alpha II engines to meet the expected demand. Gosport production was by now starting to increase as orders from overseas air forces started to materialise. It is ironic that the aircraft designed by Avros to meet the light aircraft civilian market should be seized upon by air forces as a training aircraft, but that is what happened. Ten aircraft were delivered to the Argentinean Air Force in June 1927 and a further one hundred built under licence. Estonia ordered six which were delivered by November 1928 and Peru ordered an unknown number. None of these aircraft however were equipped with Alpha engines. The first two engines had been virtually hand-built by Charles Redrup in the A.V.Roe works but the production engines started to come off Crossley Motors production line late in 1927, so were too late for the Argentinean order.

The first of these production units was used to relieve some acute embarrassment with the Lancashire Aero Club. The Gosport which A.V.Roe had donated to the Club in April 1926, G-EBNF, was fitted with a Gnome engine which gave erratic performance and had only logged eleven hours by the end of 1927. It seems that the idiosyncrasies of the rotary engine were not liked by club members, apart from John Leeming who appears to have enjoyed flying it. As this aircraft was intended to be a flagship for A.V.Roe in flying club circles they had to do something about it so in February 1928, Commission engine number three, the first Crossley production Alpha engine, was installed in G-EBNF. Thereafter the aircraft flew extremely well and it was used extensively throughout the summer of 1928. When A.V.Roe carried out a complete overhaul of the aircraft in the autumn the flying hours had leapt to 142. Unfortunately this was not the end of the story.

On 21st October the aircraft was given a thorough inspection by ground engineers and flight-tested by the Chief Flying Instructor. In the afternoon a club member took it up with a passenger and commenced aerobatics at about ten thousand feet. Descending in a series of aerobatic manoeuvres the aircraft commenced a loop at about fifteen hundred feet then dived before levelling out at about 150 feet.

At this point the aircraft stalled and dived into the ground. The front-seat passenger was fatally injured and the pilot sustained severe injuries and had little recollection of the latter stages of the flight. He did vaguely recall having difficulty with the controls. Investigation showed a deep abrasion on one of the shoes of the passenger and the inquiry concluded that the passenger had inadvertently interfered with the controls at a critical moment of flight recovery. It also concluded that there was no damage to the engine that was not attributable to the crash.

A.V.Roe replaced the written-off Gosport with an Avian II fitted with the Cirrus II engine, because by this time a major shake-up had occurred at A.V.Roe which sounded the death knell of the Alpha engine.

In a reversal of fortunes, Crossley Motors who had in 1920 rescued A.V.Roe, were by now in financial difficulties themselves. By May 1928 their shares were at an all-time low of one shilling and sixpence (seven and a half new pence) and they were ripe for take-over. On May 2nd it was announced that Crossley Motors had sold their controlling interest in A.V.Roe & Company Limited to an unknown buyer. A sum of £270,000 had been paid in cash by the managing director of A.V.Roe, Sir William Letts to Crossley Motors, and it later transpired that Letts had received this money from the Armstrong Siddeley Development Company. Control of A.V.Roe had been handed over to Charles Redrup's largest engine competitor.

John Siddeley (Plate 9-4), was born near Manchester in 1866 and was educated at Altringham and Beaumaris. His first interest was cycling and he became well known for organising cycling events. He made his own racing cycle, which even present-day bicycles would be hard to match in terms of weight and performance. He was subsequently invited to become design engineer for the Humber Cycle Company in Coventry. In the 1890s he held a number of senior appointments including the Pneumatic Tyre Company set up by John Dunlop, and Peugeot, as an importer of cars. In 1902 Siddeley Autocar was formed in Coventry. He was highly regarded by Vickers and managed their Wolseley Tool and Motor Car Company, before becoming Managing Director of the Deasy Motor Car Manufacturing Company in 1909. He acquired an interest in this company which was consequently re-named the Siddeley-Deasy Motor Car Company in 1912, and then after a merger with Armstrong Whitworth the Deasy name was dropped and it became Armstrong Siddeley in 1919.

During World War I, the Armstrong Siddeley factory produced aircraft and aero engines under licence but later on in the war Siddeley developed an engine of his own, the 230hp Siddeley Puma. Over 4,200 of these were produced for use in light bombers and several records were broken using Puma engines. Armstrong Siddeley produced the first large two-row air-cooled radial engine in 1920, the 400HP Jaguar, which proved to be the leading commercial and military aero engine of the 1920s. Armstrong Siddeley also produced numerous smaller engines for military use and was keen to sell more of these in civil applications.

The publicity surrounding the Helvellyn flight had not unnaturally aroused John Siddeley's concern. A.V.Roe was one of his biggest customers and his Mongoose, Genet, Puma and Lynx engines were installed in a wide variety of their aircraft. He was particularly incensed at the publicity given to the fact that it was a problem with the Siddeley engine in Bert Hinkler's aircraft that had resulted in him joining John Leeming in the Avro Gosport for the historic landing. The prospect of A.V.Roe going it alone with their own design of engines did not appeal to him, especially as they appeared to be proceeding with a second engine also aimed at small club aircraft, the Avro Beta. Siddeley knew that A.V.Roe had placed orders with Crossley Motors to produce another fifty Alpha engines destined to go in Gosports for the Peruvian and Estonian Air Forces. These were orders that otherwise would have gone to Armstrong Siddeley.

The weakness of Crossley Motors was a heaven-sent opportunity for him to eliminate the competition by buying their controlling stake in A.V.Roe. Siddeley promised Alliott Roe that the take-over would not result in major redundancies or affect their aircraft production. However very shortly after the coup John Siddeley appeared at the Newton Heath works and discharged Charles Redrup. Charles painfully recalled as he

Plate 9-4 John Davenport Siddeley, Lord Kenilworth

left the works, seeing the stock of Alpha engines from Crossleys being thrown from a first floor loading bay into the gutter below to be broken up. This wanton destruction of what was contemporarily described as a "miracle engine" must have broken Charles' heart, as it was a fit of vindictiveness probably unparalleled in engineering history.

Siddeley advised customers with orders for aircraft to be fitted with Alphas that only Armstrong Siddeley engines could be provided and thus the Alpha, which had been specifically designed for light aircraft such as the Gosport and the Avian, was virtually lost to the nation. The historic "Helvellyn" Gosport G-EBPH was transferred to Hamble as a company hack aircraft for a few more years but was lost in a crash in January 1930. The Alpha engine however was removed and used later to power another autogiro. It seems likely that Alliott Roe had also kept a couple of the engines at the Hamble works. For a short time he continued his work with Juan de la Cierva and these engines were used by A.V.Roe to power autogiros between 1928 and 1930. Encouraging results from work on the Cierva C.8 prompted the construction at Hamble of a new autogiro aimed at flying clubs and private owners. It was based on an Avro Avian IIIA fuselage with a 90 horse-power Cirrus III engine and was designated the Avro 612 Cierva C.17. Juan de la

Plate 9-5 Alpha-Powered Cierva C12 Autogiro Flying at Hamble

Cierva made the first flight in October 1928. It was seriously under-powered and so it was not proceeded with. A second version, the Avro 620 Cierva C.17 Mk.2, G-AAGJ was built using a 100 horse-power Alpha II engine but proved still to lack sufficient power. Yet another two-seat version was built to test a new moving head rotor design and was, confusingly, designated the Cierva C.12. It too was fitted with an Alpha II engine and this time flew successfully from Hamble in 1929. (Plate 9-5). In 1930 it was fitted with floats and flew from the River Hamble on Southampton Water, to become the first rotary-wing seaplane. (Plate 9-6). In this form it was named the Hydrogiro.

This work was well under way when to the dismay of all at A.V.Roe, Alliott Roe resigned from the Company in October 1928. He clearly could not stomach the company he had created being in the control of others. After his resignation the A.V.Roe Company's interest in autogiros declined and no further work was done for another ten years, until after John Siddeley's death.

Plate 9-6 Alpha-Powered Cierva C12 Hydrogiro

Juan de Cierva was not cowed by the A.V.Roe loss of interest and he continued to develop his autogyros. In 1929 he placed a secret contract with de Havilland to produce the Cierva C 24 cabin autogyro fitted with an inverted Gipsy engine, soon to become famous as the power plant for the iconic Tiger Moth aircraft. There were financial difficulties and the contract was almost cancelled.

Meanwhile George Dowty who was still working for Gloster Aircraft had set up a company jointly with W. S. Melville. Melville was really nothing but the owner of an accommodation address and all correspondence was signed by him so that Dowty's involvement could be kept confidential. Dowty was introduced to Cierva by Alliott Roe and made the undercarriage under contract to de Havilland for the new autogyro. This was Dowty's first contract as an independent manufacturer. His work for de Havilland came to the notice of C. G. Grey and he soon obtained work from other aircraft manufacturers. He later went on to make many undercarriages for Alliott Roe's new company Saunders Roe Limited.

One further event marked the success of the Alpha engine. Cierva C.17 Mk.2 G-AAGJ was used at Hamble for a number of years by Air Service Training Limited as an instructional airframe. In 1935 it was re-built by a team of enthusiasts from AST as an Avro 594 Avian II with its original Alpha II engine. (Plate 9-7). In this form, it was re-registered as G-ADEO and was flown for a number of years by the group, which numbered about twenty-five and which called themselves the Alpha Club. Clearly someone valued the Alpha engine! In January 1940 the aircraft was removed from the Civil Register and was impressed into the armed forces as an instructional airframe, 2075M. No further records exist of the aeroplane or of its engine.

Alliott Verdon Roe's departure from A.V.Roe was not un-premeditated. He had always had an interest in water-borne craft and had an ambition to build a large flying boat airliner. His base at Hamble had brought him into regular contact with Sam Saunders the Chairman of S E Saunders, boat-builders and aircraft manufacturers based in Cowes on the Isle of Wight.

Sam Saunders was descended from a family of engineers which specialised in manufacturing equipment for docks and locks. His grandfather Moses Saunders expanded the business to boat-building and in addition to small skiffs and punts he manufactured high speed steam-powered launches. Sam Saunders took over the business when he was in his early twenties and soon demonstrated keen business sense as well as his family's engineering skills. He was one of the first to install internal combustion engines into boats and invented a new lightweight form of hull construction which consisted of sewing plywood sheets together with copper or brass wire. He set up a factory and employed teams of women using Singer industrial sewing machines to stitch the sheets together. This technique, known as "Consuta" was immensely strong and eradicated the problems of hulls held together by fish glue. He opened the Cowes works in 1901 and prospered greatly with contracts from the Admiralty and other marine agencies.

Plate 9-7 "Alpha Club" Avro 594 Avian II with Alpha MkII Engine

Saunders adopted the Fauber design of hydroplane hull in which air is forced through tubes to the step at the back of the hull to break the suction. He adapted this technique to build a sloping-hull boat with two sidewalls between which pressurised air was forced, so that the craft would ride on a cushion of air. The approach does not appear to have been successful, probably because the air could escape too easily at the rear. It was Christopher (later Sir Christopher) Cockerill who sixty years later realised that to succeed the air had to be contained on all sides. This approach led to the Hovercraft which he patented. It is interesting to note that the first Hovercraft was built at Sam Saunders' old works at Cowes.

In 1911 at Tom Sopwith's request Saunders built a hull for a small two-seat flying-boat. (Plate 9-8). This so-called "Bat Boat" incorporated the Consuta form of construction and air injection from scoops on the sides of the hull. In 1913 the sewing-machine tycoon Mortimer Singer sponsored some amphibian seaplane trials on Southampton Water. The Bat Boat was converted to an amphibian to enable it to compete for the £500. The Bat Boat was piloted by Harry Hawker who won the trials in an aircraft sewn together on a Singer sewing machine!

Plate 9-8 Saunders "Bat Boat" Made on a Singer Sewing Machine

After this and right through the First World War the Saunders company undertook the construction of many flying-boat hulls, usually under contract to large aircraft manufacturers. Saunders decided that he ought to diversify into aircraft manufacture after the war and put in hand some designs. However after the Armistice the market for flying-boats collapsed, as with that for other aircraft. Saunders was able, so to speak, to keep his head above water in the critical post-war years through contracts from the Admiralty for re-furbishing hulls which he had supplied during the war years. His sole attempt at flying-boat construction in 1920 proved an expensive failure but he did get small orders for hulls from aircraft manufacturers. He concentrated therefore on manufacture of high-speed launches. A few attempts were made in the late twenties to make aircraft but no orders were forthcoming. By 1928, whilst the boat-building business was solvent, the aviation part was in substantial loss.

When Alliott Roe resigned from A.V.Roe, so did his long-term business partners John Lord and Harry Broadsmith. Between them they injected over forty-two thousand pounds into the Saunders business which they believed was sufficient to resuscitate its fortunes. With Sam Saunders' full co-operation they used this cash from the sale of their A.V.Roe shares to gain a controlling interest in the Saunders company. A number of other people left A.V.Roe to join the new company. Sam Saunders, now aged seventy-two became President of the company, which retained the name Saunders for a year then took on the new title of Saunders-Roe Limited in October 1929. It is typical of Alliott Roe that he insisted on the name Saunders appearing first in the title. His interests always were more in achievement than recognition. Despite this, in the New Year's Honours List of 1929 Alliott Verdon Roe was knighted for his pioneering services to aviation. In 1933 in recognition of his mother's influence on his early life he changed his surname to Verdon-Roe, as did his brother Humphrey.

The cash injection did re-vitalise the company and the next few years saw the Saunders-Roe Company, or Saro as it was popularly called, expand and grow. It manufactured water-borne and land planes of great variety, both fixed-wing and rotating wing, for Alliott Verdon-Roe continued his relationship with Juan de la Cierva. During the Second World War Saro manufactured aircraft of its own design and also under

Plate 9-9 Saunders-Roe SR.A/1, "The Squirt"

licence from other manufacturers. In July 1947 the first ever water-borne turbojet powered aircraft, the SR.A/1, .(Plate 9-9), locally known as the "Squirt" had its first flight. This became the world's fastest-ever flying boat and was capable of travelling in excess of Mach 0.8.

In 1952 Sir Alliott's vision of a large passenger-carrying flying boat for the trans-Atlantic route was realised when the first Saro Princess G-ALUN took off from the Solent just off Cowes. This was a beautiful and majestic aircraft of nearly two-hundred and twenty foot wingspan, (Plate 9-10) powered by ten Bristol Proteus 2 turboprop engines. However British Overseas Airways (now British Airways) had always been lukewarm over the project. During the war many thousands of large concrete runways had been built around the world and airlines did not see the need for flying boats, which were always at risk to semi-submerged objects in the water. The advent of the de Havilland Comet and then the Boeing 707 sounded the death knell of large flying boats. Of the three Princesses built, only G-ALUN ever flew. Despite making an impressive appearance at the SBAC display at Farnborough less than a month after its maiden flight no orders were received and the three hulls languished for many years at Cowes before finally being broken up.

In 1956 Saunders-Roe built a rocket when de Havilland Holdings purchased one third of the Saro shares. De Havilland were involved in building the Blue Streak missile and Saro had an expert rocket designer who had worked on an earlier Saro rocket-assisted aircraft the SR.53. The prototype rocket Black Knight was launched in September 1958. Sir Alliott Verdon-Roe, still Life-President of Saro, had died in January of that year at the age of eighty-one but during his career he had seen aviation proceed from the first fumblings with model gliders right through to the frontiers of space.

Charles Redrup was not at a loss after his summary dismissal from Av.V.Roe by John Siddeley. Although the Crossley Motors axial car engine project came to an abrupt halt, he had also been working on an axial aero engine version with seven cylinders. During his visits to Hamble he had become familiar with other aviation organisations in the area. He got to know Sam Saunders very well and visited Supermarine at Woolston on the river Itchen near Southampton. where his friend the pilot H D Waghorn was based

Charles became very friendly with a Supermarine employee, Oliver Simmonds who lived in Woolston and who was a founder member of the Hampshire Aero Club where Juan de la Cierva had learnt to fly. Simmonds was a design engineer at Supermarine but in his spare time had

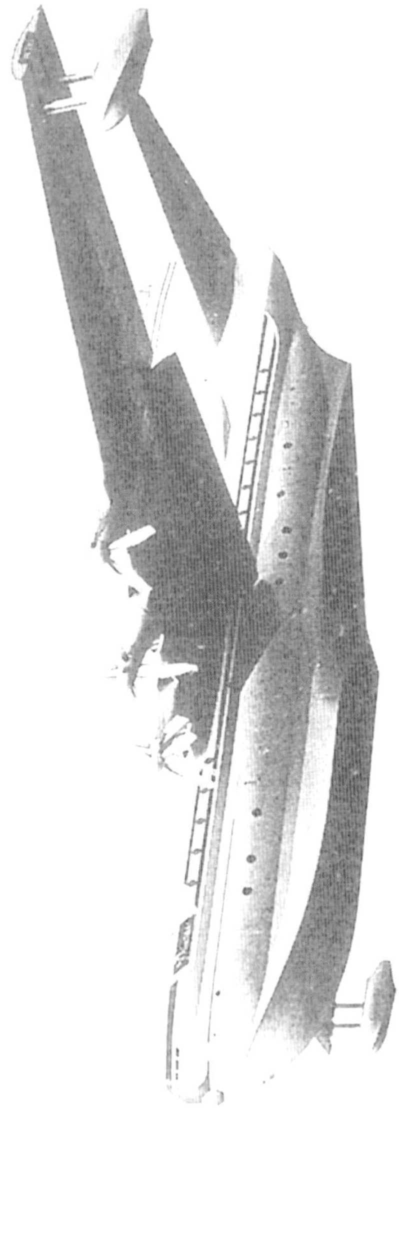

Plate 9-10 Prototype Saunders-Roe Princess Flying Boat G-ALUN

decided to design and build an aircraft of his own for the light aeroplane market. His vision was for a very light, cheap and economical two-seater aircraft that could be folded up and stored in a garage, and towed to a flying field. To reduce tooling, spares holding and maintenance costs he used a symmetrical RAF 30 wing profile so that upper and lower wings were interchangeable and left and right-hand wings could be changed merely by turning them upside down. In addition the two elevators were symmetrical and identical to the rudder. The undercarriage was also symmetrical and could be exchanged right for left.

The amazing fact about this aircraft was that it was built in his house at 65, Portsmouth Road, Woolston with the help of other Supermarine employees in their spare time. (Plate 9-11). The fuselage was built in the living room and the wings in an upstairs bedroom. When the aircraft was nearing completion in 1928 his employers got to hear of it. At first they claimed that any work he did whilst in their employ was in Supermarine's ownership, but Simmonds was able to convince them that he had worked in his own time and he left the company to complete the aircraft rather sooner than he would have otherwise! A window had to be taken out of the home so that the aircraft could be removed and it was taken to a rented property in Archway Road, Weston, Southampton, which were former Rolling Mills. Here the aircraft was assembled and the de Havilland Cirrus III 90 horse-power engine fitted. It then had to be towed from the Rolling Mills along the road to the flying field.

Plate 9-11 Simmonds Spartan Prototype and the House at Woolston Where it was Built

Oliver Simmonds first aircraft, designated the Simmonds Spartan, registration G-EBYU, was first flown from a field at Butlocks Heath on 18th July 1928. The pilot reported that it flew very well but on landing it seemed to stall suddenly and nose-dived into the field, causing minor damage. In retrospect this was probably because of the symmetrical wing section which would have had a rather nasty stalling characteristic as the airflow separates quite suddenly from such a profile. These, and other adverse handling characteristics arising from the inevitable aerodynamic compromises in the design were eventually recognised and later models had a variety of modifications such as a larger wing span and leading-edge slats, to improve handling.

The prototype was repaired, fitted with a 120 horse-power de Havilland Gypsy II engine and entered into the Kings Cup race only a few days later. Amazingly for an aircraft which had only made its first flight the previous week, it completed the gruelling course of over a thousand miles from Hendon to Glasgow and back. However it did not fare well, ending up way down the field of entrants and the winner was a Gypsy Moth, the type of aircraft Simmonds was trying to out-perform. The Spartan sold for some 5% less than the DH60 Moth, at £620, but it never achieved the performance or the docile handling of the Moth.

In October 1928 the Spartan was flown on a round trip to Berlin and back by a Flying Officer H W R Banting, bringing back on the return journey Lieutenant-Colonel L A Strange. Strange was very impressed by the aircraft and later in 1928 he and Simmonds set up Simmonds Aircraft Ltd to produce the aircraft in commercial quantities. They took over the Rolling Mills premises at Weston and manufactured a further forty-nine Spartans before financial problems caught up with them.

During his discussions with Charles Redrup, Oliver Simmonds became enamoured of the virtues of the lightweight and compact axial engine construction and decided to install one in one of the Spartan aircraft. Simmonds, Redrup, M L Bramson and a financier formed a company, the Redrup Lever Engine Syndicate, to manufacture the seven-cylinder "Fury" engine, as it became known.

Captain Mogens Louis Bramson was a Danish-born pilot and aeronautical engineer who was well known to Charles having achieved fame for his post-war sky-writing exploits in a S.E.5A. Bramson was linked to a Swiss engineer Helmuth John Stieger who was an aircraft designer and who had patented a lightweight torsionally stiff wing structure which he called monospar. (Plate 9-12).

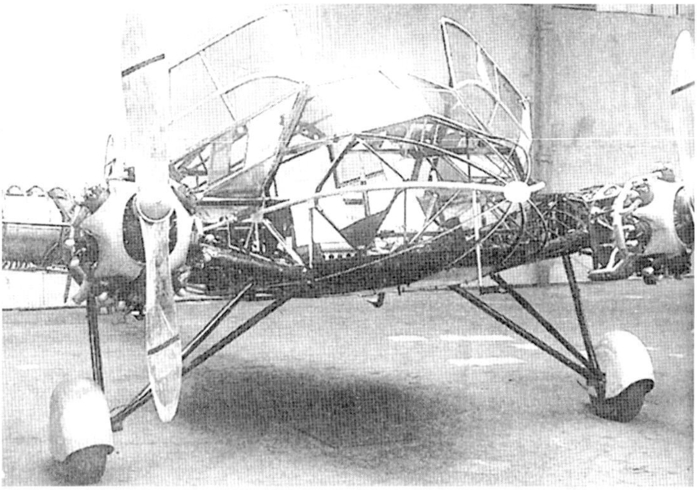

Plate 9-12 Monospar Twin-Engined Aircraft Tubular Structure

This form of construction used only one spar in the wing and the torsional strength was derived from cross-braced diagonal struts. A strengthened leading edge to the wing was used to absorb drag loads. Stieger and his colleagues interested investors in a two-engined aircraft to be called the Monospar using the novel construction and a company was formed to build it, the Monospar Wing Company. To raise finance they created The Aero Syndicate of London. They wanted engines for the Monospar and decided to back the Redrup Fury. A contract was placed with the Gloster Aircraft Company (GAC) to build the Monospar for the sum of £3,350. The Monospar would not be ready for well over a year but the testing in the Spartan would be in good time to evaluate the Fury engine. An option was taken out for the use of the Fury, with stage payments and royalties on patents due to Charles Redrup at appropriate times.

Chapter 10
Fury and Flight

Mogens Bramson was, debatably, to become the most influential man in British aviation history. Frank Whittle (later Sir Frank), a serving officer in the RAF, patented his design for a turbojet engine in 1930 but could not get the British Government to take it seriously. He was anxious to raise finance but vehemently against approaching any existing aircraft manufacture which he thought, on learning of the engine, would either, quickly find ways of getting around his patents and proceed independently, or would buy the rights then just shelve the concept. In May 1935 Whittle was approached by Rolf D Williams a former RAF colleague who was a partner in a company which manufactured cigarette making machines. He met Whittle a few days later together with his partner J C B Tinling who was another ex-RAF pilot, and they agreed to fund patent work and to help raise the necessary fifty thousand pounds finance for the jet engine project.

This proved much more difficult than expected and hopes were sinking when Whittle learnt that Bramson, whose brother was an associate of Tinling's father, was interested in the proposal. Frank Whittle knew of Bramson's reputation as an aviator and engineer and was horrified, fearing that Bramson would blab to the manufacturers. However when they met they took to each other straight away and Bramson succeeded in allaying Whittle's fears.

Bramson was very energetic and soon was able to interest a company of investment bankers in the project. Negotiations went on throughout the summer of 1935, and the bankers, Falk and Partners, engaged Bramson as an independent consultant and commissioned a report on the proposal. When Bramson reported in the November his recommendations were highly supportive. Now with bankers support, Williams, Tinling and Whittle drew up a draft agreement. Whittle was keen to get started and they sought out a manufacturer not in the aviation business. They lighted on the British Thomson-Houston Company (BTH), a well established manufacturer of steam turbines and after some initial doubts BTH started work. The choice proved to be somewhat problematical because the BTH approach to engineering was more agricultural than aerial and this later led to quality control and other problems. Nevertheless BTH had the honour of being party to the first jet engine.

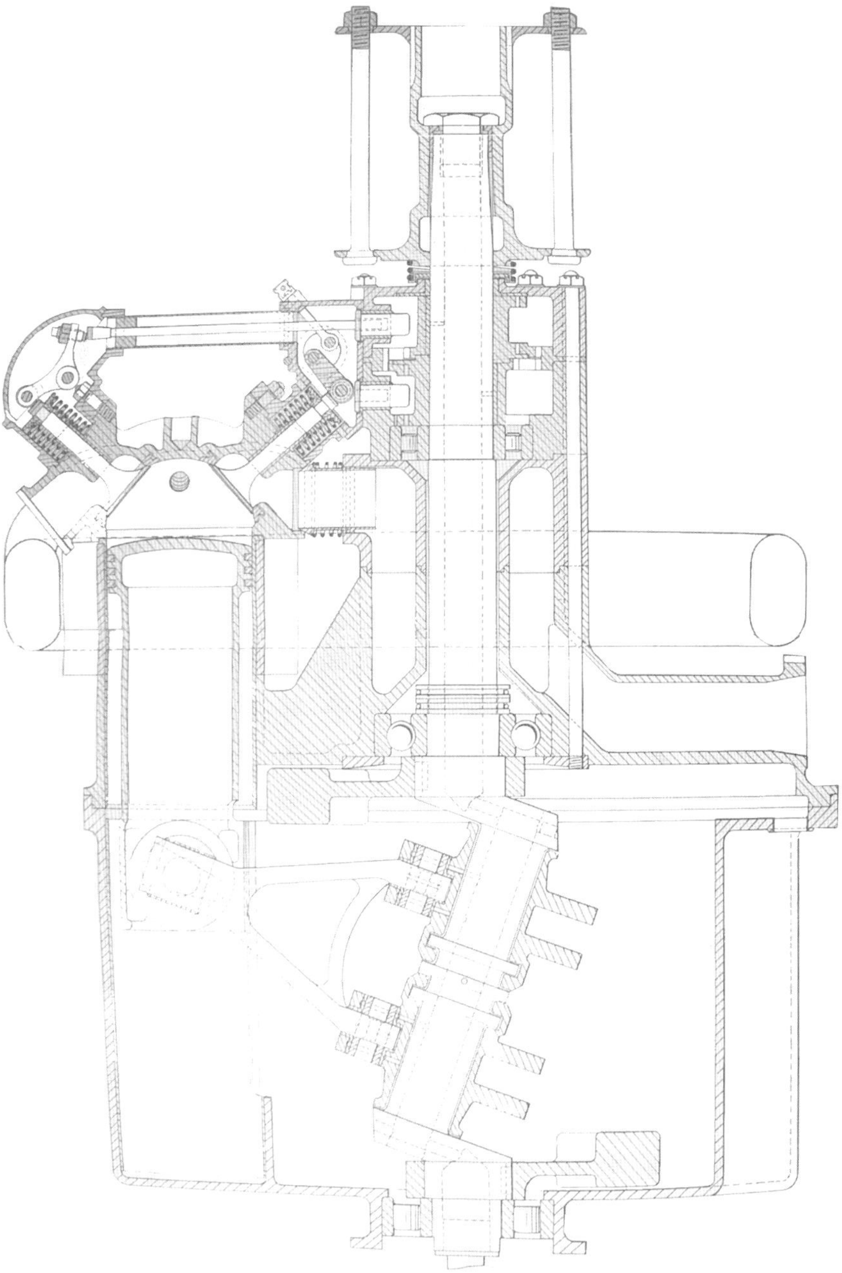

Plate 10-1 The Redrup Fury I Seven-Cylinder Axial Wobble-Plate Engine

Before the agreement could be signed Whittle had to get Air Council approval to enter such an undertaking. Now that an investment banker and a reputable manufacturer were on board, the President of the Air Council suddenly found an interest in the project and whilst proposing some amendments to the agreement decided to join in as well. Thus it was that the Four Party Agreement as it came to be known, was signed on 27th January 1936 and paved the way to Power Jets Limited and Britain's turbojet industry. Bramson was appointed Consultant to Power Jets and met regularly with Whittle. Three months later at a re-union dinner of the Cambridge University Air Squadron, Williams, Tinling and Bramson met Sir Henry Tizzard who was Chairman of the Aeronautical Research Committee and who, surprisingly, did not appear to have heard of the project. Subsequently Tizzard was sent a copy of Bramson's report and took a keen interest in developments thereafter. Tizzard had to attend many a demonstration of all kinds of developments and was not usually invited to attend until the engineers were sure that it would work. Tizzard acquired a bit of a reputation in that as soon as he turned up all sorts of problems seemed to arise!

Later on during the development of the jet engine Bramson was present at a bench test when an engine ran away and reached twelve thousand revs before it seized in the casing and screeched to a halt. Bramson, who had turned tail at the first sign of trouble, was halted by the Works Superintendent who said that it was no use running as it would soon catch him if it wanted to! However things improved and at a later demonstration to Tizzard in 1940 the engine ran perfectly, and he remarked "A demonstration which does not break down in my presence is a production job!" Tizzard would make an appearance later on in Charles Redrup's career.

In 1928 all this was in the future, but with the Aero Syndicate of London, the Monospar Syndicate and The Redrup Lever Engine Syndicate signed up Charles was confident of a market for his machine and set about manufacturing the prototype wobble-plate engine in his workshop in Milwain Drive Heaton Park. The Fury I is shown in cross-section in Plate 10-1. (British Patent 327,113). The similarity with the marine engine is apparent and it should be noted that the spider has no stabilising arm. The engine also has a very square rear casing, which differed on later models. No drawing of the axial Crossley car engine exists today but the similarities of that engine and the Fury is apparent from photographs, taking due account of the fact that the Crossley engine was water-cooled and the Fury air-cooled. (Plate 10-2).

Plate 10-2 Similarity Between the Crossley Car Engine and the Fury I

It is known that the earlier marine engine had some star-member resonance problems. This member, being mounted on bearings on the "Z" shaft tends to rotate with the shaft but is restrained from doing so by the side-loads on the pistons and connecting rods. The circumferential motion of the star-member arms was permitted by hinging them to a central spider and spigotting them into the piston trunnions. This extra degree of freedom however can lead to vibration modes at certain speeds. Whilst dynamic forces due to inertia of reciprocating and rotating parts can be compensated by balance weights, the combustion forces have to be restrained by the engine structure and put a large stress on connecting rods, spider, drive-shaft and cylinder walls. These considerations have to be carefully weighed by the designer.

Wobble plate engines are one of a family of engines generically known as "Barrel Engines". The Macomber stroke-plate and the Michell swash-plate engines have already been described, but the main characteristic of all barrel engines is that the cylinders are arranged around and parallel to the drive shaft rather like the chambers of a revolver hand gun. They have many advantages over conventional engines including compactness and balance, but they have one disadvantage, namely, friction. In a conventional engine with a crankshaft, the piston travels the length of the stroke whilst the big end travels around half the

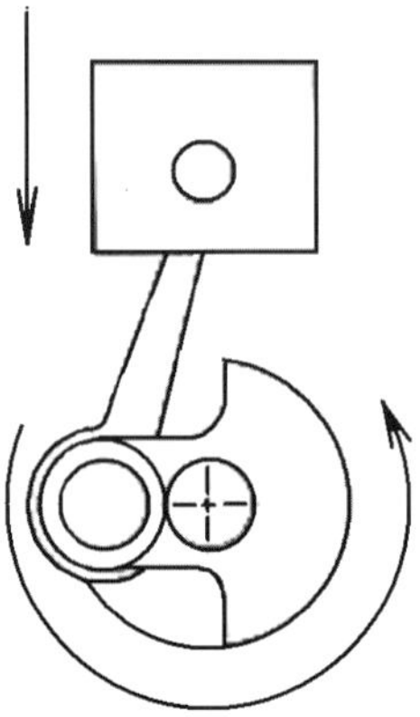

Plate 10-3 Ratio of Piston Travel to Crank Motion in a Crankshaft Engine

diameter of the crank throw. (Plate 10-3). The ratio of travel is in fact half of Pi, or about 1.57. This is the minimum mechanical advantage that has to be overcome by the piston in coping with the bearing friction.

In a barrel engine on every stroke each piston drives half way around the perimeter of the swash-plate or wobble-plate. This distance has to be greater than 1.57 times the diameter of two cylinders plus the shaft plus any cooling jackets around the cylinders. In the Fury I engine the ratio of piston stroke to diameter, the mechanical advantage, or, in this case, dis-advantage, was 4.4, nearly three times that of a crankshaft engine. Further-more, in a barrel engine during the firing stroke the piston is driving the wobble-plate at a large angle so there is a much larger reaction force, and the friction force is therefore higher. All these characteristics of barrel engines were well known and designers found different means of overcoming them. Macomber used ball-bearings and Michell used his patented design of angled thrust plates to reduce friction, but the latter were rarely trouble-free.

The motion of the connecting bosses on the spider of a wobble-plate engine is somewhat complex (Plate 10-4). They are constrained to travel over the surface of a sphere centred on the "dead point" at the centre of the "Z" shaft. In the ideal situation they all move in identical curved figure-of eight paths. In side elevation the top boss moves in an arc of a circle, whilst in end elevation it is a circle.

Plate 10-4 Motion of Spider Bosses on the Surface of a Sphere

The Fury engine for aviation use was made a much lighter structure than the marine engine. Plates 10-5 and 10-6 show the "Z" shaped crankshaft and spider for the Fury I engine and the features can be readily seen. The "Z"-shaft has flanges for bearings to carry the spider, which has a hub mounted on the shaft and articulated bifurcated tapered supports ending in oval-section arms. There were no connecting rods and the ends of the arms of the spider fitted in slots in the gudgeon-pins inside the pistons. The spider could articulate freely with the pistons through hinged joints on the arms of the star-member.

The beautiful pistons are clearly designed for lightness and ease of assembly onto the spider. (Plate 10-7). The friction forces were kept low by this direct articulation, in which the eight-inch (203 mm) long pistons ensured that the star arms did not deviate from the figure-of-eight paths.

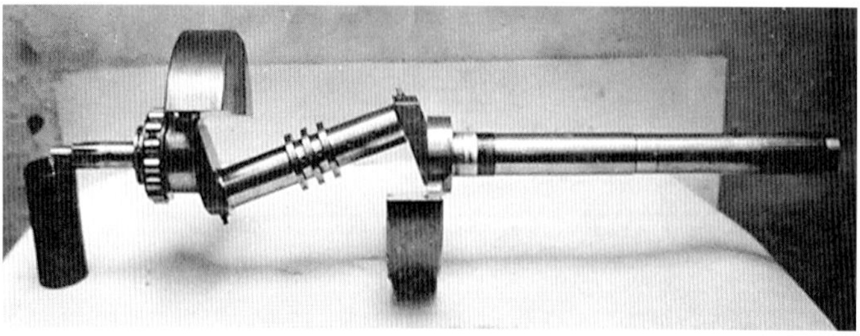

Plate 10-5 Fury I "Z"-Shaft with Balance Weights

Plate 10-6 Fury I Wobble-Plate "Spider"

The bore was 3 7/16 inches (89 mm), the stroke 4.5 inches (114 mm) and each cylinder had a swept volume of 0.684 litres giving a total capacity of 4.8 litres.

Plate 10-7 Fury I Pistons Mounted on the Spider

The engine was drawn entirely at Charles' home in Heaton Chapel. Several local first class engineering companies were given the drawings and Charles assembled the engine in the garage of his house. The crankshaft was of high tensile steel and the pistons of aluminium alloy. The cylinder block was of aluminium alloy with cast iron liners and the crankcase and spider were made of Electron, a lightweight magnesium alloy. The cams were operated from a lobed sleeve on the crank-shaft driven at half engine speed. The exhaust valves were operated by short push-rods and the inlet valves from longer push-rods, both operated directly from tappets on the cams. The crankshaft had a roller bearing at the rear, a deep-recessed ball bearing in the centre to absorb the thrust and another roller bearing at the front.

Tests on the Fury I engine showed resonance problems at certain speeds, much like the marine engine. Charles had traced this to the fact that although the piston and spider connections allowed free motion in the figure-of-eight paths, the spider was not constrained in the rotational direction and at some speeds would vibrate torsionally. He had devised a solution to this problem and patented it in 1928. (British Patent 327,161, 1928), The new design had a radial arm linking the "Z"-shaft arm to the casing to prevent the spider rotating, as can be seen in Plate 10-8. This was a very similar arrangement to that used in his very first axial engine with twin spiders, in 1922. Thus during 1929, as well as testing the Fury I, he designed a new poppet valve engine, the Fury II. It had a rigid spider constrained by a stabilizing rod. Connecting rods with trunnions on the spider had spherical joints to the pistons.

Plate 10-8 Fury II Engine with Spider Stabilising Arm

Meanwhile the Fury I was mounted in a timber frame and fitted with a Fairey Reed propeller. The frame was anchored to a heavy gun carriage from the First World War, and for testing purposes was stood in front of the garage with the doors wide open (Plate 10-9).

His son John recalls one occasion when the engine was being tested. He was only seven years old at the time and was sitting in Charles' brand new 1929 Morris Oxford watching his father run the engine. (Plate 10-10).

It was Charles' practice to start the engine by hand, firstly with the BTH magnetos switched off and then with the throttle at a fast tick-over position with the magnetos switched on. The engine would usually start at the first attempt with this procedure. Due to the limited space he would then inch his way around the propeller to the controls and gradually open the throttle. However on this occasion the engine was slow to start and he had to make several attempts, re-setting the throttle each time. He must have left the throttle partly open because when the engine did fire it leapt into life and dragged the gun carriage across the drive and the engine frame tilted forward perilously close to the car. The bonnet was fitted with a Calormeter, a visual temperature gauge fitted with short ornamental wings, just visible in the photograph. Before Charles could stop the engine the propeller caught the base of the Calormeter and chopped it clean off. It flew away complete with wings. No-one in Milwain drive ever reported

Plate 10-9 Fury I Engine on Test at Milwain Drive

a low-flying Calormeter and it was never seen again. The propeller had a slight chip in it which had to be dressed out but no other damage was done.

The tests on the Fury I engine gave it a rating of ninety horse-power at two thousand rpm and it weighed only 175 pounds (79.5 kg) dry. Charles loaded it onto a trailer and towed it firstly to a workshop in Faraday House, the home of the Institution of Electrical Engineers in London. The IEE had a ninety-nine year lease on the premises and let out surplus accommodation from time to time. During the late 1920s and early 30s the BBC had rooms adjacent to the workshop and the famous radio station 2LO broadcast from there. Charles had temporary accommodation during this time at 31, Church Road, Barnes where he and Jessie would stay whilst he was in town on Redrup Lever Engine Syndicate business. Dorothy continued to look after the children in Manchester although on occasions the whole family would make the trip to London in Charles' Morris Oxford.

Plate 10-10 The Redrup Fury and the Morris Oxford Face up for Battle

The Fury I engine was tested at Faraday House for several weeks in the summer of 1929. Charles' diary shows that it was first run on 30th May 1929 and achieved 44 horse-power at 1600 rpm. Later the same day it achieved 68 horse-power at 1775 rpm. It was worked progressively up to its full power rating over the next few weeks and thereafter it was towed down to Southampton and fitted into the second Simmonds Spartan aircraft. (See colour plate C14). The Syndicate was particularly anxious to test-fly the engine so that they could present it at an exhibition in Olympia during July.

This aircraft was the first off the production line at the Rolling Mills and had to be towed by road to Hamble where Oliver Simmonds had agreement to fly his aircraft. Simmonds claimed that his aircraft could be towed along the road at a steady twenty-five miles an hour. Plate 10-11 shows the aircraft fitted with the Fury I engine being fuelled up with Shell petrol for the first time at Phipps Garage in Netley on its way to Hamble. This garage still exists today as Netley Garage, being virtually unchanged, except it no longer sells fuel! In the photograph of the aircraft the push-rod guides can be clearly seen, as can the ring-type exhaust. The metal Fairey Reed propeller had a diameter of 6" 6 inches. (2 metres). The symmetrical wing-section is also clearly visible.

The aircraft was flown by Captain Mogens Bramson himself on the 15th of July 1929 and Plates 10-12 and 10-13 show it just as it gets airborne and in a flypast at about one thousand feet. It was flown directly to Hendon where it made a flypast on this, its maiden flight as part of the Olympia Aero Show. On landing back at Southampton, Bramson was not entirely happy with the Fury I engine during this first flight and suggested that more work was required to improve balance at certain speeds. Alan Jones, a colleague of Charles' son John painted a picture many years after the flight to commemorate it. (See colour plate C15).

It is interesting to note that at the Olympia show Charles Redrup's previous employers exhibited a model of their Avro 618/10 three-engined high wing monoplane. This aircraft was the result of a license agreement with the Dutch company Fokker and the Monospar Syndicate and had a wooden one-piece Monospar cantilever wing and a welded steel fuselage, both of which were very advanced for their time. The basic wing and fuselage structure would be taken a few years later by A.V.Roe to produce the Avro 652 Anson, an aircraft which surpassed the Avro 504K in numbers, and with which Charles would have some involvement later in his career.

Plate 10-11 Fury-Powered Simmonds Spartan Fuelling-Up at Phipps Garage, Netley

A sectioned model of the Fury II engine was displayed at the International Aero Exhibition at Olympia from July 16th to 27th 1929 where it aroused a lot of interest. The engine was turned over slowly by an electric motor to show how it worked. (Plate 10-14). Clearly the first flight of the Spartan on 15th July was aimed at capturing interest at the exhibition.

Plate 10-12 Redrup Fury I-Powered Simmonds Spartan Taking off from Butlocks Heath, Hamble

In the late summer of 1929 the Fury II was put on test in Charles' workshop at Milwain Drive. Plate 10-15 shows another photograph of this engine and its clean and compact lines are clearly visible. The exhaust stubs are beautifully curved to couple to the annular exhaust ring which was so typical of Charles' designs. A special demonstration was given to a potential investor, Grover Loening, who had been the Chief Engineer of the United States Air Service and now owned his own aviation company, the Loening Aircraft Engineering Company. Loening was born in Germany but emigrated to the United States whilst still quite young. His background was all in aviation and he had designed aircraft and pioneered aviation in his early days, designing and building the first monoplane flying boat in 1918. Loening was on a tour of Europe seeking ideas for his next investments and he had seen the Redrup Lever Syndicate's stand at the Olympia exhibition and witnessed the flight of the Spartan. He had been put in touch with Charles by Mogens Bramson.

Loening was intrigued by what he saw of the engine and agreed to discuss further the possibility of developing and manufacturing the engine. However he was travelling on to France and Germany and wanted to wait and see what else there was on the market.

Charles wasted no time after the visit and drafted out a proposal for Loening which he forwarded via Bramson. The proposal was for Loening's company to manufacture the Fury II, which Charles explained was a big improvement on the engine flown in the Spartan. Charles had re-designed the casing, reduced the mechanical advantage to 3 and fitted a stabiliser arm. The stabilising arm was the same length as the spider arms and the end fitted into a trunnion in the spider and into another fixed guide bolted to the bottom of the crank-case. Thus as the shaft rotates the stabilising arm held the spider steady in the vertical plane and reduced the side-loads on the pistons so that the engine torque was transmitted to the engine casing equally by the pistons and the stabilising arm. This arrangement constrained the bottom of the spider to move purely in an arc of a circle, and consequently the top boss moved in a larger figure-of-eight and the other bosses in somewhat smaller paths. The engine had "bottle"-shaped cylinders with twin sparking plugs arranged along the neck.

Charles analysed the motion of the wobble plate mathematically, and derived the relationship between the dimensions of the engine and the

Plate 10-13 Fury-Powered Spartan Setting off for Olympia Aero Show

shape of the figure-of-eight motion. He showed that the figure-of-eight when viewed from the front looked like a circle. He deduced that if the wobble-plate could be constrained so that one point on the periphery moved in such a circle at twice engine speed, the spider could be stabilised.

Plate 10-14 Sectioned Redrup Fury II Engine at the Olympia International Aero Exhibition, July 1929

In September 1929 Grover Loening replied to Bramson concerning Charles' proposals for the Fury II from Berlin, where he was continuing his European tour. He explained that he had seen many interesting developments in France and Germany and would prefer to wait until the Fury had completed its Ministry type tests before investing.

The performance of the ninety horse-power Fury I engine in the Spartan had met its targets, and in October 1929 a performance fee was paid to the Fury Syndicate, of which Charles received one hundred and twenty pounds! It was intended to install the improved Fury II in the Spartan. However Simmonds had found that the prototype Spartan aircraft with its symmetrical wing profile was somewhat under-powered with the ninety horse-power Cirrus engine and having fitted it with a 120 horse-power Gypsy for the Kings Cup in 1928 was planning to fit more powerful engines to production aircraft. Later Spartans were fitted with 100 horse-power Gypsy I or ADC Hermes 100 or 105 horse-power engines. Thus Charles did not manage to sell any engines to Simmonds.

*Plate 10-15 General View of the Redrup Fury II
Seven-Cylinder Axial Aero Engine*

The Aero Syndicate patented its engines in several countries and in 1930 Bramson patented on behalf of the Syndicate a double-ended opposed-piston version of the engine based on some of Charles Redrup's designs.

Oliver Simmonds' company got into financial difficulties during 1930 and by mutual agreement was taken over by Saunders-Roe. The company still manufactured under the Spartan name for a few years and produced two and three-seaters and larger aircraft many of which were sold abroad and played a significant part in establishing international postal services. Oliver Simmonds went on to invent the locking "stiff nut", of which many millions were used during the Second World War. The nut had a unique design in which cross-cuts were made near the top end of the nut, and the flanges so created were then crimped slightly so as to tightly grip the thread as the nut was tightened. By carefully controlling the angle of the cuts in the nut, it was made to be very difficult for it to come undone accidentally. The nut was made of softer material than the stud so that when the nut had to be removed for dis-assembly, it was damaged and so had to be thrown away and replaced. Thereby Simmonds created for himself a lucrative on-going after-sales business! He became an MP in 1931 and served on a number of government committees until 1945. He was particularly influential in the years just before the war in helping to determine foreign policy and in preparing for the inevitable conflict. He was President of the Air Raid Protection Institute formed in 1938 to consider the precautions necessary to protect citizens from bomb attacks and he was eventually knighted for his services.

Meanwhile in late 1929 Charles Redrup's career took a series of abrupt turns. At the International Aero Show at Olympia the Fury II engine had attracted the attention of several potential investors, not only Grover Loening, but also directors of the Bristol Tramway and Carriage Company Limited. The Bristol company were particularly attracted to the compact size of the engine and the vibration- free behaviour compared to the existing J W six-cylinder in-line petrol bus engine which was particularly noisy and heavy on fuel. They had in mind the construction of a low-deck bus where the engine was recessed below the chassis, enabling more passengers to be carried. As talks with the Tramways company proceeded, Loening decided to act and offered a contract to Charles to take his engines to America and for him to work for them, moving his family lock, stock and barrel across the Atlantic.

For a time Charles was in discussions with both organisations and eventually decided to take up the American offer. He discussed the options in great detail with Jessie and their children, some of whom were reaching critical stages in their education. Both he and Jessie were no strangers to the idea of working abroad as we saw just after they were married. Charles had travelled in his youth and Jessie's father had worked overseas as a mining engineer. Moreover Charles knew from his apprenticeship with Richard Stephens how much he had valued his experiences in Australia, Canada and America. After careful consideration they decide that with the depression still taking its toll on work in Britain, America offered a better future for them and their children, and now was the right time for them to be re-located in new schools.

Loening made all the arrangements for him and the family were booked on the Mauretania to sail from Southampton in November 1929. However disaster struck on Monday 28th October, when the Wall Street Stock Market crashed by over twelve percent in one day. This "Black Monday" was followed by further collapses as credit was called in by the banks. The aircraft company was in severe financial difficulties within a few days and Charles and his family had to call off his emigration. Loening eventually had to merge with another company and lay off staff. One consequence was that a number of staff made redundant by the merger went on to set up their own company, Grumman, which became a very successful American aircraft manufacturer in its own right.

A highly disappointed Charles returned to the development of the more robust Fury II type of spider and connecting-rod arrangement with a stabiliser. The intention was to offer the option of a poppet -valve or a rotary valve engine to the Monospar syndicate. However the development work on the Fury engines had taken longer than expected and they were still not certified when the prototype Monospar was ready in autumn 1930. It was called the Gloster-Monospar SS1 and was scheduled to make its debut at the Paris Air Show on 27th November but it was not until after the Show had started that the 38 foot (15 metre) wingspan, twin-engined Monospar had its maiden flight. This took place at Gloster Aircraft's airfield at Brockworth, Gloucester, which was to be the airfield at which Frank Whittle's first jet engine would make its first short hops in the Gloster-Whittle E28/39, (fitted, of course, with a Dowty undercarriage).

The Monospar was fitted with 45 horse-power Salmson engines for this flight and it proved a successful if under-powered aircraft. It went on to father a long line of Monospars fitted with Pobjoy 90 horse-power engines, manufactured by General Aircraft Limited. (GAL). As already mentioned Gloster built for £4,100 a sixty-three foot (sixteen metre) span monospar wing for an Avro-Fokker FVIII tri-motor aircraft. The wing weighed only one tenth of the aircraft's total all-up weight, a tribute to its strength of construction. Glosters, GAL and some other aircraft companies decided to pool their expertise on building metal structures and formed Aircraft Technical Services Limited (ATS) in May

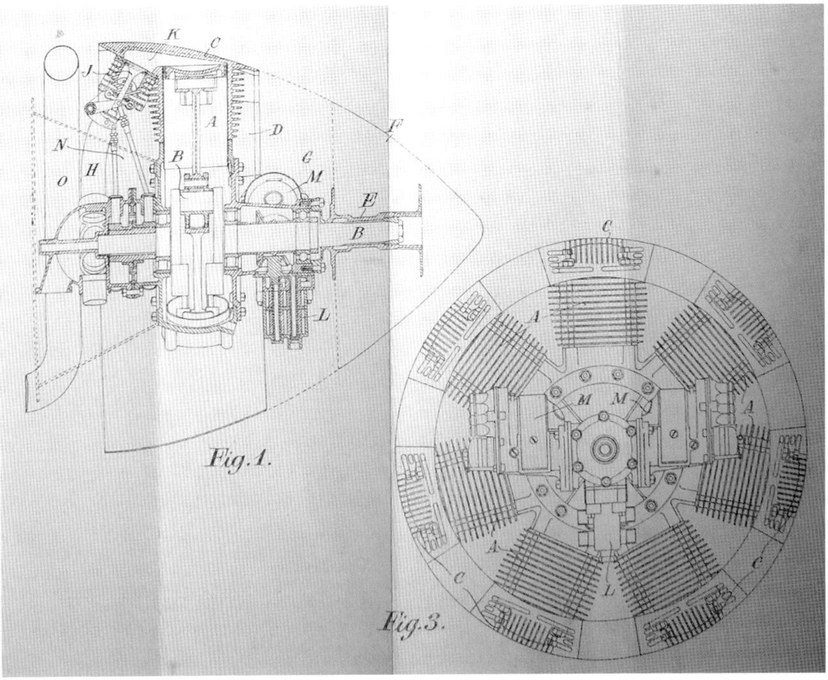

Plate 10-16 Redrup Patent for a Streamlined Radial Engine

1931. Amongst other things this company invented pop-riveting.

During 1930 Charles continued with his engine development work on the Fury II engine with "wine bottle" cylinders. He also lodged a patent for a streamlined cylinder head arrangement for radial engines, UK Patent 346,054. (Plate 10-16). This design incorporated rear-mounted poppet valvegear so as not to interfere with the smooth airflow over the top of the cylinder heads, but was also well-suited to sleeve-valve engines lacking any poppet valves. Aspects of the design contributed to the clean lines of the Bristol Hercules and Centaurus engines later in the decade.

Later in 1930 Charles resumed his discussions with the Bristol Tramways company who still wished to engage him to design a water-cooled axial engine for them. They were particularly keen to purchase

Charles' patent No. 327,161 incorporating the stabiliser arm design. Negotiations began and because of the protracted time in getting the aero engine certified and the consequent falling interest by the Monospar Syndicate, the Redrup Lever Syndicate sold out their interests to the bus company. The members of the Syndicate were paid off and in the autumn of 1930 the Fury II aero engine was transferred to the Tramways Company works in Brislington, Bristol. Before signing a contract with Charles Redrup the company wished to see his engine demonstrated on a test bed.

The Bristol Tramways staff fitted the engine into their bus engine dynamometer. The Works Manager was a Major Christopher George Nevatt and it soon became apparent that he and Charles Redrup were not going to get on well. Nevatt had worked on internal combustion engines during and after the First World War and had patented a carburettor design as early as 1916 whilst working in Chester. At the end of the War he left the army with the rank of Captain (Acting Major), and received an OBE in the January 1919 Honours List for services in France. By 1921 he was living and working in Bristol where he patented a spring suspension system for vehicles and in 1922 he also patented a rotary type of engine using opposed pistons which ran around a curved tube. This type of engine was used with some success in Russia for pumping gas but suffered from a virtually insuperable problem of sealing the joint where the piston arm came out of the cylinders.

Nevatt had worked for the Bristol Tramways company since 1928 and was driven by a desire to impress his directors and pushed hard all the time to rush matters along. The Bristol works dynamometer was a fairly crude device with a large diameter stiff shaft and large-clearance journals, adequate for heavy bus engines but too crude to be rigidly coupled to an aero engine. When the Fury engine was first run the dynamometer vibrated badly because the alignment was not set up properly. As a result the engine was given a bad shaking. Despite Charles' protests Nevatt insisted on running the engine for several hours. In this configuration there was very little cooling as the air-cooled engine was normally cooled by a propeller and its slipstream, and Charles had rarely run it on his own test stand for more than an hour at a time, even with a propeller.

Eventually Charles persuaded Nevatt to allow him to install the engine in his own test stand with a propeller and Charles shipped this into the works from Stockport. Once installed the engine was run up and was soon running smoothly. However Nevatt insisted on doing a ten-hour run and Charles got very concerned as the temperatures increased. Because of the small diameter of the engine most of the propeller slipstream passed around the engine and it was only when in flight that the engine was fully cooled by the airflow. After about four hours running Charles observed that vibration levels were increasing rapidly and insisted on shutting down. On examination it was found that one of the arms on the base which held the cylinders had fractured due to fatigue. This caused the stabiliser arm for the spider to become bent. Charles attributed this to the earlier running on the dynamometer with high vibration and to the high temperatures leading to lowering of the tensile strength.

The stabiliser arm was removed and Charles returned to his workshop in 7, Milwain Drive and re-designed the arm for the more arduous duty. He returned to Bristol and re-assembled the engine and resumed testing. After a further ten hours without incident Nevatt invited the Bristol Tramway directors to observe the engine test. They were very impressed and offered Charles an option on his engine patent, to run for one to one and a half years during which they would employ him to design a water-cooled bus engine. If when the option matured they were satisfied, they would purchase the rights to the design.

Chapter 11
On the Road Again

The beginnings of the Bristol Tramways and Carriage Company can be traced back to the middle of the nineteenth century when urbanisation and industrialisation of the country's towns and cities started to lead to congestion and restrictions on suburban growth. These problems were alleviated to some extent by the use of horse-drawn carts and omnibuses for public transport but the slowness and cost of such methods was in itself restrictive, leading to congestion in the narrow city streets. From about 1850 onwards horse tramways started to emerge whereby the carriages rode on iron rails. This was more efficient as friction was lower and horses could pull twice the load on rails compared to roadway surfaces. However legislation did not exist for the construction of tramways and local authorities and residents alike proved obstructive in providing wayleaves and so growth was slow. In recognition of the problem visionary Parliamentarians introduced the Tramways Act in 1870 which simplified the process. From then on entrepreneurs and investors started to take an interest in providing capital for tramway construction.

In Bristol a young law clerk became instrumental in promoting tramways and other forms of transport. George White was born in 1854 to a painter and decorator, Henry White and his wife Eliza in Kingsdown. He was apprenticed at the age of fifteen to Stanley and Wasborough, a Bristol law firm and his industrious work on bankruptcy cases together with his burgeoning business acumen resulted in his quick advancement. Within a year of his appointment the firm became involved in drafting enabling documents for tramway development. At the age of sixteen George was set the task of assisting clients to form tramway companies. Whilst the new legislation simplified the process it was still a planning minefield as vested interests tried to block schemes or to turn them to their own advantage. A group of London investors employed Stanley and Wasborough to launch a company to build a two-mile long tramway from Redland in Bristol to the city centre.

There was much debate at the time as to whether transport should be in public or private ownership and Bristol City Council refused the proposal and decided to build the line itself. However whilst legislation at that time allowed local authorities to own public transport, they were not allowed to operate or maintain them, so before the scheme could be built they had to find an operator and grant a lease. The only takers were Stanley and Wasborough who, realising that the single line scheme was uneconomic, put forward a proposal to operate the Redland line, and to build two more lines which would link together to provide a network which would be much more attractive economically. The Council were reluctant to accept but did not have the reserves to build further lines themselves, so after much heated debate they agreed to the scheme. George White drafted the Company Articles and late in December 1874 at the age of twenty he became the first Secretary of the Bristol Tramways Company.

George White was an extremely personable, but determined and dogged man with powers of persuasion and logic which quickly charmed and won around the diverse interests with which he had to deal. At the age of 21 he set up his own stock-broking company whilst remaining as Secretary to the Tramways Company and worked closely with entrepreneurs, business men and investors in a wide range of activities. He built up his own portfolio and soon became very wealthy, by a careful choice of investment, borrowing and takeovers. His experience in dealing with failing companies stood him in good stead as he purchased run-down companies, turned them around and sold them on.

The Redland line proved a great success when it opened in 1875 and carried half a million passengers in the first six months. It was the first public tramway to be opened under the new legislation. Over the next decade tramways spread throughout the whole of the city suburbs, although Clifton fought a long battle to keep the tramway and its "working class" customers away from the village. Instead White ran a horse-drawn omnibus service to the village which, being slower and noisier, was only used by the residents. By 1880 the Company had purchased the Redland line and owned seven lines around the city. A year later the Company acquired the rights to all public transport in and around Temple Meads Station and in 1886 set up a taxi cab company to operate services from the station around the city. A year later the two companies merged to form the Bristol Tramways and Carriage Company.

Despite their great success horse-drawn trams were not highly popular with citizens, nor were they highly profitable for investors. Fares were considered high and carriages were dirty, smelly and noisy. The huge stock of horses required meant that stabling, fodder and replacement costs ate up over half the revenue. At its peak the Company owned nearly nine hundred horses. The working life of a horse was only four years and it took five horses in shifts to service each tram because they could only work a few hours each day. Furthermore in a city like Bristol with many steep hills the horses had to be doubled up at times and so service outstations were also required. Added to that, the city cleaning costs and offensive smell all detracted from the popularity. On the other hand, the convenience of public transport for thousands of workers to move across the city was a major factor in Bristol's growth, and at weekends the population could travel for recreation to Durdham and Clifton Downs which the City Council had purchased for the population.

The Company, and in particular George White, were not averse to new technology and built a steam-driven tram and tested it on the Horfield line. However it proved noisy and smoky and was unpopular with the public. Furthermore it took a crew of five instead of the one-man operated horse-drawn trams so was also uneconomic. The Company also looked into the use of cable-drawn cars which had been used in other cities such as Edinburgh. However these worked well in long, straight streets with little gradient but would have proved horrendously complicated in a city like Bristol with its many intersections and hills. However serendipity seems to play a large part in the affairs of men and the invention of the first practical electric motor in 1870 and the construction of the first power generating station in 1891 lead to a revival of the tramways systems in the country and a new construction boom in the 1890s.

In late 1893 the Board of Trade published regulations for the construction and operation of electric tramways and George White, who was appointed Managing Director of the Bristol Tramways company in 1894 commissioned a review of the use of electric trams in Bristol. Just over a year later, in October 1895 the country's first publicly operated electric tramway opened between Kingswood and Old Market. Within five years the existing lines had been electrified and the network was increased by over sixty percent of new lines, and the Company owned nearly two hundred and fifty electric trams. A major workshop and depot was constructed at Brislington in the south of the city, and a power station constructed next to Temple Meads Station.

In 1900 George White was appointed Chairman of the Bristol Tramways and Carriage Company. He was knighted in 1904 for his services to public transport but he did not rest on his laurels. He invested in motor buses and taxicabs and in 1906 the Company started motor bus services on an experimental basis although acknowledging that they were as yet of doubtful commercial viability. As the efficiency and performance of internal combustion engines improved, the Company expanded motor bus and motor taxi services and in 1913 built a manufacturing works with an annual capacity of three hundred vehicles at the Brislington depot, selling motor buses all around the world. Motor buses became an integral part of the Bristol Tramways and Carriage Company's business and extended their network to well beyond the city boundaries and to other towns and cities. (See colour plates C17 & 18).

Meanwhile the Company came under political threat. Bristol City Council had tried to take the electric tramways into partial public ownership in 1895 by insisting on owning the new electricity generating station, but George White had fought off that attack. Again in 1913 the Council tried to take over the whole Company and obtained an Act of Parliament for this purpose in August 1914 but Sir George's sterling defence and the outbreak of war put the scheme into abeyance.

Road transport was not the only interest of Sir George White. He was a visionary where new technology was concerned and very early in his career he had invested in and directed various railway schemes, and he was also instrumental in creating Bristol's own aircraft manufacturer, which would have some influence on Charles Redrup's later career. In 1909 whilst visiting a car manufacturer in France to finalise details of his purchase, the designer introduced White to Wilbur Wright who was making flying demonstrations having failed to sell his aircraft to the British government. Sir George witnessed Wright's expert flying and saw several other French aircraft in flight. At that time aviation was still seen as a very risky business but in 1910 Sir George surprised The Tramways Board of Directors by announcing his intention to use family funds of twenty-five thousand pounds to create the British and Colonial Aeroplane Company. Whilst most aviation enthusiasts were dilettantes, he saw the potential of aviation as a commercial business.

The tramway system had at its northern extremity a terminus in the village of Filton, and it was here amongst open fields that Sir George established his aircraft factory. His vision was that the population of Bristol would stream out in their thousands, using the Tramway, to see his air displays. He first of all built aircraft under licence but was soon disappointed in their performance and used a Farman biplane as the basis for developing his own aircraft, the Bristol Boxkite. He recruited George Challenger, the son of the Tramways Company General Manager as his draughtsman and designer and it was Challenger who drew up the Boxkite. Over eighty of these aircraft were sold. Whilst most aircraft manufacturers operated on a shoestring White ensured that sufficient capital was put into the business to place it on a firm footing. He also ensured that the company had excellent staff such as test pilots Eric England and from France, Henri Jullerot and Maurice Tetard, and recruited designers such as Frank Barnwell and Clifford Tinson.

The Company went on to design and manufacture large numbers of aircraft including the famous Bristol Fighter of the First World War. Sir George died suddenly in 1916 and was succeeded by his brother Samuel White. In 1920, for tax efficiency reasons, the Company's assets were transferred to another, dormant company set up for £100 in 1910 by Sir George White, the Bristol Aeroplane Company. In the same year it took over the Cosmos Engineering Company and with it Roy Fedden (later Sir Roy) who had designed the Jupiter radial engine and who would play a not insignificant part in Charles Redrup's later career.

The Bristol Aeroplane Company went on to become a major aircraft manufacturer of aircraft and engines during and between the wars with aircraft such as the Bristol Fighter, the Blenheim, the Beaufort and the Beaufighter and sleeve-valve engines such as the Hercules and the Centaurus. After the Second World War the huge government-sponsored Brabazon aircraft, powered by eight Centaurus engines failed to grasp the changing trend of the market which was moving rapidly away from luxury travel for the few towards the mass leisure market. The company responded and made the highly successful Britannia aircraft powered by their own Bristol Proteus turbo-propeller engines but these filled a slot for only a short time as the market changed rapidly with the arrival of pure-jet passenger aircraft such as the Comet and Boeing 707. The Company ventured into helicopters and freightliners and participated in government research programmes which saw such impressive experimental supersonic aircraft as the Type 188. However changing government policies saw such developments scrapped in favour of unmanned craft and the Company was involved in developments such as the Thor and the Bloodhound missiles.

The Type 188 research was not wasted as the British and French governments signed an agreement in 1962 to build a supersonic passenger aircraft. The Bristol Aircraft Company (BAC as it became known) undertook a major part of the research work on materials and structure and when the aircraft went into production as the Concorde, BAC had forty percent of the work in making the forward fuselage with its drooping nose, the air intakes and the rear fuselage and tail. Rolls Royce supplied the Olympus engines. The second prototype flew from Filton in April 1969 and the first passenger service took place in 1976.

Concorde flew for over thirty years with an unblemished accident record until debris on the runway at Paris Charles de Gaulle Airport caused a total destruction crash in 2000.

In January 1978 the British aircraft industry was totally reorganised and BAC became part of the much larger British Aerospace. Collaboration with France continued after Concorde production ceased and a highly successful series of commercial airliners resulted, the Airbus family. After several changes of name the company is now simply called Airbus, and the British part of the company is responsible for the design and manufacture of the highly sophisticated wing structures. Filton, together with the sister factory in Chester comprise Airbus UK. The latest and largest Airbus, the A380 made its maiden flight in 2005 and is a two-deck aircraft capable of carrying up to 750 passengers and is the largest commercial aircraft in the world. It paid a courtesy visit to the place of its origins when it made a slow flypast over Filton in May 2006. Sir George White's vision of commercial air traffic has developed further than even his visionary dreams had imagined and his companies for road and air transport live on, albeit in very different forms.

Such then was the background to the Tramway company that Charles Redrup joined. The company was by then chaired by Sir William Verdon Smith who in 1928 took over from his uncle Samuel White, Sir George White's brother, when he died. Sir William's brother Colonel Sydney Smith was the Managing Director. The White family sold a large interest in the tramway company to the Great Western Railway in 1929 and the GWR in turn sold their shares to the Thomas Tilling group of transport companies in March 1932. Tilling then had the majority interest and took overall control but the White family still retained the chairmanship and other seats on the Board.

Charles Redrup started work with the Bristol Tramways and Carriage Company on May 16th 1931 and the contract was drawn up by Major Christopher Nevatt the Brislington Works Manager and approved by the board of Directors. It was signed by Charles Redrup and V Parsons, Clerk on behalf of the company and had two elements.

Firstly it granted the company an option to purchase the rights to Charles' 1930 Patent No. 327,161 and the equivalent foreign patents which embodied his axial engine design. Charles received a lump sum of five hundred pounds in respect of the option which was to run for one year and he was to receive a further sum of five hundred pounds on 15th November 1931 in respect if these options. The company had the right to extend the options by a further six months on payment of a further five hundred pounds. If the company decided to exercise its options before the due date it would pay Charles five thousand pounds for the British patent rights and five thousand pounds for the foreign patent rights.

Secondly, the company would employ Charles as a design engineer at a salary of five hundred pounds per annum and he was to design, manufacture and test a prototype axial engine for use in the company's omnibuses. If the design resulted in sales of the engines made by the company Charles would receive four shillings per litre of engine capacity sold. If the company subsequently licensed others to manufacture the engines Charles would receive fifty percent of the license lump sum and fifty percent of the royalties up to a maximum of four shillings per litre.

With a contract of employment in his pocket, and his eldest son John Arnold just leaving primary school, Charles moved his family from Manchester down to Bristol. Dorothy moved to Bristol with Charles and Jessie and the three youngest children and the other twin Marjorie moved to London to train to go to Africa as a missionary. However she failed her medical examination as she was considered too frail for the arduous duty involved. Disappointed, she obtained a post as a secretary to a married couple who were doctors and worked for them for many years. When the wife had a baby at the age of forty, Marjorie looked after the child. She was treated as a member of the family and when the son went to school she resumed her work as secretary. The family was very good to her and eventuality the son and his family looked after her until she died in 1999. Charles and Jessie's eldest daughter Florence did not move from Manchester but stayed on, running her junior school for a few years before selling up and becoming a maths teacher at a private girls' school. Violet also remained, well established in her work as a draughtswoman with A.V.Roe. Charles' two youngest children Jessica and Ray, still of primary school age, went to St Ursula's school.

John Arnold went to Bristol Grammar School where he was educated to prepare for the Matriculation examination. During his time in Bristol he was to form some strong enduring friendships with his schoolmates. His best friend however was not from his school but was the son of a neighbour. Rex Pollock lived in the house backing on to the Redrups' garden and he and John soon became close friends. They were always interested in scientific subjects and soon rigged up a "cocoa tin" telephone between each other's bedrooms. Later they went on to tinker with real telephones and also to build radios from magazine articles they had read.

Once established with the Tramway company Charles set to with a will and working alone, designed a nine-cylinder water-cooled axial bus engine with poppet-valves, designated RR1, for Redrup Rotary. The engine was of a much more sturdy design than the Fury engine as weight was of less importance for road vehicles. The engine incorporated Charles' patented design as used in the Fury II for a stabiliser which ensured that the star member was constrained to move in a fixed path. (Plate 11-1). This design restrained the bottom of the star member to oscillate backwards and forward whilst the other connecting rod bosses moved in figure-of-eight paths.

Plate 11-1 Bristol RR1 Nine-Cylinder Bus Engine with Stabiliser Arm Fixed to the Base of the Casing

Charles knew that perfect swashing, as he called it, required all bosses to move in an equal figure of eight. His 1922 patent had approximated this by using two half-star members, with diametrically opposite arms restrained to move in an axial plane. This gave perfect balance through symmetry. He devised a model with two meshing gears inside the wobble-plate to demonstrate to the Bristol staff how perfect swashing could be achieved. However he knew that as the stabiliser arm had to take the full torque load of the engine, the gear tooth arrangement would not withstand the forces and consequent wear in practice. He instead had ideas for achieving the same ends on later engines using a sturdier, simpler, eccentric drive, for which he prepared a patent.

The star member stabiliser as used on the Fury II aero engine was also used on the first Bristol engine, the RR1 and consisted of a Y-member

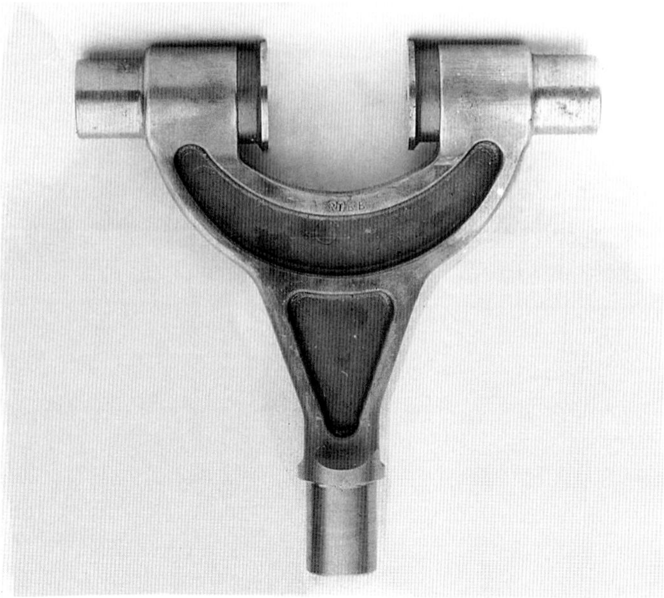

Plate 11-2 The RR1 Engine Stabiliser Arm

mounted on the shaft by a sleeve bearing with the leg of the "Y" locating in a peg in the base of the engine casing. (Plate 11-2). A longitudinal slot in the star member was just wide enough for the leg to protrude through, and the edges of the slot provided the sliding bearing surface to take the transverse torque load from the star member to the casing. The pistons had spherical little-end connections so that the piston heads could rotate freely and even out wear and also allow the connecting rods to follow the figure-of-eight motion. (Plate 11-3).

The big-end connections were by means of gudgeon pins between flanges onto the star member. As discussed earlier this did not give perfect swashing but enabled the star member to be effectively stabilised and balanced. The valves were operated by short push-rods operating directly from cams mounted on the shaft. The engine had a bore of 3.5 inches (89 mm) and a stroke of 4.92 inches (125 mm). Charles used the same pistons and connecting rods as the Fury II engine, although the stroke was longer. The stroke of an engine has a direct effect not only on the size and weight, but also on the thermal efficiency of the engine. The longer the stroke, the more energy is extracted from the expanding gases and the cooler the exhaust. In the Fury aero engine where weight and size was at a premium Charles Redrup opted for a stroke of 4,5 inches (114 mm). In scaling up to nine cylinders for the bus engine he kept the

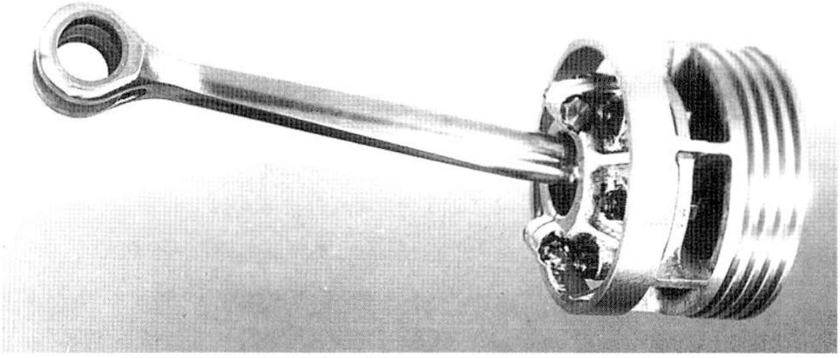

Plate 11-3 Connecting Rod and Piston

same "Z" crank angle which meant the cylinders were proportionately closer together but the stroke was increased to 4.92 inches (125 mm) thereby increasing the swept volume per cylinder to 0.778 litres giving the total capacity of 7.0 litres. The compactness of the engine can be seen in Plate (11-4). The size and weight were less than half that of the J W engine. (Plate 11-5).

Within six months, in September 1931, this first engine RR1 was on the test bed and performed very well in comparison to the six-cylinder J W engine currently then in use, both in terms of weight, size and fuel consumption :-

Average fuel consumption per BHP-Hour 1,000/2,400 rpm

J.W.6-cylinder engine	.666 pints	Standard Carburettor
R.R. 9-cylinder engine	.629 pints	Standard Carburettor
R.R. 9-cylinder engine	.528 pints	Special Carburettor

BHP per litre of total piston displacement, and weight per BHP :-

J.W. 6-cylinder engine	15.3 BHP,	11.7 lbs per BHP
R.R. 9-cylinder engine	20.0 BHP	5.2 lbs per BHP

Plate 11-4 The Compact Bristol RR1 Redrup Nine-Cylinder Axial Engine

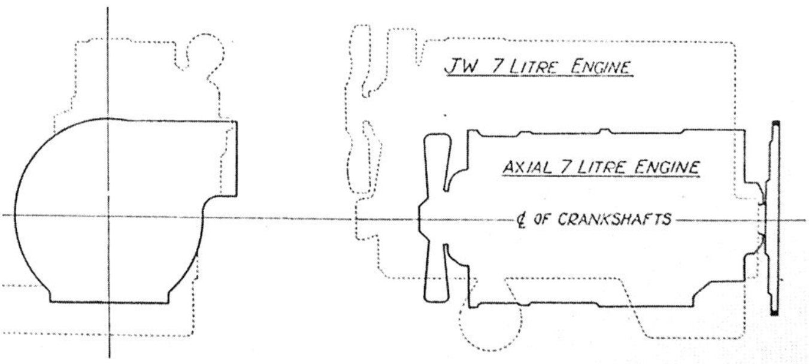

Plate 11-5 Comparative Sizes of the RR1 Engine and the J.W. Engine

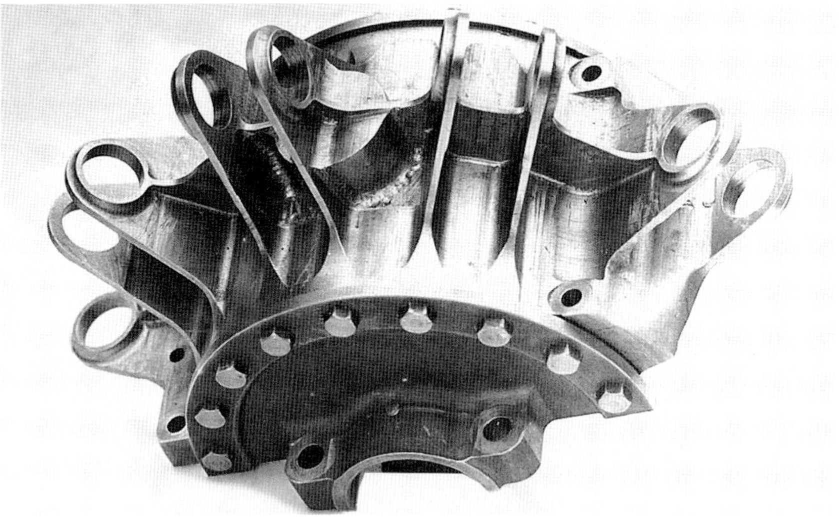

Plate 11-6 One Half of the RR1 Spider

The Bristol Tramways and Carriage Company wanted the engine to have the same capacity as its standard seven litre R W engine for direct comparison purposes. The spider was made of two half castings and finished to a high standard. (Plate 11-6). All the bearings were of the journal type with white metal linings.

During these tests it was observed that there was a slight vibration from the front of the engine and Charles had the engine removed and checked. He deduced that the asymmetrical swashing was causing an unbalance and he devised a dynamic balancing apparatus using springs and a counterbalance in the form of a plumb-bob to enable the spider to be balanced in all planes. (Plate 11-7).

Plate 11-7 Spider Balancing Apparatus

By adding small weights in the form of welds to the spider he was able to cure the unbalance. Subsequent testing proved that the unbalance had been cured.

Christopher Nevatt was overjoyed at the performance and invited the Managing Director Colonel Sydney Smith to witness the tests, who was equally impressed. Sydney Smith's uncle, Sir Stanley White was at this time Managing Director of The Bristol Aeroplane Company, whose chief engine designer was Roy Fedden, and Sydney Smith had at one time been a Bristol Aeroplane Company test pilot. Smith invited Fedden to send an engineering representative to witness the axial engine on test and this was done. The representative was very congratulatory and went away enthused. However from Charles' recollection it appears that Fedden was very jealous of the new development. Fedden had spent many years trying to perfect the sleeve-valve radial engines for which he was famous.

Plate 11-8 Charles Redrup with the First Bus Engine Installation

These engines were based on the Burt and McCollum sleeve valve which were similar in operation to the reciprocating sleeve valves used by Charles Redrup in the "Barry" engine in 1904 but incorporated the part-rotating motion which he had so narrowly missed patenting in 1911. The sleeve-valves eliminated all poppet valvegear and were extremely quiet because of the smooth rotary and reciprocating motion. Fedden's team had needed to hand-select components in building their engines as the sleeve had to fit snugly between the piston and the cylinder liner and tolerances were difficult to match. Furthermore during the final grinding operation distortion of the sleeve would often occur. A suitable choice of materials with compatible expansion coefficients eventually helped solve the problem.

When the Bristol engines had to be mass-produced in shadow factories during the Second World War, the (probably apocryphal) story is that an inexperienced operator in one of these factories performed the grinding operations in reverse order, starting with a fine new wheel and finishing with an old wheel. He never produced distorted sleeves and once the reason was understood, the technique was adopted for all sleeves. This kind of behaviour is often found in milling processes. Taking a finishing cut that is too fine can cause tool chatter and spoil the finish. Charles Redrup feared that the intrinsic simplicity of his engine, with its much reduced diameter and drag would be seen as a threat by Fedden and in a report to his Board at Bristol Aeroplanes, Fedden was very negative about the axial engine.

RR1 engine bench tests were completed in 1932 and the engine was fitted into a J.MW.2 chassis, and designated J.A.X.1. (Plate 11-8).

Plate 11-9 Charles Redrup's Rotary Valve for The Bristol RR1 Axial Engine

The free space above the engine is clear to see, hence the interest in employing it for under-floor use. During this time Charles put in hand the design of a rotary-valve engine modification for the RR1 engine and when the parts were ready the vehicle was returned to Brislington works and the engine removed. This rotary valve was very ingenious and had four sets of double ports cut into it which alternately lined up with the inlet manifold and the exhaust. (Plate 11-9).

By rotating the valve at a fractional speed equal to one less than the number of cylinders it was possible to achieve the correct timing for a four-stroke engine, and also to have very low wear rates. Thus with the nine-cylinder Bristol engine the valve was rotated at one-eighth engine speed. The RR1 engine was modified to take this new rotary valve and mounted again on the test-bed. (Plate 11-10). It gave more power than the poppet-valve version and when re-fitted in the bus chassis was operated again for several weeks without incident. (Plate 11-11).

Plate 11-10 Preparing the Rotary-Valve Version of the RR1 for Test

In May 1932 the Bristol Tramways and Carriage Company exercised their option to purchase Charles' UK patent and he received his lump sum payment. Nevatt obtained Board approval to start engine manufacture but they wanted to see a direct comparison of the two engines first of all, to see which one was best suited to road service.

Charles had meanwhile had further thoughts on the design of the engines. In 1932 he lodged his patent for an eccentric-driven stabiliser

Plate 11-11 Charles Redrup at the Wheel of the J.MW.2 Chassis

mechanism. In this the stabiliser arm is oscillated laterally at twice engine speed, and synchronised with the star member motion to give a true figure-of eight motion, thereby giving perfect swashing. He explained the figure-of-eight motion in the patent and it was granted the next year. (Plate 11-12).

He also wanted to replace most of the bearings with roller and ball-thrust bearings. He was concerned particularly about wear at the faces where the star-member bearings faced onto the crankshaft. There was considerable axial thrust at these points arising from the torque reaction from the star member. By fitting ball-thrust bearings here he hoped to reduce wear. Thus he drew up two further engine designs incorporating ball bearings, a simpler and cheaper star member and using big-end connections with spherical seatings to reduce frictional forces further. (Plate 11-13). These two engines, designated RR2 and RR3 had poppet valves and the rotary valve, respectively.

Charles was having great difficulty in getting these engines manufactured. The Tramways company shop was full of other work and he had to battle to get work carried out. What he did not know was that by this time Major Nevatt was pursuing his own agenda. Sometime during 1932 he called Charles into his office and asked him whether or not the ball and socket joints on the star member should be patented. Charles' view was that it was not particularly novel as it had been used in the 1911 Macomber engine. Later he learnt that Nevatt went ahead and patented it in his own name and that of the Company Secretary E G Kingston. Furthermore he had seen Charles' earlier models of an internally-geared swash-plate and he and Kingston patented this as well without Charles' knowledge. Nevatt put into manufacture a set of gears based on this principle. Charles had strongly advised against this design as he knew that the asymmetrical loading on the gears would cause high tooth loads and wear because the gearing gave a high torque on the gearwheel shafts. Nevatt took a draughtsman, Colin Campbell, with no experience of the axial engine from the Drawing Office and set him to work to do the modifications and also gave instructions to the Works to give his own work priority.

When Charles' next two engines were finally ready after much delay early in 1933, the RR2 poppet valve version was ready first by just a few days, and Charles erected it on the test stand and ran it up. It was immediately obvious that the cylinder-head joint had a leak. When the cylinder head was removed it was found that the faces of the head and cylinder block had deep scores with indentations in the shape of a nut. It

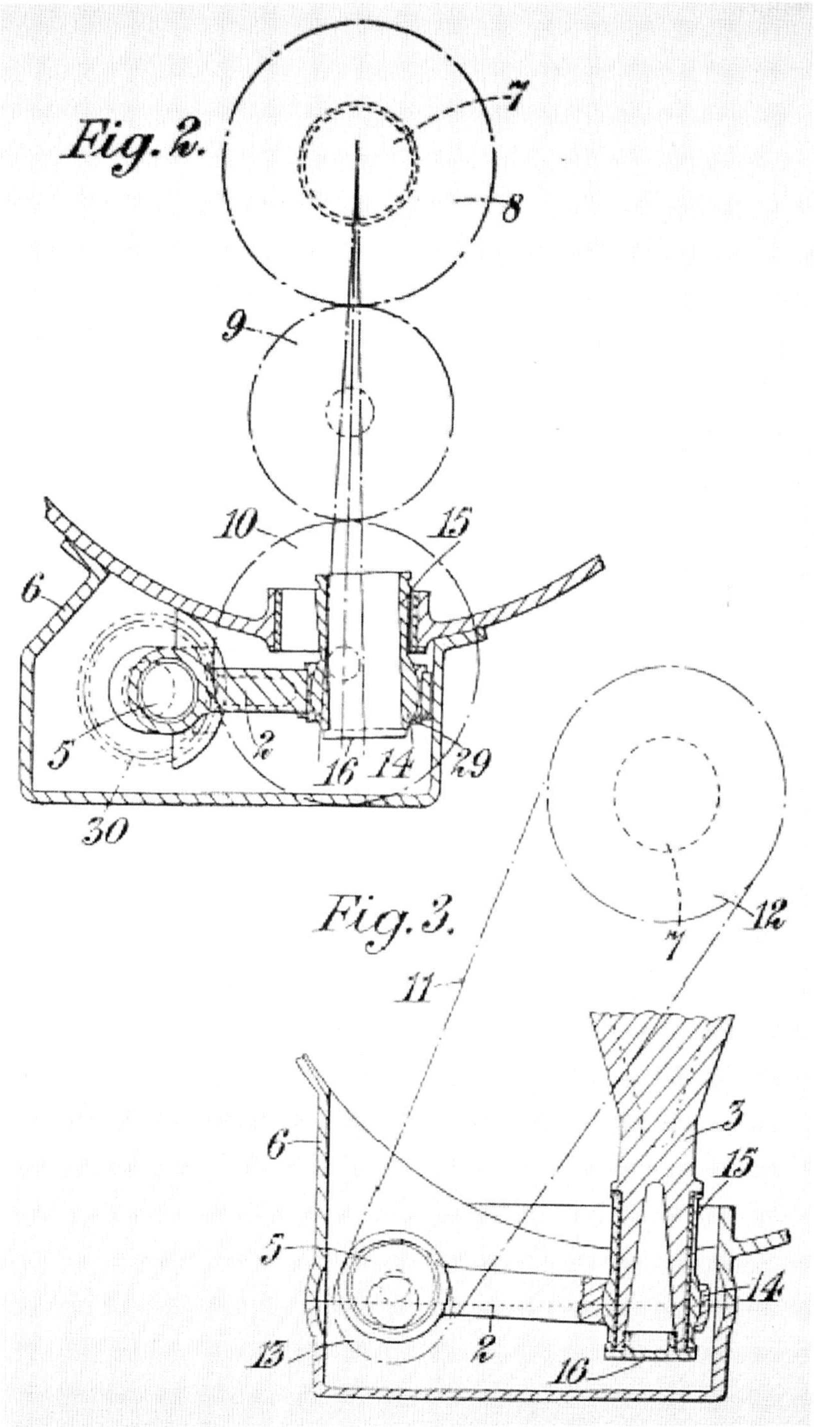

Plate 11-12 Extract from 1932 Patent on Eccentric Drive for Stabiliser Arm

Plate 11-13 Ball and Socket Spider Connections for RR2 Engine With Ball-Race Main Bearings

appeared that the engine had been assembled for a check-fit at some stage and the head had been tightened down onto a vagrant nut. The engine had to be completely dismantled and the faces re-machined.

The RR3 rotary valve engine was now finished so this was mounted on the test stand and turned out to be a great improvement on the previous engines. Losses were lower owing to the use of ball bearings, oil consumption reduced and petrol economy improved.

Whilst these tests were proceeding, unknown to Charles, Nevatt took the parts of the dismantled RR2 engine and modified them to take his own gear-type stabiliser. In particular he took the star member and cut much wider slots in it to accommodate the gear mechanism and in doing so destroyed its strength and balance.

The modifications involved installing a ring of machined teeth around the inside of the star-member and fitting a complex gear into the stabiliser bar, an arrangement against which Charles Redrup had strongly advised. (Plate 11-14). It took many months before this engine was put on the test stand and it ran for just a very short time before the stabiliser arm broke free. Nevatt then did a re-design and after more months delay the engine was tested once more. It was operated at tick-over for about three-quarters of an hour and then seized solid. The engine was re-built several times with the same result after which Nevatt

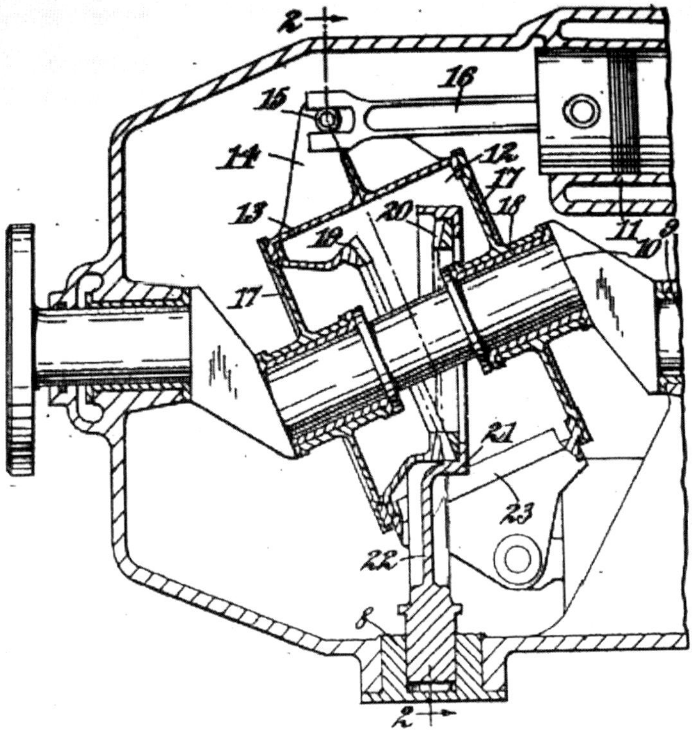

Plate 11-14 The Nevatt Gear-Type Stabiliser

abandoned the gear-wheel stabiliser. Over a year had been lost and the opportunity to do a comparative test of the RR2 and RR3 poppet and rotary valve engines was lost.

Meanwhile the RR3 was undergoing extensive development testing in J.A.X.1 prior to production. The cooling of the rotary valve faces had to be improved and the single annular plate was replaced by hardened steel segmental valve-plates. The size of the valve openings was increased to give greater breathing and lands were fitted to the big-end spherical bearings to prevent the connecting rods hitting the star member at critical speeds. By the end of 1934 the engine was considered suitable for putting into service and the Board authorised the manufacture of four production engines designated RR4.

Chapter 12
Avro-Again!

The Redrup family were well settled in Bristol and enjoyed the city and its surrounding countryside. At weekends Charles would take the family for drives around the area in his Armstrong Siddeley. His antipathy to John Siddeley did not extend to his cars! Plate 12-1 shows Charles and Jessie on one such trip, with Dorothy still helping to look after the younger children.

Plate 12-1 The Redrup Family on a Day-Trip

They particularly liked to drive to Sidmouth in Devon for the day, as they found the little seaside resort relatively unspoilt compared to other towns. (Plate 12-2). Charles and Jessie of course could not resist visits to their relatives and old haunts in and around Clevedon and often visited Clevedon Court, the home of Sir Edmund Elton.

As stated previously, the Thomas Tilling Group purchased a controlling interest in The Bristol Tramways and Carriage Company. Early in 1935 Sir William Verdon Smith and Sydney Smith resigned from the Board to go to the Bristol Aeroplane Company where their

Plate 12-2 Charles and Family on Sidmouth Beach

knowledge and skills were required in preparation for the looming war effort. In conjunction with Sir Stanley White, still at the helm, they helped re-organise the firm and turn it into a public limited liability company in June 1935. Sir William was replaced at the Tramways company by J Frederick Heaton of the Thomas Tilling organisation. With Sir William gone and another Tilling man Major Chapple replacing Sydney Smith as Managing Director, Nevatt seems to have seized the opportunity to further expand his influence. The RR3 engine was described in an article in *The Engineer* in May 1935 and Charles Redrup was appalled when he read it. Nevatt was quoted extensively, taking all credit for the engine and Redrup was not mentioned at all. Nevatt made slighting comments about earlier versions of the engine used for aircraft and personally took all credit for solving the "figure-of-eight" problem. This was despite the fact that this had been solved years earlier with Charles Redrup's 1925 marine engine and was a main feature of Charles' patent that the Tramway company had purchased!

Charles wrote a letter of protest to the journal but got little redress. The RR3 chassis was also displayed at the Commercial Motor Show in the autumn and details of the engine were reported in *The Commercial Motor* in November 1935. This time there was no reference to Nevatt but then, neither was there to Charles Redrup. However, the company were clearly gearing up to start marketing the engine.

The Bristol Tramways and Carriage Company produced a glossy brochure for the Commercial Motor Show based on the RR3 performance and compared it directly with the six-cylinder 7 litre R W which was their current operational engine. (Plate 12-3). The RR3 weighed 7 cwt (356 kg) and developed one hundred and fifty horse-power (112 kw) at 3,000 rpm, at which point the power curve was still climbing. The maximum torque at 1250 rpm was 320 ft-lb (442 newton-metres) and fuel economy at economy and full power carburettor settings was 0.5 pints and 0.6 pints per BHP-Hour respectively at 1700 rpm. (0.21 and 0.25 litres per kw-hour) This fuel economy was 21 percent better than the R W engine. The RR3 weighed 1.90 kg per kw whilst the R W weighed 3.97 kg per kw, more than twice as much. The RR3 was measured as having a thermal efficiency 5.3 percent better than the R W engine, and a mechanical efficiency 23.5 percent better.

By spring of 1936 the first of the production RR4 engines was on test. (Plate 12-4). The engine was a virtual copy of the RR3 engine with sleeve valves but the valve plate was made of hardened steel. A plate was also made using the relatively new material Stellite, a very hard-wearing steel alloy. In addition the gear train and eccentric drive to the stabiliser bar was strengthened. This drive system was a very clever arrangement, with an auxiliary shaft driven at twice engine speed coupled to a block into which the stabiliser bar fitted. This block could move transversely in lubricated slides. The shaft had a crank section offset by a distance equal to the semi-diameter of the circle of rotation of the curved figure-of-eight motion of the star member extremities. A stout bearing fitted onto the crank section and was coupled to the sliding block. As the main engine shaft rotated the auxiliary shaft rotated at twice the speed and the crank gave a transverse eccentric motion to the sliding block and thereby to the stabiliser shaft which fitted into it. (Plate 12-5). The gears connecting the two shafts were synchronised to ensure that the resulting figure-of-eight motion was in the correct relationship to the piston motions.

The works tests on the RR4/1 engine passed without incident and it was fitted into a thirty-two seater front-entrance "B" Type omnibus and extensively road-tested during the summer. With registration BHW 429 it was fitted with the KS five-speed gear-box and the speed had to be

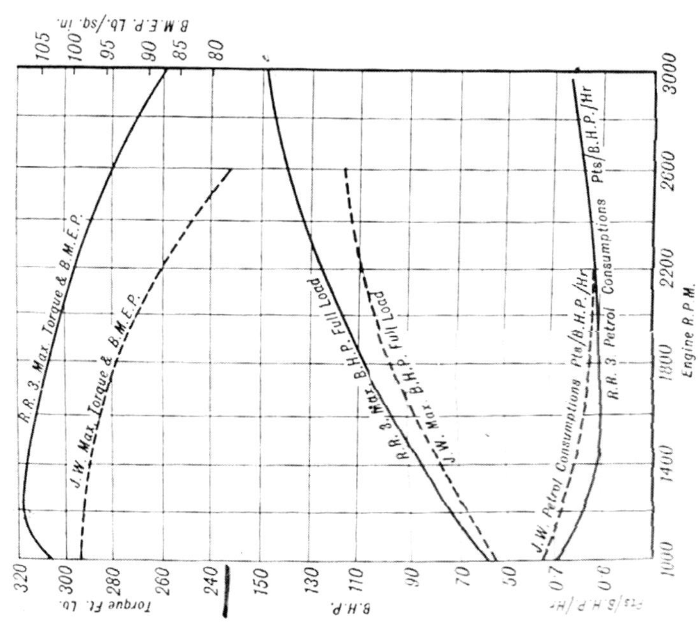

Fig. 10 Comparison of Full Power and B.M.E.P. Curves

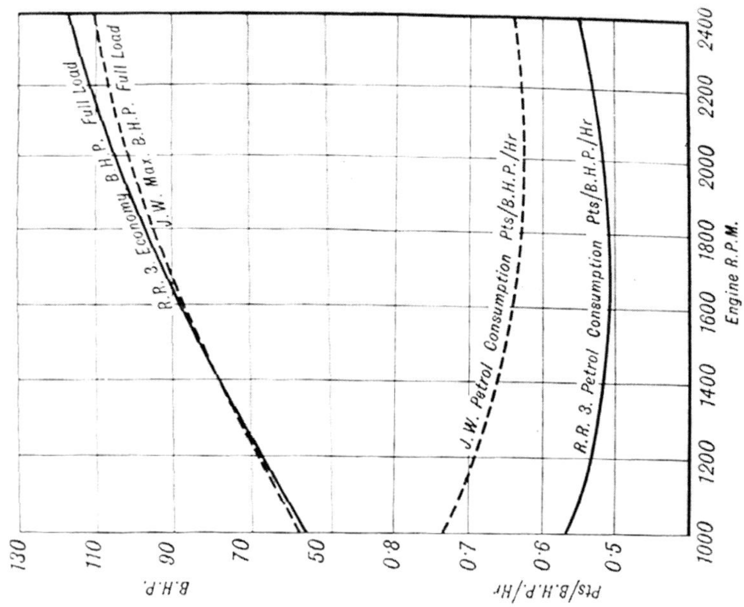

Fig. 11 Comparison of Characteristic Curves

Plate 12-3 Comparison of Redrup RR3 Engine and J.W.Engine

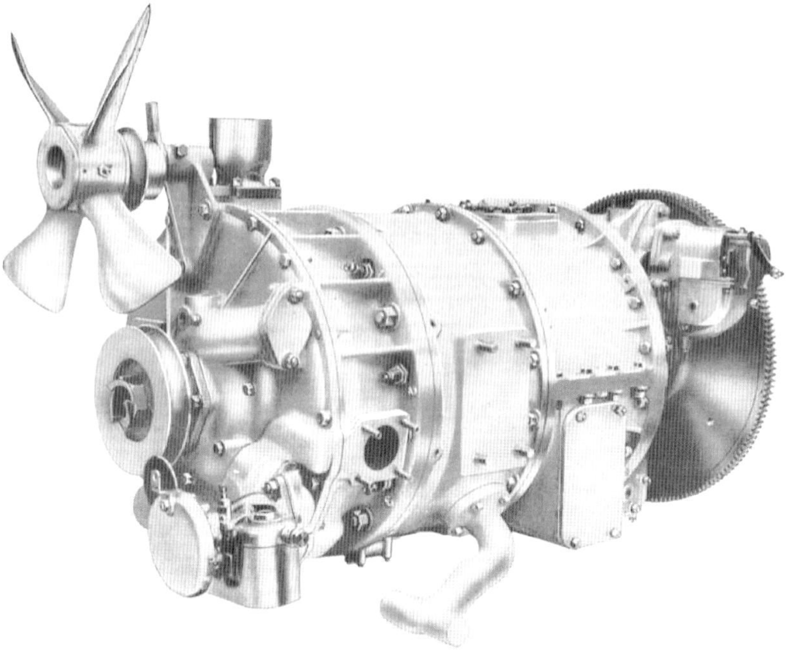

Plate 12-4 First Production RR4/1 Engine

Plate 12-5 Eccentric Drive for RR4 Engine Stabiliser Bar

kept down to use the existing ratios. (Plate 12-6). The second production engine RR4/2 was put on test in the Brislington Works and ran for about four and a half hours over the last weekend in August. Fortunately some test results have survived and show that the engine was run up to an output of about 137 horse-power 102 kw) at 2,700 rpm. At low load a slight tremor was noted at the front of the engine but the rear end was very steady. The engine was then fitted into the J.A.X 1 chassis with a loaded weight of 3 tons (148 kg). On the first day, Wednesday 2nd September, the vehicle was run around the circular Chelwood route for a total of 84 miles. Over the next two weeks the vehicle travelled nearly three thousand miles. Many adjustments were made to the carburettor jets and to seals and a number of problems with ancillaries were solved to obtain final reliable running. Final figures for fuel consumption up to 18th September were excellent. On hilly routes the vehicle achieved 20 miles per gallon (8.0 km per litre). And on the flat it achieved over 45 mpg (18.0 km per litre). However the engine oil consumption during the tests was 400 mpg (160 km per litre) compared to 700 mpg (280 km per litre) for the R W engine.

On 18th September the engine stopped suddenly and this was found to be due to a broken water hose clip leading to overheating. The engine was taken back to the Works the next day for inspection and it was found that the phosphor-bronze valve plates had distorted and the valve plate springs had lost their temper due to the overheating. The valve plates were replaced with hardened steel ones taken from the RR4/1 engine and the springs replaced and testing re-commenced on 30th September. During October the vehicle was operated for several more hours but a large increase in oil consumption was observed and the cooling fan appeared to be fouling its casing. On dismantling the valve plate it was found that the hardened steel had cut a deep groove in the plate which broke through the sealing ring, causing high leakage. The damage was repaired and the engine re-assembled.

After the RR4/2 engine had been bench tested in September the RR4/1 engine had been returned to the Works for detailed examination and analysis. Wear on the big-end connecting rod spherical joints was observed and these were replaced. No other significant wear was observed, with the valve faces well bedded-in. The engine was assembled on the test bed and run up for several minutes. After a while tapping noises were heard from the casing. The engine was stopped and the side inspection plates removed and a damaged connecting rod could be seen. The engine was therefore dismantled and it was found that one of the new connecting rods had broken at a metallurgical defect near the big-end stem. The rod had flailed around and damaged its cylinder skirt and several other cylinder liners. A second connecting rod had been hit and broken, driving its associated piston right through the cylinder head. The engine was rebuilt with parts from the next production engine and the hardened steel valve plates were transferred to the RR4/2 engine as described above, and the new Stellite-faced valve plates were fitted instead. The engine was put on test again late in October 1936 and after about ten hours running the valve faces were examined for wear. Slight running-in scoring was noted but the seal was good and the valve was re-assembled. The engine was then given a test up to full power and at 2,900 rpm an output of 145.5 horse-power (109 kw) was held for one minute. The engine was considered satisfactory, and it was decided to keep it in the test shop until required at some future date.

Plate 12-6 A Bristol "B"-Type Bus

Like his friend Oliver Simmonds, Charles Redrup could never be satisfied with just a day job. Although, to use the actual words from his contract with the Bristol Tramways and Carriage Company :- "The Patentee shall during the employment devote the whole of his time and attention to the Company's business". Charles had spent a lot of his "spare" time pursuing other designs and inventions. During his lifetime he took out sixty-seven UK patents either alone or jointly with others, and many more international versions of these patents.

The Fury Mark II engine which he had demonstrated to Christopher Nevatt was a poppet-valve engine and had identical cylinders to the RR series of bus engines. He had however developed and patented a design for a seven-cylinder one hundred and twenty horse-power rotary-valve aero engine, the Fury III (Plate 12-7). This engine incorporated two new major features intended to improve the stability of the star member. Charles was not happy with the eccentric drive motion used on the RR3 and RR4 series of engines, which, although giving perfect swashing, was complicated, heavy and a source of potential wear and not considered suitable for aero applications. In addition the rubbing speed between the star member and the stabilising arm was considered high and he wished to reduce it.

Charles designed a new “W” shaped crankshaft, which had a central section angled to the main axis at half the angle of the star member shaft. The stabilising arm was mounted on this central section and its bottom end slid in a trunnion with a longitudinal slit. The consequence was that the stabiliser arm slid backwards and forwards in the star member at half the previous speed, and also slid backwards and forwards in the trunnion at a similar speed. Thus the rubbing area was doubled and the rubbing speed halved and wear correspondingly reduced. This engine also had a different mounting arrangement for the rotary valve. The valve plate was much smaller and lighter than that on the bus engines and was mounted on a large-diameter ball-bearing at the front end, with a face seal onto the cylinder head and eliminated the earlier compromise between high oil consumption or high face wear.

Charles also retained his interest in radial engines and during this period he designed a novel form of main crankshaft spider which eliminated the master rod/slave rod arrangement. In this design he replaced the master rod with a symmetrical bearing having connecting rods which interlocked over a spherical surface giving a lighter but stronger assembly. (Plate 12-8).

During 1936 he also patented a side-valve nine-cylinder radial engine which used the symmetrical valve and head arrangement which he had used on the three-cylinder Boyle and Redrup engine in 1920. The main feature of this engine was that the pistons were all linked to the hub via identical connecting rods which were bolted to the hub and piston via a parallel-action arrangement. This was a development of the patented Redrup design of valve with a double-pushrod used on the Alpha engine, to relieve side-loads on the tappets. The advantage of this system for connecting rods is that the tendency of the pistons to cant in the bores and produce higher friction is eliminated. (Plate 12-9). The side-thrust on the pistons was thus uniformly distributed along the piston length giving less wear and preventing the oil film from breaking down. There

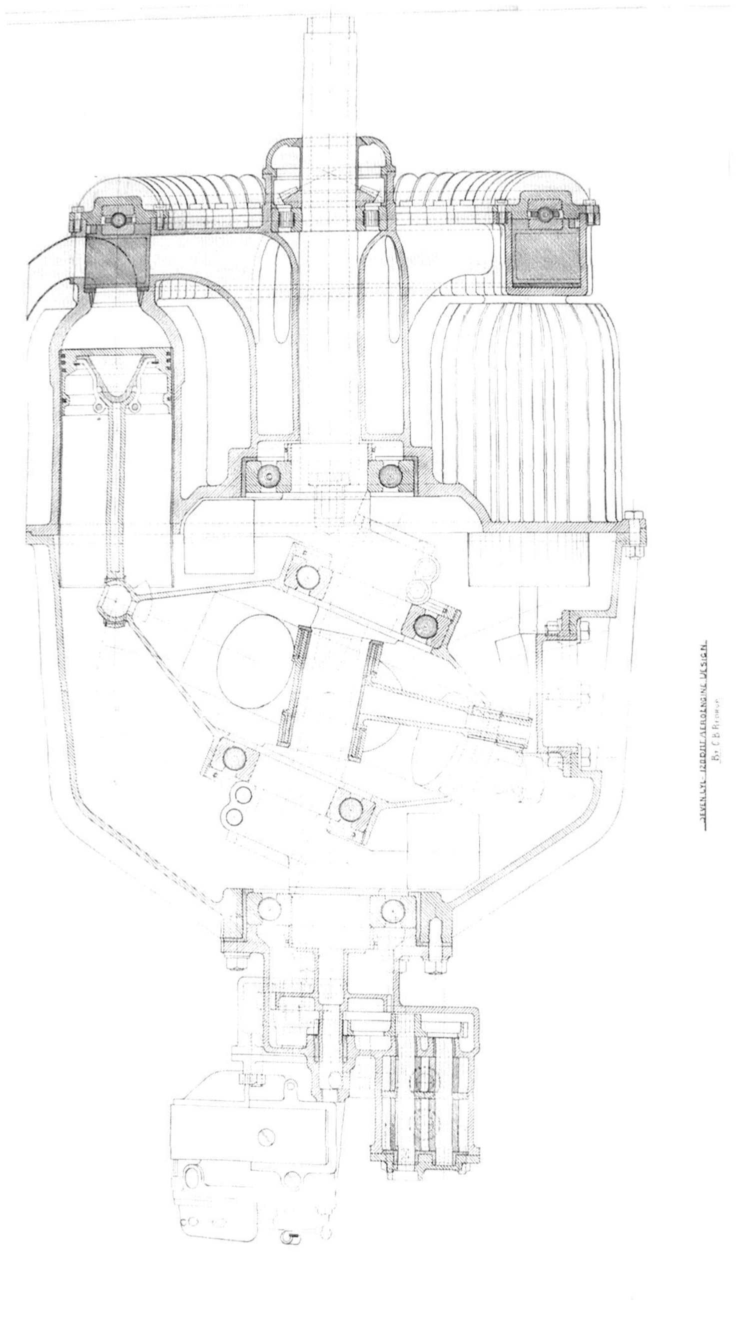

Plate 12-7 Redrup "Fury III" 120 Horse-Power Rotary-Valve Axial Engine

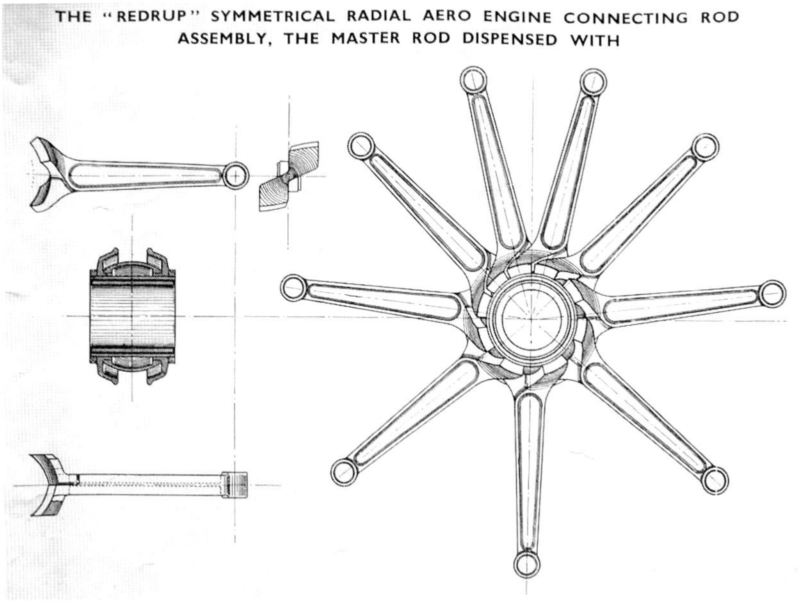

Plate 12-8 Redrup Lightweight Con-Rod Spider for Radial Engines

does not appear to be any evidence that this design was taken further, and one factor may have been the use of side valves

The space in the cylinder head occupied by the valves sets a limit on the compression ratio that can be used. As new fuels were developed with higher octane ratings it became possible to move to higher compression ratios without the fear of pre-ignition. Aero engine designers were more conservative in adopting these changes as reliability was more important than efficiency at that time but the Second World War was to change all that and ensure much more rapid development on all fronts. With higher compression ratios the un-swept volume at the head of the cylinder had to be kept small and so overhead valve designs were evolved which did not have the dead-space of a side-valve engine. They did however have the added complexity of a longer push-rod, rocker and tappet assembly. It was always a feature of Charles' design strategy to reduce the parts count and his use of side-valves, sleeve valves, rotary valves and axial engines were all part of this philosophy.

When the Thomas Tilling Group took overall control of the Bristol Tramways Company in 1935 they did not immediately make large changes. One of the reasons for the White family selling out was that public ownership was again on the agenda. The 1913 Act of Parliament gave Bristol Corporation the right to return every three years and exercise

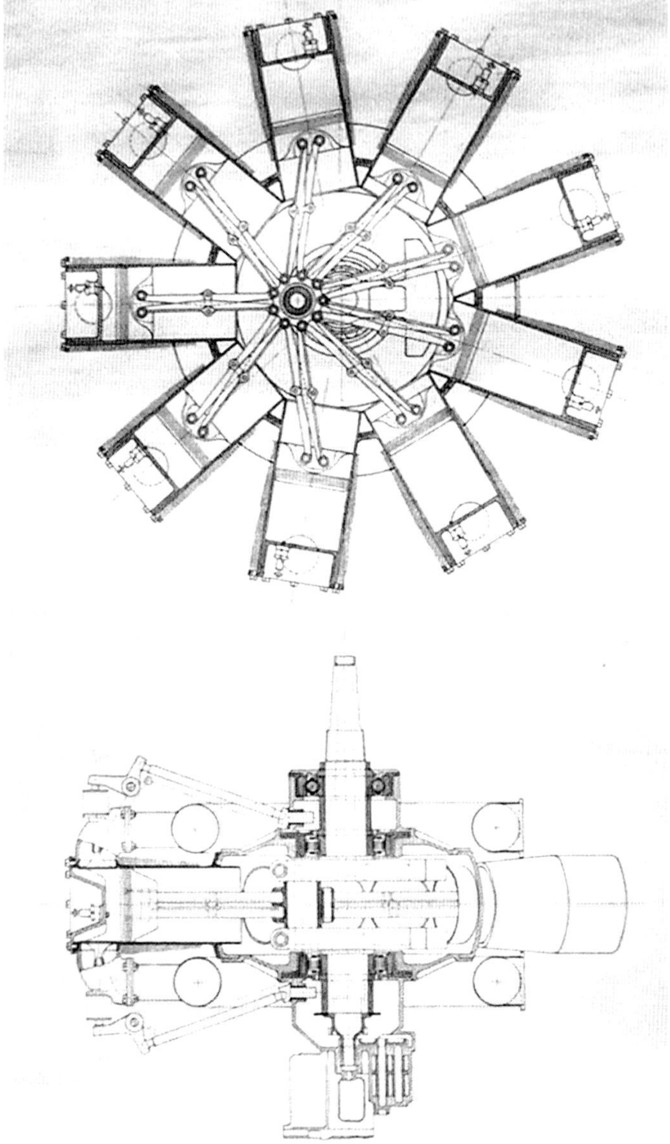

Plate 12-9 Patent for Parallel-Action Connecting-Rod for a Radial Engine

their option to purchase the company. The First Word War had deferred any such plans in 1913, 1916 and 1919 but in 1922, 1925, 1928,1931 and 1934 the White family had successfully fought an increasingly acrimonious fight to retain the company in private ownership. However in 1934 the writing was clearly on the wall and the take-over was only prevented when the company produced a report valuing it at about £1.8 million, which the Corporation could not afford and its valuers would not accept. Subsequently a committee was set up to prepare for the 1937 option date.

It seems likely that the White's had grown tired of the battle whilst at the same time seeing the future in aviation, as the country rather belatedly started to accept the inevitability of another war. Thomas Tilling, on the other hand probably saw a forced sale as a way of realising a quick profit on their investment. Tillings had large fleets of vehicles in many parts of the country and these were mainly diesel-engine powered. The Bristol Tramways and Carriage Company had no such engines although, in keeping with the White family's tradition of embracing new technology, they had fitted a five-cylinder Gardner oil engine to a chassis, number J05G1 and exhibited it at the 1933 Commercial Motor Show. The chassis was sold to an overseas customer and the concept was not pursued further. The chassis was last heard of in the Chinamora Tribal Trust Lands of Rhodesia, where it served as a draining-board in the outdoor kitchen of one of the owners three wives!

Thomas Tilling who was born in 1825 was first heard of when he started a horse-bus service between Peckham and Oxford Street in 1850. This, the Number 12 route, is still used by thousands of commuters today, although it is probably slower now than it was then! He soon built up a fleet of such buses and was noted for the fact that he employed only greys. He introduced the concepts of Mandatory and Request bus stops in agreed locations instead of casual hailing and thereby improved timekeeping and reliability. By 1897 the Thomas Tilling Limited Company was established and at this time owned about four thousand horses. The company put its first motor vehicle into service in 1904 and was a pioneer of the combined petrol-electric vehicle which it first put on the roads in 1911. These "hybrid" vehicles were used for many years, and go to show that there is little new in technology! During the next twenty years the company was involved in many mergers and takeovers and grew to have control or interests in about nineteen bus companies.

Thomas Tilling had eleven children and his son Richard who had overseen the conversion from horse-drawn buses to motor buses took over when his father died. Richard had seven children but he himself died

Plate 12-10 Redrup RR4 Axial Bus Engine in the Bristol Industrial Museum

at an early age in 1929. Two of his three sons failed to attend the Board meeting to appoint his replacement and to their subsequent chagrin, instead of a family member, J Frederick Heaton was elected. The Tilling brothers resigned in pique leaving no family member in the company. The company continued to flourish under Heaton who masterminded the purchase of Bristol Tramway shares and the eventual takeover.

By mid-1936 the remaining members of the White family had departed and the Thomas Tilling management at Bristol started to flex their muscles. They wanted to rationalise their fleet and cut costs and so decided to purchase only diesel-engined vehicles henceforth. Frederick Heaton permitted the RR4 tests to continue but let it be known that the work would ultimately stop. Once the road and bench tests had concluded in October 1936 no further use was made of the axial engines. As early as 1934 Charles had started to draft a diesel version of his axial engine and patented fuel injectors for it but Heaton gave instructions to stop this work and to design a conventional six-cylinder in-line diesel engine. This eventually went into production in 1938 but by this time Charles Redrup had left the company.

Frederick Heaton entered into negotiations with Bristol Corporation. These proceeded smoothly and eventually in October 1937 the Bristol Tramways and Carriage Company was sold for £1,125,000. All but one of the RR engines were sold to the Royal Navy who were interested in them for submarine and torpedo use. RR4/1 still exists today and is on display in the Bristol Industrial Museum. (Plate 12-10 and colour plate C16).

Charles Redrup left the Bristol Tramways Company late in 1936 and returned to his old love, aero engines. He had on occasion whilst designing his engines consulted a graduate of Imperial College, Hedley J Thompson who ran an engineering consultancy business and was an expert in gear transmission systems. In April 1936 Charles had a visit from Thompson who was on a business trip to Bristol. During their discussion Charles mentioned that he had draft designs for an air-cooled opposed-piston version of his engine which was a two-stroke. He stated that an eight-cylinder version should be capable of developing 2,000 horse-power (1,500 kw) at 1,500 rpm. (Plate 12-11). The problem was that the engine relied on features which were in the 1930 patent No. 327,161 and overseas equivalents which Charles had sold to the Bristol Tramways Company in 1932. As the company were now stopping further development of the bus engine, Thompson thought they might be amenable to selling the patents back.

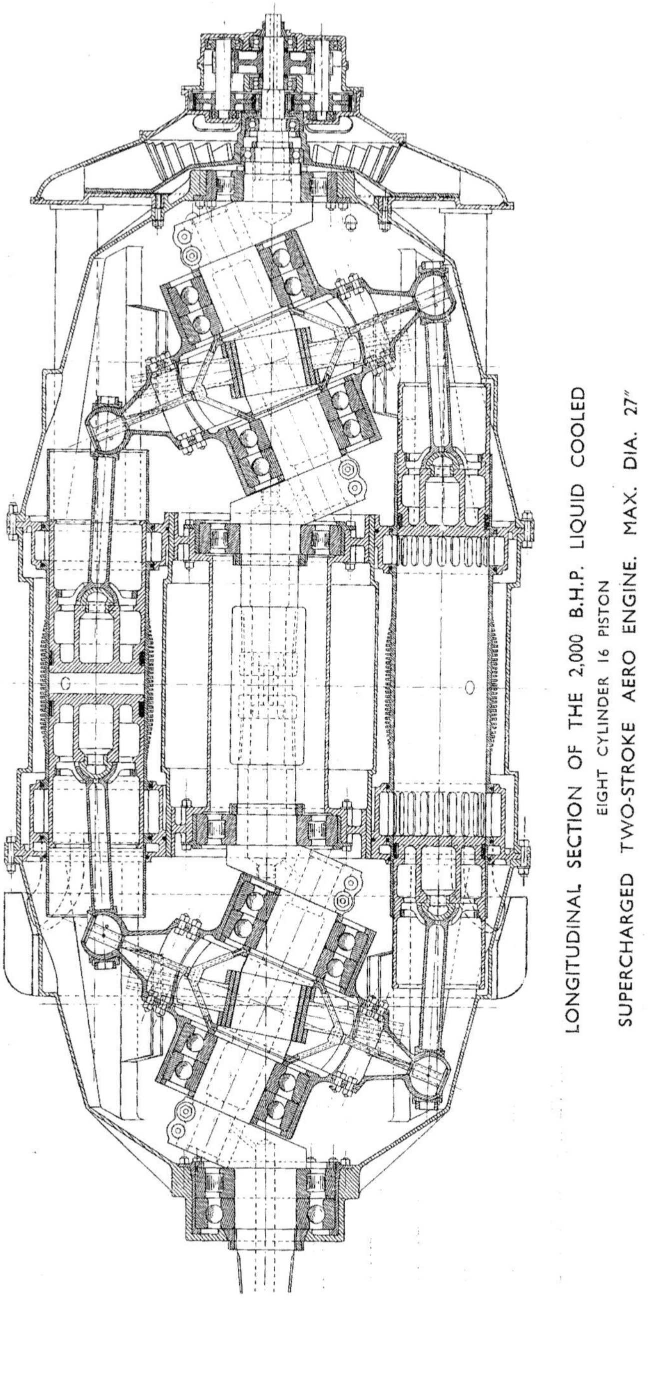

Plate 12-11 Eight-Cylinder Opposed-Piston Two-Stroke Aero Engine.

Charles was concerned that if Nevatt got to hear of it he would prevent it happening because of his continued close links with the White family and with Fedden at Bristol Aeroplanes. Thompson undertook to act as intermediary and to write to the new Tilling Managing Director Major Chapple to see if the buy-back was possible. He also thought that an engine of such performance would be attractive to the Air Ministry and undertook to try to interest his contacts at the Ministry in the engine. Meanwhile Charles agreed to detail the 2000 horse-power (1500 kw) design of the engine for proving trials.

In June 1936 Thompson wrote to Chapple but still had no reply by September, when he wrote to Charles giving him some information about the Napier "Dagger II" aero engine, which was still highly confidential. This was a very complicated engine with four banks of six air-cooled

Plate 12-12 The 24-Cylinder Air-Cooled "Napier" Dagger" Engine

cylinders arranged in an "H" formation (Plate 12-12). With all the complication of valvegear and twin ignition plugs this still only had a capacity of 16.84 litres and produced only 750 horse-power (560 kw). Clearly if the Redrup engine's promise was realised it would be a major advance on current technology. Thompson was later proved right as the RAF found that the Dagger engines fitted to the Hereford bomber required such non-stop maintenance that they eventually withdrew the aircraft from service.

Thomson sought an interview with Chapple and negotiating on Charles' behalf, was successful in obtaining an agreement in principle for him to purchase a licence option. He also asked Charles to see copies of his contracts with the Tramways Company to see what he had actually sold them. During November 1937 Thompson set up a meeting between Charles and financiers from the Pacific Trust and also had a preliminary meeting with a Major Ross of the Air Ministry. He advised Charles that the Ministry were unlikely to fund the prototype engine but might be interested if the promised performance materialised. This was the same vicious circle that Frank Whittle had been caught up in with his jet engine proposals. The Air Ministry seems to have invented "Catch-22" long before Joseph Heller wrote his famous book!

The Ministry also said that they were looking for an engine in the 450-500 horse-power range (340-370 kw), and gave Thompson some guidelines on Ministry requirement standards. Thompson advised Charles to continue with the engine development and that if the financial backing materialised he would arrange manufacture and a fifty-hour endurance test which the Air Ministry required. On behalf of his own transmission-drive interest, he also found that the Ministry required that all engines should be fitted with an end-plate with standard attachments for take-off drives for ancillary services, and he advised Charles to ensure his engine design could accommodate this. At the same visit to the Ministry Thompson had picked up intelligence about the Bristol Aeroplane Company's concerns about the potential development of the axial engine and he warned Charles to be very wary of releasing information to the Bristol Tramways Company.

During 1937 the Redrup family had a surprise visit from Jessie's cousin Ada, daughter of Richard Stephens. The next time Ada saw her brother Dick, with whom Charles Redrup had spent so many happy times whilst working in Clevedon, she told him that Charles was now living in Bristol and he immediately wrote to renew their acquaintance. Just before Christmas 1937 Dick visited Jessie and Charles at their house in Henleaze whilst on a business trip. Dick was still living in Norwood in

North London and carrying on his garage business. After visiting the Redrups he went on to spend a few days with his relatives in Clevedon.

Charles continued to prepare drawings for the 2000 horse-power (1500 kw) engine and he seems to have been confident of obtaining a licence agreement as his drawings from this time have a notice saying "Incorporating the BTTC Co. Patents". Charles wrote to several engine manufacturers including Alvis and Armstrong Siddeley trying to interest them in his engines but to no avail. Meanwhile Thompson had been advised by Chapple at the Bristol Tramways Company to deal direct with Nevatt on the licence issues and so he wrote to Nevatt asking for a progress update on the Tramways work. Nevatt replied in early December 1937 stating that he was leaving the company and setting up his own company, Nevatt Axial Engines. He said that he had bought licences to the patents from the company to build his own engines, had applied for further patents and expected to have the first engine running by January 1938.

Hedley Thompson saw Mr Wardman a member of the Pacific Trust a few days later and reported back to Charles that they wanted the patent situation resolved in preparation for setting up a limited company. Charles did eventually obtain an offer of a licence agreement from the Bristol Tramways Company which would cost him fifty thousand pounds. Considering that he had sold his original patents to the Bristol Tramways Company for two payments of five thousand pounds each and had also patented his later developments on their behalf, had worked for them for six years and designed and built them four successful bus engines, this was a very high price, and represented a huge return to the Tramways Company, particularly as they had sold licences to Christopher Nevatt as well!

However, once again serendipity played a part in Charles' career, for as one door closed, another opened. Late in 1937 Charles' old adversary Sir John Siddeley retired from A.V.Roe and shortly afterward Charles' old colleague Roy Dobson, now Managing Director, approached him and asked him to rejoin the company. Charles therefore did not proceed with the licensing agreement but purchased an option on it, which he hoped to take up at a later stage. The post with A.V.Roe was in the Experimental Department, to set up an Experimental Armaments Division to enable the company to equip its aircraft for the forthcoming war. Charles agreed to the offer with alacrity.

This upset Nevatt's plans. He had intended to ask Charles to join him in his own axial engine company, but from what we know of Charles' views

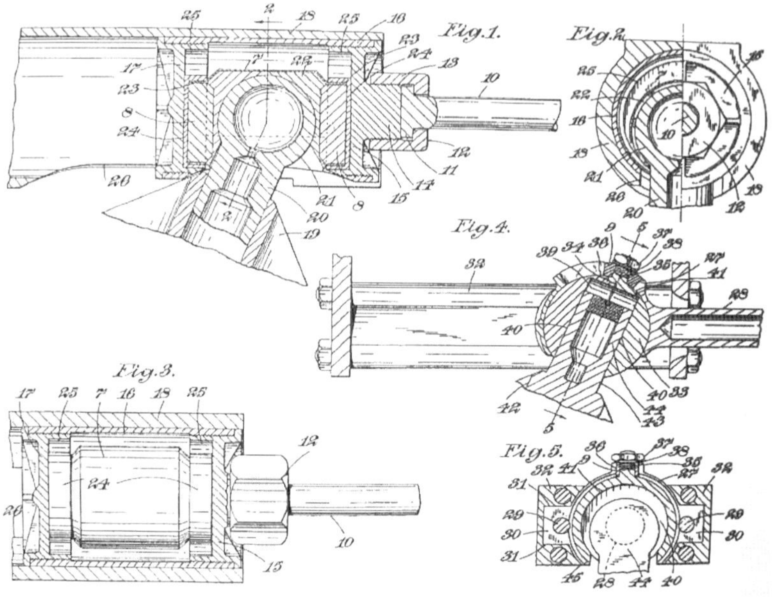

Plate 12-13 Nevatt Axial Engine Patent of 1938

of Nevatt this was never an option. In subsequent business dealings with potential customers Nevatt tried to give the impression that he was still working with Charles Redrup. Nevatt published further patents on a stabilised axial engine of ever increasing complexity. (Plate 12-13). The design had complicated fittings on the ends of the star member that articulated directly with the ends of the pistons via a complex linkage. It was somewhat reminiscent of the Redrup Fury I engine, but more complex.

In 1935 a small struggling electrical manufacturing group The Ray Engineering Company in Southmead, Bristol circulated a letter to a number of companies in the city offering their services as an engineering manufacturer. The company was owned by two brothers Robert and Harold Joy and within a year Ray Engineering had become one of the founder members of the Bristol Engineering Manufacturers Association BEMA, and their fortunes improved dramatically. Ray Engineering greatly extended their range of products, doing, amongst other things, sub-contract electrical and mechanical work for The Bristol Aeroplane Company. They soon were able to take on apprentices and five were appointed in 1936. One of these, Arthur Ogborne started with Ray Engineering at the age of fifteen and worked for the company for forty-three years. He trained as an electrical engineer and designed and made switchboards for the Middle East oilfields and for other clients. He also designed electrical and mechanical switches for the undercarriages of Bristol Aeroplane Company aircraft. He still lives in Filton less than a mile from the Southmead works of the Ray Engineering Company. Arthur recalls that shortly after he started work, a short, dapper man of military bearing and wearing spats appeared at the works and started looking around. Soon afterwards the visitor was given an office in the Ray buildings in which he lodged himself and his only member of staff. Christopher Nevatt had left the Bristol Tramways Company and brought with him the draughtsman Colin Campbell. The office in the Ray Engineering works now constituted the Nevatt Axial Engine Company. Nevatt and Campbell set about designing an axial engine based on the Tramways RR4 engine but incorporating Nevatt's patented ideas, to get around Charles Redrup's patents. Arthur Ogborne remembers Nevatt as an incessant tea-drinker and smoker who would spend a lot of time in the office chatting to one of the Ray Engineering Company secretaries, who also doubled as Nevatt's secretary. Nevatt was in the habit of smoking his cigarettes only half-way down and then throwing the remainder onto the shop floor. The apprentices soon caught on to this and would rescue the half-smoked remnants for their own use. Nevatt in his turn soon came to realise what was happening and would snap the partly-smoked stub in half before throwing it away!

Nevatt contracted the manufacture of his engine to Ray Engineering and also had some components made by his former colleagues at the Bristol Tramways Company. One of the Ray Engineering handymen, "Johnny" Walker did most of the work on the engine and Arthur Ogborne worked on some minor components including the ball and socket joints at the end of the pistons. He was amazed that the vertical miller used to make the joints, which had a rather flexible main pillar, could produce such precision components. He remembers that Robert Joy would put on a foreman's coat and go onto the shop floor and using only a file, would fashion journal bearings several inches long. The Nevatt engine took much longer to complete than planned, by which time the Second World War was under way. Because the Ray Engineering Company were by this time very much involved in aircraft component manufacture many of their staff, including Arthur Ogborne, were excused military service. Instead, Arthur doubled in the evenings as a Medical Courier distributing antibiotics, blood serum and other medical equipment to First Aid Posts after air raids. Through his work on the control gear for aircraft undercarriages Arthur often visited the Dowty works in Cheltenham to collect drawings and on at least one occasion met George Dowty.

When the Nevatt engine was finally completed it was erected on a test stand and it started up straight away, to everyone's joy. However this was shortly followed, in Arthur's words, by 'an ominous clanking' and the test had to be stopped. The engine hung about in the works for a few weeks then was spirited away and it never went into production. One of the Joy brothers, Harold, worked for the Admiralty at Bath and there were suggestions that the naval authorities took an interest in the engine, but nothing more was heard of it and the Nevatt Axial Engine Company slid into obscurity.

There now took place a most acrimonious saga between Nevatt and Charles Redrup that dragged on into the war years. In the winter of 1937 the Western Graduate Section of *The Institute of Automobile Engineers* published their 1938 programme. It included a forthcoming lecture in March on the subject of axial engines by Colin Campbell. Charles heard of this and requested, through his former employers, to see a copy of the paper. Arnold John Romer from the company wrote to the Institute requesting a copy which was sent on 23rd January 1938. Charles was extremely upset when he saw the paper. It re-iterated many of the errors about the Redrup aero engine published in 1935 in *The Commercial Motor* magazine, but went on to publish the details of Charles' analysis of the wobble-plate figure-of-eight motion. Charles had protected this in his 1932 patent GB398,553 in which he had laid down the basic equation for the motion, but had not gone into the detail of its derivation. Campbell's paper made several scathing and inaccurate references to Charles' earlier engines and gave a detailed, but somewhat convoluted analysis of the figure-of-eight motion. No acknowledgement was made to Charles Redrup, but only to Christopher Nevatt. By the time Charles saw the article it was too late to affect the programme and the paper was read at a meeting of *The Institute of Automobile Engineers* on 17th March 1938 in Carwardine's Café in Bristol.

Later on, in 1941 the issue re-surfaced when an article by Campbell was published in *The Automobile Engineer*. This again re-iterated the myths about Charles Redrup's earlier engines and went on to say that it would be many years before axial engines would surpass conventional engines like the Merlin. Perhaps this was a hint that Nevatt was having as little success with stabilisers in his own company as he had experienced when he started to dabble with them at the Bristol Tramway Company. Campbell also stated that with advances in materials

Plate 12-14 Jessica Redrup (right) with RAF Colleagues

properties conventional engines would be able to achieve even greater performance. With the earlier reading of the paper in an unpublished graduate members' section of a learned society Charles was unable to reply, but on this occasion he was able to respond. Through Messrs. Iliffe and Son the publishers he wrote to the journal and pointed out that the Bristol RR3 and RR4 engines had achieved consistent performance over thousands of miles and were only taken out of service when the company decided to standardise on in-line diesel engines. He made the point that the development had taken just a few years between 1931 and 1935, and that any improvements in material properties could just as equally be exploited by axial engines.

Charles Redrup took up his post with A.V.Roe Limited late in 1938 but because his son John's education was at a critical stage did not move his family back up to Heaton Moor, Stockport until August 1939, where they took a house at 25, Clifton Road. At the outbreak of war Violet, who was still working for A.V.Roe, moved from the Newton Heath works to Chadderton when Charles started there. Jessica got a job as a secretary in Manchester but at the outbreak of war she joined the RAF (Plate 12-14), and served in the Plotting Rooms at Stanmore and Duxford, directing fighter aircraft to interceptions with enemy bombers. Dorothy left home and trained as a nurse at Calderstones Hospital for wounded soldiers at Whalley in Lancashire and ended the war as a nursing sister. Ray went to Heaton Moor College until he was seventeen when he too joined the Army and served as a corporal in the stores. (Plate 12-15, middle row, second from right.)

When the family moved back to Cheshire John Arnold was seventeen

Plate 12-15 Ray Redrup and No. 5 Platoon at Duxford

and had just matriculated at the end of the summer term at Bristol Grammar School. He was interested in aeronautical engineering and his best friend Rex Pollard had just obtained an apprenticeship at the Bristol Aeroplane Company. Charles had no difficulty in arranging for John to obtain a post with A.V.Roe as a "Gentleman Apprentice" or GA and over the next five years John went through every office and production shop in the company and finally ended up with a permanent post in the Design Office. He started his apprenticeship at the beginning of September 1939 and had to start work at 7.30 am whilst his father started at 9 am. John therefore needed his own transport to travel the twelve miles between Chadderton and Heaton Moor and so Charles bought him a brand new 250 cc Lee Enfield overhead valve Model L. E, which cost £42 10 shillings.

John already had years of cycling and off-road motorcycling experience and so took to the road very easily, riding the bike back from

Alexanders Ltd, the dealers in Ardwick. Being his father's son, he had taken the magazine *The Motor Cycle* for fourpence a week from a very early age and so was already very knowledgeable on the subject. He also started to drive the family car after his seventeenth birthday. John ran the Enfield until early 1943 when he acquired a low-mileage 250cc Rudge. Later that year he bought an almost new Triumph 350 from a friend in Kendal. In 1945 he upgraded to a 500cc Triumph, also of very low mileage for which he paid £85. Thus he was gaining experience of more powerful motor cycles and of their maintenance which was very much do-it-yourself during the war years. Eventually he bought himself a smart sporting Ford tourer car.

John started work at Chadderton just a few days after war was declared on 3rd September and worked six days a week and the seventh day went to Stockport Technical College. He found the ride to and from work good survival training as much of the road had granite sets which were treacherous when wet, far worse than frosty road surfaces. For good measure most of the roads had tramlines down the centre and in winter had to be ridden in the blackout with only a very dim headlamp and even dimmer single tail lamps from the vehicles in front. Throughout this time he kept in touch with Rex Pollard and they would visit each other from time to time as the petrol ration permitted.

Chapter 13
War Work

Charles Redrup went to work in the Experimental Department at the Chadderton Factory in August 1938 where the Head of Department was known universally as "Cock" Davies. Cock asked him to pull together a variety of miscellaneous projects which were already under way and Charles immediately set about creating the Experimental Armaments Division. Production of military aircraft was now stepping up and many of the components were subcontracted. Items such as machine guns, bomb loads and gun turrets were manufactured by specialist armaments firms for a wide range of aircraft and had to be capable of being installed with great ease in a variety of types. The hydraulic systems used in aircraft grew in complexity as new functions were added and they placed heavy loads on the engines. This was further compounded by the need for the systems to have redundancy in the event of damage from enemy aircraft. Charles' role was to design equipment and systems for A.V.Roe which would enable these objectives to be achieved.

Plate 13-1 Roy Chadwick, Avro Chief Designer

Together with many other aircraft manufacturers A.V.Roe were bidding for large military contracts and in 1936, in competition with Handley Page, had won a contract to develop a large twin-engined bomber. This was to be equipped with the new Rolls Royce twenty-four cylinder Vulture engine. This was an untried engine with four banks of six cylinders arranged in an "X" formation. It was in effect two Merlin engines coupled together back to back, or, as events transpired, "cobbled" together! The specification called for aircraft to be equipped with a formidable array of nose, tail and ventral gun turrets. It was also to be fitted with a large bomb-bay running the length of the fuselage, and retractable undercarriage. All these were to be hydraulically operated as well as the flaps. The company had never produced such a large, complex aircraft before and needed all the help it could get.

Since the first few years of the A.V.Roe Company's formation it had in its employ two very capable but formidable members of staff. Roy Chadwick, (Plate 13-1), started off as Alliott Verdon Roe's first draughtsman in 1911 but soon rose to be the Chief Design Engineer.

Roy Dobson (Plate 13-2), started in 1914 working for Chadwick, who was only twenty-one at the time but by now had one hundred staff working under him. Dobson's organisational talents were soon apparent and by the end of the First World War he was Works Manager.

The immense pressures of war work forged a strong link between "the two Roys" as they came to be called, and by 1918 A.V.Roe had probably

Plate 13-2 Roy Dobson, Avro Managing Director

the strongest design team under Chadwick and the most efficient production organisation under Dobson than any other aircraft manufacturer. When Charles Redrup worked for A.V.Roe on the Alpha engine in the mid 1920' he found both men hard task-masters. We have seen in Chapter 7 how Dobson, who became General Manager in 1934, pushed him in regard to engine testing and materials, but we have also seen his decisiveness in putting the Alpha engine into production once he was satisfied as to its performance. Now in 1938 when his company needed expertise, he remembered Charles and called upon his skills.

The new A.V.Roe bomber, named the Manchester, was the result of a 1936 Air Ministry specification P13/36 and a contract was placed with A.V.Roe later in that year for two prototypes to be built at Newton Heath. Incredibly, the Manchester was only the second A.V.Roe aircraft for the RAF to be both a monoplane and to have a gun turret and a retractable undercarriage. The first was the Anson but in that aircraft, all except the later versions had a turret and undercarriage that were operated manually. The Avro 652 Anson was designed in response to a 1933 specification from Imperial Airways for a small but fast long-range aeroplane suitable for charter work. This requirement was in response to the growing number of American aircraft of this type. Roy Chadwick took the design of the Avro-Fokker 618 three-engined aircraft and using the same wooden wing and basic welded steel tube fuselage produced a low-wing twin-engined monoplane which used the relatively new Armstrong Siddeley Cheetah radial engines.

Even before the prototype of the new transport aircraft had flown, A.V.Roe received an Air Ministry specification for a fast twin military patrol aircraft. It was so similar in requirement to the Imperial Airways civil aircraft that Chadwick had no difficulty in producing a design for the military version, the Avro 652A. This was fitted as an option with a manually-controlled Armstrong-Whitworth dorsal turret having a single Lewis machine gun and also a forward-firing Lewis gun operated by the flight crew. (Plate 13-3). It had a bomb load capability of 360 pounds (164 kg) and a retractable undercarriage. This was manually operated by a chain drive and required one hundred and forty painful turns of the very low-geared handle. From 1936 all subsequent Ansons were fitted with hydraulically-operated Schrenk flaps and so became the first Avro aircraft to be so fitted.

Civil and military Ansons were produced in their thousands and as the Second World War approached versions were adapted for gunnery and bomber training. The author's uncle William Dawson Fairney was a

Plate-13-3 Avro Anson with Armstrong Whitworth Gun-Turret

Pilot Officer in the RAF and trained on Ansons in Rhodesia in 1943 before being posted to Northern Italy to fly Liberators bombing the Ploesti oilfields in Poland. He was shot down over Hungary in August 1944 and is buried in a beautifully maintained cemetery just outside Budapest. (Plate 13-4). The author himself also has fond memories of the Anson for it was in one of these aircraft that he had his first flight whilst a member of the school Combined Cadet Force in 1955. He vividly remembers having to take his boots off to enter the aircraft as it had a fabric-covered floor!

The Anson has three combat "firsts" to its credit. On the fifth of September 1939, two days after the outbreak of war a Coastal Command patrol Anson bombed a "U" Boat. Later in that month another Anson shot down a Dornier flying boat. The main claim to fame however came in June 1940 when three Ansons on coastal patrol were being attacked by three Messerschmitt Me109 fighters. The Ansons, with a top speed of one hundred and sixty-five miles per hour (300 km per hour) were difficult targets for the attacking aircraft which had to fly close to their stalling speed to have a chance of hitting it. However the Anson pilots throttled back at just the right moment and the Me109s had to overshoot at a slow relative speed. The gunners of the Ansons destroyed two of the fighters and damaged the third, an incredible performance for such an aircraft.

To design the Manchester's undercarriage Roy Chadwick called in his old friend George Dowty, who after leaving A.V.Roe in the 1920's to

Plate 13-4 1939-45 RAF War Cemetery on Outskirts of Budapest

work for Gloucester Aircraft for a short time, had set up his own company in Cheltenham to specialise in undercarriage and propeller systems. Thus it was that in 1939 Charles Redrup found himself working once again with the man whose Gosport landing gear had made the Helvellyn landing possible.

One of Charles' first jobs was the design of hydraulic pumps and motors for bomb-doors and gun-turret drives. Because all of his work was security classified very little remains of what he did, but he kept a few drawings, and recently, a clutch of secret patents taken out by him and A V Roe Limited during the war have been released. Charles had a senior assistant, an engineer named George Beardshall who was also very inventive and a number of patents were also taken out in his name. The secret nature of the war work was such that very few engineers knew exactly what it was that they were working on. There were about twenty people in Charles' Department which was located at Chadderton up a flight of stairs on a small mezzanine floor with drawing boards and a few machine tools.

All of the jobs were split up in such a way that very few people saw the complete picture. Probably only Roy Chadwick and Roy Dobson themselves knew all that was going on. Only by piecing together information from Charles Redrup's former staff and his son has it been possible to understand his role at A.V.Roe. Dick Marsh who was in his early twenties at the time recalls working with Charles on the Lancaster hydraulic systems, whilst Dennis Wilde who was one of about six draughtsmen in the department, worked with him for about eighteen months on a project to install 20mm Hispano-Suiza cannons into the Lancaster.

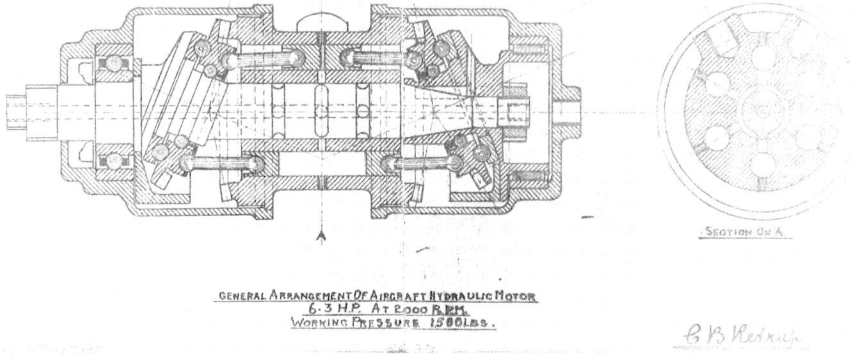

Plate 13-5 A 1500lb Hydraulic Pump Designed by Charles Redrup

Not surprisingly, Charles used axial designs for his hydraulic pumps and motors as these were positive-displacement devices capable of developing the high pressures which were becoming standard for supplying the aircraft systems. (Plate 13-5). The optimum pressure for a hydraulic pump was in the range of one to three thousand pounds per square inch but the standardised pressure used on the aircraft systems was two hundred and twenty pounds so Charles developed and patented a pressure-reducing valve for A.V.Roe.

The first prototype Manchester was built without gun turrets and first flew in the summer of 1938. It proved to have some handling problems in yaw and the second prototype was fitted with larger span wings and modified fin and rudder. This aircraft was fitted with nose, tail and ventral retractable gun turrets but still proved laterally unstable and so after the first few flights a central dorsal fin was added. If the old engineering adage "If it looks right, it is right" is true, then so is its corollary and that was the case here. The shark-like fin looked anachronistic against the other two elliptical fins, giving the aircraft a cobbled-together appearance. (Plate 13-6).

Plate 13-6 Second Prototype Avro Manchester I with Triple-Fin

However it largely solved the problem of stability and the aircraft was put into production. The gun turrets were of Frazer-Nash design and were integrated into the aircraft's hydraulic system. In the event of hydraulic failure each turret could be rotated manually but this made simultaneous training, elevating, aiming and firing very difficult. Each engine had hydraulic pumps attached to the auxiliary pads at the rear and these fed accumulators connected to the turrets. With only two engines two of the turrets had to be operated from one engine and the ventral turret was coupled up to the tail turret hydraulic lines. The FN21 ventral turret had the added complexity of being retractable into the belly of the aircraft and was ungainly and difficult to access. It was aimed from a periscope operated by a gunner lying on the fuselage floor. It was eventually discarded on later models of the aircraft as it reduced airspeed by about fifteen knots when deployed.

The Vulture engines on the Manchester proved unreliable and the early versions were also underpowered. Handley Page's bid for the P13/36 contract also proposed the twin Vulture engines but when they lost the contract they re-designed it to take four Merlins. This aircraft eventually became the Halifax which first flew in 1939 and went on to be very successful although suffering higher losses than the A.V.Roe aircraft. The Manchester, even when fitted with the upgraded Vulture Mk II engines still suffered from engine reliability problems and after several thousand hours service experience this was tracked down to overheating due to the composite arrangement. Further modifications improved the situation somewhat and in total over 200 Manchester Mk Is were constructed up until late 1942. A further version was fitted with the new Bristol Centaurus engines and designated Manchester Mk II but it never flew because it was superseded by the immediately-successful four-engined Mk III.

Roy Chadwick never stood still and neither did his thinking. Even when the Manchester was just coming off the drawing-board, he had started to sketch out a four-engined version, the Avro 680. Thus when in March 1939 the Air Ministry issued Specification B1/39, Chadwick was ready for it. The Ministry envisaged a large four-engined bomber of such lifting capacity and range that it would replace all existing bombers within five years. The specification required an aircraft with a short take-off and landing run to accommodate existing airfields. For the same reason the Manchester had been designed with a strong thick, stubby wing as the earlier specification required the aircraft to be suitable for catapult launching. Although the Manchester successfully undertook catapult trials this requirement was subsequently dropped.

Thus Chadwick was free to design a thin, high-lift elegant wing of greater span which combined with generous flaps gave the required take-off performance. In addition a larger tailplane of greater span with enlarged fin and rudder were designed so that the central fin could be dispensed with. The new aircraft was designated the Avro 683. However by mid-1940 the Air Ministry were having second thoughts and hinted that UK manufacturers should all concentrate on building Halifaxes under contract. The two Roys at A.V.Roe immediately sprang into action and travelled to London and invaded the Ministry of Aircraft Production with detailed designs and performance estimates for the Manchester Mk III. Their combined powers of persuasion were such that they were granted a stay of execution on the promise of delivering two prototype aircraft by July 1941. The meeting was followed up by a contract, which in addition to the first two prototypes required a third and fourth with Bristol Hercules engines, as it was thought that Merlins would be in short supply.

Chadwick and Dobson knew that they could only deliver on the July date by converting an existing Manchester with its thick wing, to four engined operation. The story goes that Dobson returned to Newton Heath and commandeered a production Manchester. He cleared a space in the production shop and assembled jigs and components to accommodate the MK III layout. Through a contact at Rolls Royce he conjured up four Merlin Mk Xs, which were like hens teeth. All Merlin production at the height of the Battle of Britain was supposedly dedicated to fighter aircraft. Because the Vultures and Merlins came from the same stable the engine-mounting jigs were almost identical and the assembly was completed in a remarkably short time. Wider-span outer wing panels and flaps were also fitted.

On test in the works the larger flaps required more power, so whilst turrets, bomb doors and undercarriage were all operated from hydraulic pumps on the two inboard engines, the system had to be modified to use further hydraulic pumps on the outer engines for the flaps. Dobson had set 31st December 1940 as the date for the maiden flight but these changes caused a slight delay and the first flight took place on 9th January 1941. Over the next two months the aircraft was extensively tested, then it was returned to Manchester to have the wider tail surfaces fitted and the central fin removed. This proved to be a remarkable success, eliminating the yaw instability once and for all and the aircraft looked as if it meant business with the anachronistic shark's fin removed. The modification was so successful that it was retrospectively fitted to many operational Manchester Mk I aircraft to become the Mk 1A.

During the previous months in the workshops the Manchester Mk III aircraft had acquired by common usage a name of its own and on 28th February 1941 it was formally recognised as what was to become the most remarkable and successful bomber aircraft of the Second World

War, when it was renamed the Avro Lancaster. The second prototype was constructed as close to the production standard as possible, with thinner wings and Merlin Mk XX engines. It had dorsal and ventral gun turrets as well as those in the nose and tail. It first flew on 13th May 1941 and after further proving trials and modifications was ready for delivery to the Air Ministry in July 1941 as agreed less than a year earlier. (Plate 13-7 and colour plate C19). The Hercules-powered third aircraft first flew in November 1941 but by then the success of the Merlin-engined aircraft was plain to see, the anticipated shortage of Merlins had not materialised and so the second Hercules-powered aircraft was never built. Earlier contracts for Manchesters already in production were amended to require remaining aircraft to be made as Lancasters and later un-started Manchester orders were cancelled in favour of new Lancaster orders.

Plate 13-7 The Legendary Avro Lancaster

Dobson's experience with construction of the Manchesters and with the Lancaster prototypes meant that by the time the latter went into full production the design had been refined to allow for mass production techniques. The aircraft was assembled from five fuselage sub-assemblies, two inner wing and two outer wing-tip assemblies. Each section was fully fitted out with all its equipment and they could be connected together in a relatively short space of time. As production progressed sections were manufactured at a range of factories all around the country and eventually overseas, but the standardisation meant that there were relatively few compatibility problems. The sub-assembly philosophy also meant that whole sections could be kept as spares on

Plate 13-8 Modular Production of Avro Lancasters

operational airfields and damaged aircraft could swiftly be re-built and returned to service. In addition several damaged aircraft could be dismantled and sections re-connected to make a new aircraft. The philosophy was to continue in post-war years and is now widely adopted in the aerospace industry, especially by Airbus Industries where whole aircraft sections are manufactured at factories all over Europe and taken to Toulouse for assembly.

The heart of the Lancaster was the centre-section, which consisted of the central wing section with forward and rear spars together with the inboard engine nacelles complete with retractable undercarriage. This fuselage and wing centre-section contained all the main services; fuel, electrical, hydraulic and pneumatic. As most of the operating systems such as hydraulically-operated flaps, inner engine cooling vents, connections to outboard ailerons, fuel lines and connections to the engine-driven generators and hydraulic pumps were in this section the number of connections to the forward and rear fuselage sections was minimised. The forward sections of the Lancaster, (Plate 13-8). consisted of a nose, complete with turret and bomb-aimers position, and a cockpit and crew section which housed all of the remaining crew apart from the operators of the three aft turrets. These two sections were transported as an assembled unit. Aft of the centre section was an intermediate centre section housing the dorsal and ventral turrets and a walk-way to the rear section. This rear section was twenty-one feet in length and carried the thirty-three foot span tailplane with its twelve foot high rudders, and the tail gun turret.

The fuselage frames extended from the roof down to the floor which formed the ceiling of the bomb bay. Experience with the Short Stirling which first flew in 1938 had shown the wisdom of this. The Stirling had fuselage frames which extended right down to the bottom of the bomb bay with the result that the bay was divided into relatively short sections. This was satisfactory at the time of the design of the Stirling when the largest bombs were of about four thousand pounds in weight, (1800kg), but it severely restricted its ability to carry the larger bombs as they were developed. By making the Lancaster's bomb bay run the full thirty-three feet length of the underbelly without frames to restrict it, much larger bomb loads could be carried, right up to the massive twenty-two thousand pound (10,000kg) "Grand Slam" bombs of the later war years.

The aircraft systems were carefully laid out so as to facilitate ease of assembly but also to provide redundancy and minimise the effects of damage from enemy action. The hydraulics for flaps, landing gear, bomb doors, fuel jettison system, carburettor heating and engine cooling shutters were operated from pumps on the inner engines. Flaps and landing gear could be operated by compressed air in an emergency and the latter could also be dropped under gravity in the event of loss of all systems. There was a main hydraulic reservoir in the centre section and smaller reservoirs in the nose section and near the dorsal turret. These could also be pressurised as a last resort by a hand pump. The four gun turrets were each operated from an additional hydraulic pump on each engine so that loss of one engine still left the aircraft with three fully-operational turrets. Each turret could however also be operated manually. This high degree of redundancy made the Lancaster capable of taking a tremendous degree of punishment and countless aircraft limped home with major damage after being in action but still able to land safely.

The modular arrangement resulted in there being only fourteen hydraulic connections between the centre section and the nose assembly, and only ten connections between the centre section and the rear section. These connections which had to be coupled together as the sections were assembled gave some initial trouble. Each joint was made with a proprietary coupling which had a steel conical olive which was squeezed up onto the pipe section to give a leak-free joint. However the hardness of the olive often produced a circular indentation around the pipe which would soon fail due to fatigue under vibration in service. Charles Redrup developed a technique to guarantee a perfect joint each time and he patented this (No. 546,306) with A.V.Roe in 1941.

Roy Chadwick was concerned about the difficulty of manual operation of gun turrets in the event of hydraulic failure and wanted to explore an independent means of driving the turret. One technique was to have a hand-charged accumulator near the turret which the turret operator could pump up whilst en route to the target. However once this was discharged it was not practicable for the gunner to leave his turret in the middle of combat to pump up the pressure. A further concern was that the hydraulic connections to the turret had to be flexible enough to cope with the rapid rotation and these connections became worn and sometimes failed. Furthermore in some designs of turret the flexible lines reduced manoeuvrability inside the turret owing to the already restricted space.

Charles Redrup patented with A.V.Roe a self-contained turret which drew its power from the slipstream and which powered a hydraulic pump attached to the turret. (Plate 13-9). The patent (No. 561,933) was

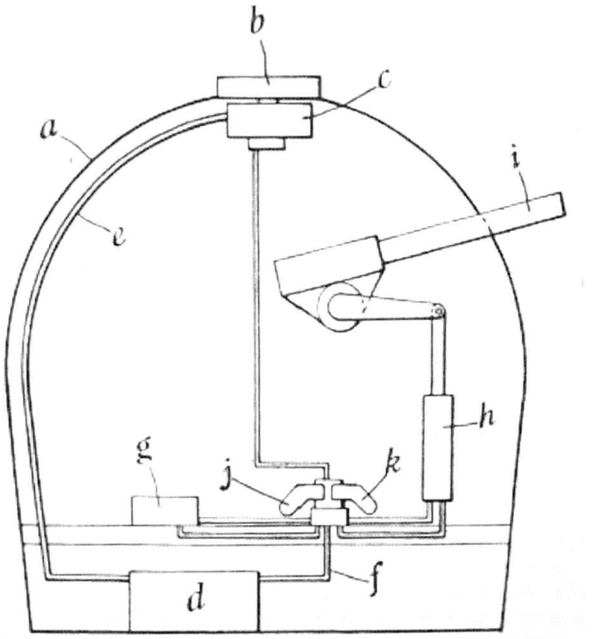

Plate 13-9 Aero-Hydraulic Drive for Aircraft Gun-Turret

for a retractable propeller-powered pump which could be dropped out into the slipstream whenever the turret was to be operated. It is not known if this system was ever installed as the vast majority of Lancaster gun turrets were of standard Frazer-Nash manufacture, although experiments were carried out with other types.

Charles throughout this period was working closely with George Dowty, who did not forget the concept and in later years his companies manufactured drop-down ram-air driven hydraulic pumps for emergency operation of aircraft hydraulic systems. These were fitted to Concorde but never needed to be used in anger. However a similar installation fitted to Lockheed Tri-Stars was put to the test on one occasion when an aircraft suffered simultaneous flame-out of all three engines. The drop-down ram-air system enabled all flight control systems to be maintained whilst engine re-starts were successfully carried out, thus saving the aircraft and crew.

Soon after the beginning of the war many enemy aircraft fitted with 20mm cannon which had a long range were able to outgun the allied bombers. Charles worked on a project to replace the twin 0.303 inch machine guns in the Frazer-Nash mid-upper gun turrets on the Lancaster with 20mm Hispano-Suiza cannons. These developments were put into effect very quickly and at times, too quickly for Charles' satisfaction. In one internal A.V.Roe memo he strongly advises against using live ammunition for the first test as the risk of jamming in the breech was too great. Special butts were constructed at Chadderton for these tests. The problem was clearly resolved, as a later report from A.V.Roe's agent Major H N Wylie dated 1st March 1940 showed that the first firing trials had proved successful. This same Major Wylie was the Chief Engineer of the Aircraft Technical Services Company (ATS) set up back in 1931 to exploit the metal-working techniques used in producing the Monospar wing. Charles worked closely with him whilst at A.V.Roe during the war years.

The cannon installation in the Frazer-Nash turrets however posed other problems as the recoil was too great for the gun mounting rings. Stouter rings were tried but this resulted in the space within the turret becoming too cramped. Eventually Martin turrets with 0.5 inch guns were fitted on many aircraft to replace the .303 machine guns but the 20mm cannons were never fitted to the manually-operated turrets. Of the 7,377 Lancasters produced 610 were fitted with the Martin turrets.

One other concept which did reach the experimental stage was to fit two remotely-controlled turrets or "Barbettes" with 20mm cannons in the dorsal and ventral positions and for one man to operate them from a small cockpit in the rear of the aircraft. A Lancaster LL/780G was fitted with this equipment and test flown but the scheme was abandoned in late 1944 when the German defences were crumbling and posed less of a threat to British bombers.

The installation of gun turrets into the Lancaster provided additional problems in terms of the large amount of ammunition it was desired to carry. The Frazer-Nash turrets fitted with the Browning 0.303 inch (7.7 mm) machine gun were generally renowned for their reliability but liable to jam under conditions of high rate of fire, either due to the cold, the drag of the long feed cartridge-belts, or to poor assembly of the belts themselves. The gun fired at a rate of 1,150 rounds a minute and in the FN 5A front turret had a supply of 1,000 rounds for each of the two guns, arranged in ammunition boxes on either side of the gunner.

The FN 20 tail turret had four guns with 2,500 rounds per gun but these were in ammunition boxes located in the rear fuselage. The ammunition had to be fed to the guns via long flexible tracks to accommodate the rotation of the turret. The FN 50 dorsal turret had twin guns with 1,000 rounds each and the ventral FN 64 turret fitted to early

Lancasters and then again to aircraft produced towards the end of the war also had twin guns but only with 500 rounds each. It was found that with high rates of fire the drag of the ammunition belts caused jamming and so Charles designed and patented an automatic feed system using a hydraulic motor to pull the cartridge belt forward towards the gun breech in such a way that the feed speed matched the firing rate of the gun. In other patents he dealt with the problems of disposal of the used belts and cartridges which otherwise very rapidly filled up the already cluttered turret.

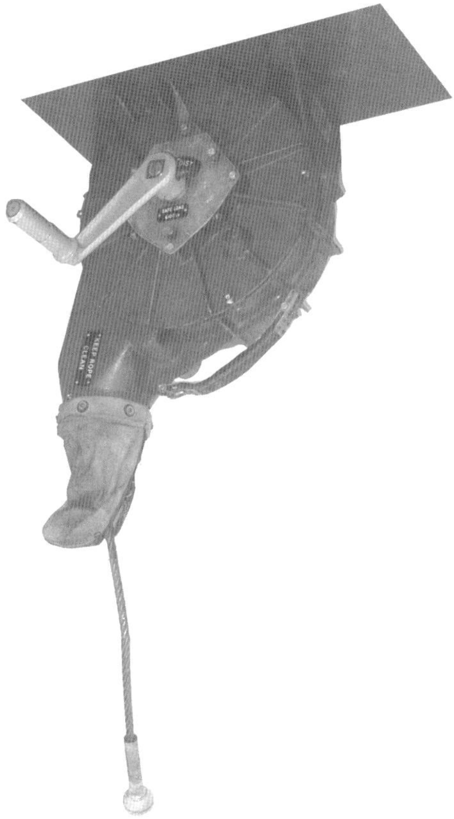

Plate 13-10 Redrup 6,100lb Bomb Winch

The Lancaster was in advance of its competitors in other ways. Not only did it have a full-length bomb bay clear of frames and other encumbrances but it had a grid of hard points for the location of bomb attachments. The bombs could be attached in a large variety of combinations and the attachments also had self-contained winch points.

Early bomber aircraft could be loaded up by hand, but as bomb sizes increased they became too heavy for one or two men to lift and so later aircraft had winches fitted. These clearly added to the all up weight of the aircraft and led to a corresponding reduction in bomb load. The time taken to load bombs also became prohibitive. The Stirling aircraft had manually operated winches and took half a day to load.

The RAF had been concerned by the time required to fuel an aircraft and instituted an operational research project into the preparation of a squadron for action. They found that it took half a day to fuel a squadron of heavy bombers for a long sortie but were surprised to find that it could take this long to load weapons into a single bomber. A.V.Roe fitted the Lancaster with portable winches and this speeded up the operation considerably. (Plate 13-10). The winch could be connected to any one of the hard point bomb attachments and used singly, in pairs or, for the larger bombs fours, to raise each bomb or bomb crate into place. Charles and the company patented many features of the winch design to ensure smooth reeling of the cable onto the drum over many cycles of operation, including helical grooves into which the cable reeled, and guides to prevent fouling and damage due to over-winding. Furthermore the company used transportable bomb crates which could be winched already fully-loaded into place in the fuselage, to reduce loading times. This was a development of the system which Charles had worked on twenty-five years earlier at Avros. For the later huge "Tallboy" and "Grand Slam" bombs of up to 22,000 pounds (10 tonnes) 6,100 pound (2.8 tonnes) rated winches were attached to the frames of the bomb transporter and used both for loading up in the armoury, and transferring to the Lancaster. (Plate 13-11).

In 1942 the Anson aircraft was upgraded as a gunnery training aircraft and Charles worked to install hydraulically-operated Bristol B1 turrets to replace the Armstrong-Whitworth manual turrets. The new turrets had under-floor electric motors driving a hydraulic pump. Later still, in 1944 a further upgraded version of the Anson, the Mark 11 came into service and this and subsequent models had in addition hydraulically-operated undercarriages. All these changes required development and the main works at Chadderton together with satellite works at Failsworth and Ashton-under-Lyne were kept very busy. Over eleven thousand Ansons were built and the type went on in service for many years after the war. The last Anson was withdrawn from RAF service in 1967 and many transferred to the civil register. Only two airworthy Ansons are still flying, one by courtesy of Atlantic Air Services, based at Coventry, and one at Old Warden airfield, maintained by the Shuttleworth collection. They both make appearances every year at air shows around the country.

Plate 13-11 Winched Transporter for the "Grand Slam"

During this very productive time in his career Charles Redrup was starting to become handicapped by failing eyesight. Since boyhood he had virtually no sight in his left eye, but now a slowly-growing cataract was starting to affect his right eye. Medical advice was that it would take over six weeks of resting after surgery before he could resume work. In the existing wartime climate Charles felt that he could not afford this loss of time and so he struggled on with his handicap, much to Jessie's concern. As they advanced into old age they were just as devoted to each other as ever and still spent as much time together as possible despite Charles' war work and his continuing development work at home.

It was in this period that he also developed improved machine-tool attachments for A.V.Roe. The aircraft structures now being manufactured required long lengths of alloy materials to be held and machined to fine tolerances and the usual method of manually clamping the parts at different stations along the machine bed were too slow and cumbersome. In addition the raw material was often twisted and needed to be straightened. This was not easy to do manually and so Charles devised and patented an automatic device using hydraulics to simultaneously clamp and straighten the material. (Plate 13-12).

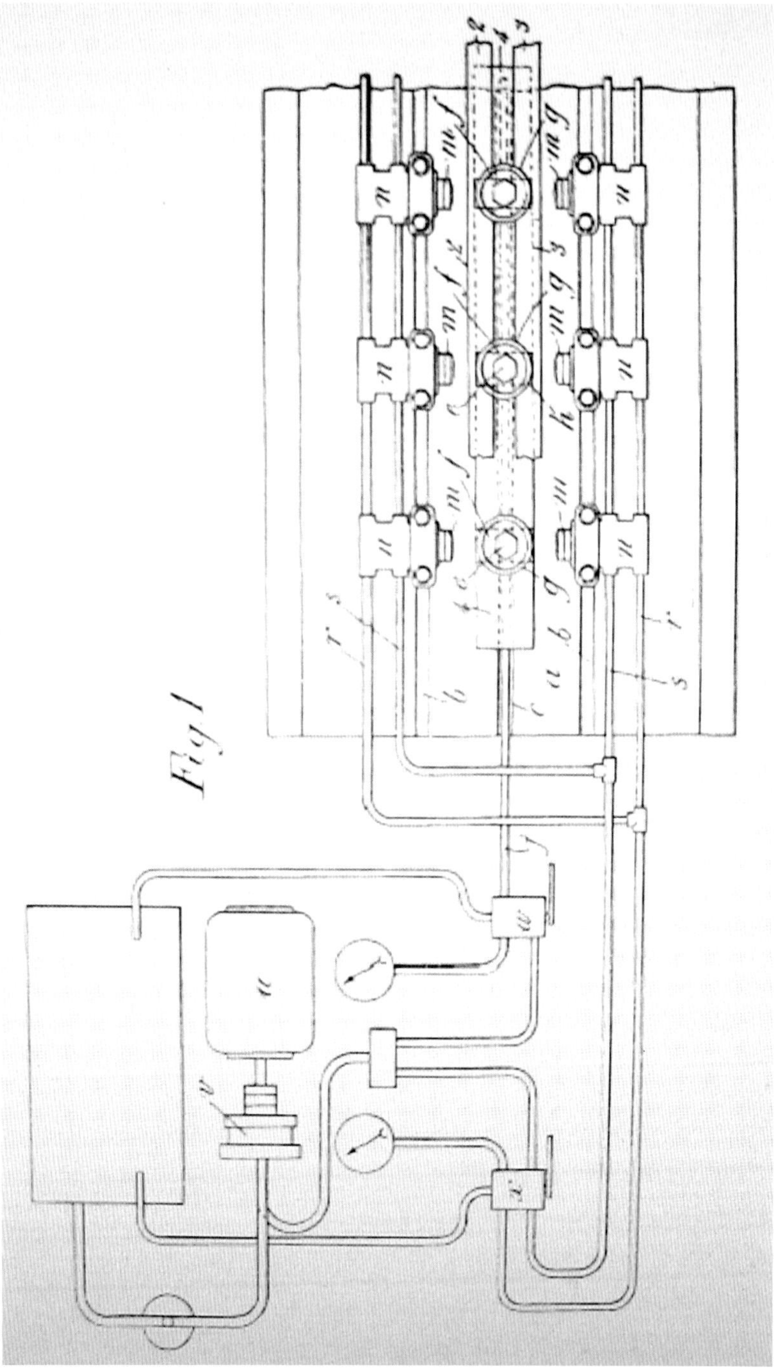

Plate13-12 Extract from Patent for Hydraulic Clamping and Straightening Machine

Chapter 14
Bouncers and Bounders

Charles had not ceased to promote his aero engine and tried to persuade Roy Dobson to let A.V.Roe develop it. Dobson did not wish to embark on engine manufacture but in late 1941 when a Mr B Bucher from Armstrong Siddeley Motors in Coventry was in Manchester to discuss some development work Charles took the opportunity to provide him with a copy of a pamphlet he had produced on his axial engine. Bucher was very interested in the concept and asked Roy Dobson for a further meeting to discuss whether the engine could be put into production. The meeting never materialised, no doubt because Dobson was pre-occupied with other matters, but in January 1942 Bucher wrote Charles a very complimentary letter stating that his engineers had reviewed the design and found stress levels most favourable. He believed that given the resources his factory would have no difficulty manufacturing the engine which would be ideal for RAF use and for post-war civilian aircraft. He concluded that if it was decided to pursue the engine further with A.V.Roe then he, Bucher would give the engine all the support he could. In April 1942 Dobson enquired from Charles as to the licensing arrangements with the Bristol Tramways Company and Charles advised him about the option to purchase British rights for aero engines for fifty thousand pounds, but nothing appears to have happened after that.

The power and carrying capacity of the Lancaster was progressively increased during the war years and a large variety of bomb loads carried. Apart from the twenty-two thousand pound "Grand Slam" penetration bombs already mentioned the most spectacular and effective bombs carried were the "Upkeep" bouncing bombs used in the "Chastise" raid on the hydro-electric dams of the Ruhr valley in 1943. Even before the war started studies had been carried out to see how the dams could be attacked in the event of war. Each study concluded that the dams were virtually impregnable because of the huge amount of explosive needed to be dropped from a suitable height, and because of the defence systems available. To destroy a dam with a bomb or aerial mine dropped into the water even a few yards from the dam wall would require explosive power much greater than any aircraft could carry. Even if such a load were available the precision required meant that a very low level approach would be required and the attacking aircraft would be destroyed by the explosion. The alternative of a high-altitude attack would not give the required precision. The matter was therefore left in abeyance until the advent of the war forced a re-think.

Plate 14-1 Dr Barnes Wallis

The engineer Dr Barnes Neville Wallis born in 1887, (Plate 14-1), had worked for the Vickers companies since 1911. During the First World War he worked on airships and was responsible for the design of the R80.

Although involved in different aspects of aeronautics he and Charles Redrup became acquainted during this period when Charles was visiting Vickers factories and offices during the development of the Hart engine. After the war Wallis went on to work on the R100 airship project where he worked with another engineer, Neville Shute Norway, later to become famous as the author Neville Shute. The R100 (Plate 14-2), was a private venture competitor to the government-sponsored R101. Lord Thompson, the Minister for Air had proposed that the UK should have an airship to match the large airships such as the Hindenberg being manufactured by Germany and the United States, and the Air Ministry issued a specification for a prestigious passenger-carrying airship capable of flying non-stop across the Empire to Montreal and India. He contracted with the

Royal Aircraft Factory and a private venture consortium which included Vickers Aircraft, to work on the design and construction of two airships and huge hangers were constructed at Cardington in Bedfordshire to house the R100 and R101. The R101 was constructed at Cardington in the light of full government publicity whilst the R100 was built quietly at Howden in Yorkshire.

Plate 14-2 The Vickers R100 Airship

Throughout, C.G. Grey led a vociferous campaign in the columns of *The Aeroplane,* railing against public expenditure being used in unfair competition with private enterprise. After the R101 crashed so disastrously in Beauvais, France on its maiden flight to India in 1930 killing Lord Thompson and Air Vice-Marshal Sir Sefton Brancker in the process, the R100, which had made a very successful flight across the Atlantic to Montreal, was scrapped. This was much to the exasperation of both the young Vickers design engineers as they believed that their airship was superior in every way. It also played straight into the hands of C. G. Grey who damned the R101 as a major public folly. During construction the R101 had been successively increased in weight and length as work progressed, probably leading to the poor buoyancy and handling problems which led to its crash. The lightness and strength of the R100 (Plate 14-3), compared to the R101 was due to Wallis's design of a lightweight "geodetic" truss. This truss was to be used to great effect in the Wellington Bomber which he designed for Vickers, incorporating this patented structure. (Plate 14-4). At the beginning of the Second World War he was employed by Vickers-Armstrong at their Brooklands airfield works in Surrey as Deputy Chief Design Engineer.

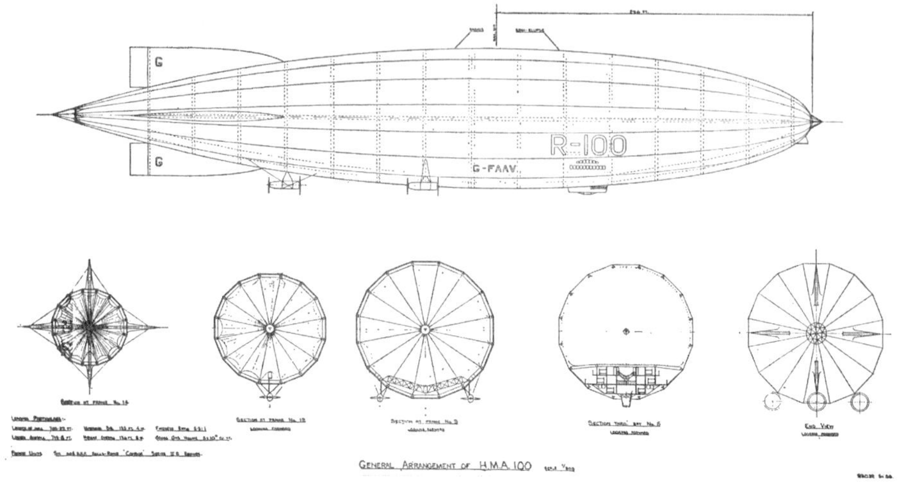

Plate 14-3 Structure of the R100

Purely in a private capacity he had already taken an interest in how to destroy strategic enemy targets and had proposed a massive "earthquake" deep-penetration bomb dropped from high altitude to the Air Ministry, which turned it down as impracticable as no aircraft existed capable of lifting the weight. He turned his attention to precision bombing. He knew that Nelson's gunners had bounced cannon balls off the surface of the sea to increase their range and he experimented in his own garden with a catapult and marbles. Having determined the basic rules of bouncing objects off water he was able to have some bomb models made of different shapes and sizes and have them tested in the large tanks at the National Physical Laboratory at Teddington. There he found that by spinning the dummy weapons around a horizontal axis, not only was the axis stabilised by the gyroscopic forces but the distance of travel could be increased or decreased, depending on the direction of spin.

Wallis' ensuing struggle with the bureaucracy at the War Department to plan a raid on the Ruhr dams is now well documented elsewhere and I will not repeat it here. Eventually however Winston Churchill's adviser Sir Henry Tizzard learnt of the proposal and Wallis was allowed to demonstrate his theories with a scaled-down bomb dropped from a Mosquito aircraft. After much prevarication the raid on the Ruhr dams was finally approved on February 26th 1943. The timing of a suitable raid was critical. Clear weather was essential as was moonlight with which to see. It was necessary to attack when the water levels in the lakes behind the dams were at their peak to ensure that the pressure would be sufficient to rupture the dams after they had been weakened by

Plate 14-4 Wellington Geodetic Construction

the blast. The Air Ministry knew from earlier reconnaissance that the water would be highest at the end of May and so the date was set for night of 26th/27th May.

Barnes Wallis' theory was that by giving a spherical bomb backspin, it would stabilise the bomb onto a straight path and create aerodynamic lift as it fell and so hit the water at an angle shallow enough to prevent it breaking up. In addition, on hitting the water the spin would generate hydrodynamic lift, thus lengthening the bounce. On reaching the target dam the residual backspin would then generate hydrodynamic thrust pushing the bomb against the wall as it sank, thus ensuring that it the explosive force would be directed right into the dam structure. The backspin would also ensure that the bomb slowed its forward movement in the air thus enabling the aircraft to escape without being caught in the blast. Wallis' calculations, confirmed by experiments with a model dam showed that with this technique an explosive load of about six thousand pounds (2,730 kg) would be sufficient to weaken the German Ruhr dams to the point of collapse.

A new squadron, No. 617 was created, based at Scampton in Lincolnshire and it was equipped with specially modified Lancasters to carry the bombs. Thirty Lancaster Mk IIIs were allocated to the project and were designated "Provisioning" aircraft and given the identification letter "G" with the intention of confusing enemy agents into thinking they were merely for carrying heavy supply loads. The Mk III Lancaster was a Mk I fitted with Merlin 28 engines which were Merlin 22s manufactured under licence by Packard Motors of Detroit because Roll Royce could not meet the huge demand for engines for fighters and bombers. The Merlin 28s were built to American standards and differed in detail for installation in terms of pipe and hose connections. The Lancasters had to be extensively modified in great secrecy to carry the bombs. Barnes Wallis started in late February to design a mounting arrangement for the bomb and also a hydraulic drive to rotate it at the right speed, which would be derived by experiment to be five hundred revolutions per minute. On 3rd March Roy Chadwick and Barnes Wallis agreed the changes and Chadwick dispatched Design, Drawing Office and Armaments personnel, including Charles Redrup, to work with Wallis's Vickers staff in Weybridge.

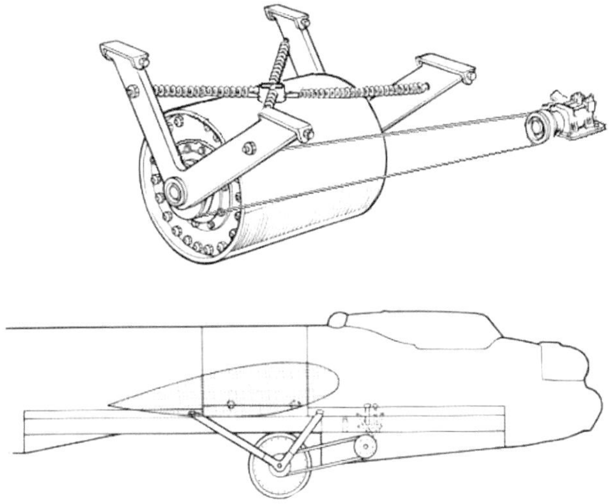

Plate 14-5 The Bomb Release Mechanism

So great was security that Charles was prevented from showing Wallis actual drawings and so Wallis had to make certain assumptions. The agreement was that Vickers would manufacture the release mechanism and the bomb drive system and build the bomb casings. A V Roe would provide the structural hard points for the holding arms, would remove the dorsal turrets to reduce weight and drag, and modify the airframe by cutting away the bomb doors and belly. They would also modify the hydraulic bomb door mechanism to give the necessary coupling points for the bomb release and the drive motor to spin the bomb. This motor was fortuitously an off-the-shelf four-cylinder swash-plate item for submarines from the Vickers shipyards in Newcastle. Whilst the hydraulic system normally operating the bomb doors also operated other services, its duty was fairly light as all these services required only intermittent operation of a few seconds. To operate the bomb-spinning motor the system had to operate for several minutes during the bombing runs and so the reservoir and accumulator systems had to be re-inforced in capacity. The conversion was further complicated by the American Packard hydraulic fittings on the engine-driven pumps.

For speed it was also agreed that Vickers would do the conversion of the first three aircraft which would be used for trials with the full-sized bomb and A.V.Roe would convert the remaining twenty-seven for delivery direct to Scampton. When the A.V.Roe staff were working with Wallis they eventually found to his dismay that his assumption about the width of the Lancaster bomb bay was incorrect, and the bomb casing had to be cut down in length by about an inch. (25.4 mm). Several bomb casings had already been made so this caused some delay and modified bombs only became available for test drops late in March.

Plate 14-6 The Bouncing Bomb In Situ

Wallis' design for the bomb release mechanism was a pair of large "V"-shaped arms on either side of the fuselage, with ball-bearing mounted wheels which engaged flanges in the ends of the bomb. (Plate 14-5). The arms were held closed onto the flanges against the pull of large springs which were released by the bomb aimer at the target so that the arms sprang apart. The wheel on the starboard side was driven by a long "v" belt driven by the hydraulic motor forward of the bomb bay. (Plate 14-6).

Plate 14-7 Bomb-Spinning and Drop-Test Rig

Wallis was very concerned that any unbalance in the spinning bomb or the act of releasing the arms with the belt drive attached would destabilise it and that it would cause havoc as it fell from the fuselage. Tests were carried out on a test rig in the Weybridge works with a scaled-down bomb for use in Mosquitos and they showed that these problems could be solved by dynamic balancing of the bomb using a similar balance technique to that used by Charles on his bus engine. Wallis's experienced test engineer Humphrey Jeffree performed these tests to resolve the problems and was responsible for analysing the test results and also the results of the field trials. (Plate 14-7).

These trials were carried out off the North Kent coast at Reculver with reduced-size bombs using a modified Vickers Wellington bomber and

Charles' first project after retirement was to make a three-cylinder axial motor-cycle engine based on the wobble-plate principle. (See colour plate C21). This had a stroke of two inches (50.8mm) and a similar bore.

The engine used a rotary valve plate based on exactly the same principle as his rotary-valved bus engine. (Plate 15-2). With only three cylinders the valve plate had four sets of ports and revolved at one-eighth of engine speed.

Plate 15-2 Cylinders and Rotary Valve

The induction air was fed into the central shaft chamber from a carburettor attached to a port between two of the cylinders. The connecting-rods were made of magnesium and were constrained to move axially by cheek-plates set in the side of the crank-case and the figure-of-eight motion was enabled by the spherical bosses on the wobble-plate being attached to the spider via sliding plates which enabled lateral motion. (See colour plate C22). The result was a beautifully compact machine which would have produced about ten horse-power (7.5kw).

Early in 1948 John Redrup suggested to his father that they should design and build a motorcycle based on the very successful Redrup Radial engine of the 1920s, but with overhead valves. John undertook to design and build the motor cycle whilst Charles set out to design a new engine. Work on the engine progressed rapidly and incorporated features and improvements from the lessons learnt on the earlier machines. As in all his designs, Charles produced an engine with maximum rigidity, efficient cooling and minimum weight. The engine consisted basically of three cylinder castings all identical and three detachable overhead valve cylinder heads with one exhaust and one inlet valve. The engine capacity was reduced to 248ccs to benefit from the reduced Road Tax. A single throw crank had the big end pin tapered and keyed and bolted to the outer webs of the crank shaft. (See colour plate C23).

All the connecting rods were identical with big end roller bearings. The flat topped aluminium alloy pistons each had three rings. The gudgeon pins were fully floating and retained by circlips. The valve gear, without gear wheels, was on the same principle as that used on the 1920 side valve Redrup Radial. However the engine was mounted in the frame horizontally with the crankshaft vertical, with side bearer plates forming a box which contained the main drive. Spiral bevel gears provided the connection to the cross shaft and the lower end of the engine crankshaft. This cross shaft also provided drives to the distributor and oil pump and also to a chain sprocket for a standard Lucas six-volt dynamo.

Mounting the engine in the frame with the crankshaft vertical has several major advantages. With one cylinder facing forward and the other two at one hundred and twenty degrees all the cylinders were fully in the air stream, thus providing excellent air cooling and a low centre of gravity. The horizontal cylinder block position enabled equal lubrication for all three cylinders, overcoming one of the problems of the earlier Redrup Radial where the top cylinder would sometimes overheat due to oil starvation, whilst the lower cylinders would get oiled-up plugs. As the overall design used a drive shaft to the rear wheels this position therefore simplified the installation.

The engine was arranged with the inlet valves at the top connected to a multi jet carburettor of Charles' own design via three short induction pipes meeting at the centre above a small flywheel. The whole was enclosed by a cast aluminium cover which incorporated a flange connection for the carburettor. The cover also provided enough heat retention for the induction pipes to promote rapid warming up from cold and ideal running conditions. The exhaust valves and ports are at the bottom provided a straight run to the main silencers and efficient cooling. All Charles' previous experience with motor cycle, aero and bus engines had proved to him the importance of adequate carburettor warming.

The connecting rods were identical and mounted side by side with their roller bearings on the case-hardened big end pin. As all the cylinder castings were identical there was enough material allowed on the cast iron flanges for the required staggering of the cylinders to provide for the side by side conrods. This was a deviation from the earlier design with forked connecting rods. Assuming the forward cylinder is No.1 and the right hand cylinder is No.2 with the left hand cylinder No.3, the No 2 cylinder was machined so that the connecting rod and piston were on the correct centre which would be below No.1 cylinder, and No.3 cylinder had the flanges machined and drilled to allow it to be below the No.1 cylinder and on the correct centre for its connecting rod and piston. When the 3 cylinders were bolted together they also accurately locate the inlet and exhaust valve gear assemblies. The cylinder heads were bolted on in the normal manner with the push rods enclosed within the cylinder castings. Any one cylinder could be removed easily if required for inspection. (Plate 15-3).

Plate 15-3 Arrangement of Cylinders and Con-Rods

A simpler and more easily manufactured multi-cylinder engine for mass production would be hard to imagine. All the patterns were made in the workshop at Clifton Road, Heaton Moor, All the casting and all the machining was done by Charles in the same workshop.

For the motor cycle frame John did some design work on a modern machine which was to have telescopic front forks hydraulically damped,

Plate 15-4 The 1948 Redrup Radial Motor-Cycle

swing arm rear suspension with hydraulic shock absorbers and shaft drive. At this time George Dowty was producing such shock absorbers for motor cycles as a diversification to compensate for the fall-off in post-war aircraft orders. The whole machine was to be covered in with light alloy panelling readily detachable with an attractive air intake grill for the engine. The petrol tank and oil tank were to be all simply finished and completely enclosed as is the case now over fifty years later with most advanced machines.

However this design work took much longer than anticipated and so in order to get the engine on the road as quickly as possible he decided to make the prototype from readily available new parts, frame, gear box, etc. He made the frame from standard Enfield 350cc parts with which he was very familiar. The wheels were standard with chromium plated rims which he painted with a central strip in light maroon cellulose. The brake drums were standard. The mud guards were also sprayed with light maroon cellulose, as were the side and top panels on the chromium-plated petrol tank. He used the four-speed Albion foot change gear box with his own design of multi-plate clutch of much smaller diameter than the standard clutch as this made it easier to provide the chain drive to the gear box.

The machine and engine were finished and assembled at Clifton Road. The completed machine was then registered as a Redrup Radial with the local taxation authority Reg. No. DDB 248 in 1948. (Plate 15-4). Road tests were carried out in the local streets. After trying a single Amal carburettor and also a version with an Amal for each cylinder, they finally settled for a single multi-jet carburettor of Charles' own design which gave the best overall very satisfactory performance. After running the machine for approximately two years without any mechanical failures or problems the total mileage was approximately forty thousand. This was very good considering that only rationed pool petrol was available. Throughout this period Charles and John tried to interest British manufacturers in the design but in these years of austerity they were not interested in investing in new machines but only concerned in selling their established designs, so the Redrups had to abandon the project, at least in Great Britain.

In September 1948 John and Joan were invited to Bristol to attend the wedding of John's old friend Rex Pollard and Gloria. Unfortunately they could not get the time off to attend the wedding as it was on a Friday. However they visited Rex and Gloria a few weeks later after they had returned from honeymoon and would spend several weekends together thereafter. (Plate 15-5).

Plate 15-5 Rex and Gloria Pollard with Joan and John

However, only six months after his marriage, in March 1949, Rex was on a test flight over the English Channel in a new variant of the Bristol Freighter which the Bristol Aeroplane Company had developed. The particular test was to determine the aircraft's climb performance with one engine stopped. For some reason, at that time not determined, the aircraft crashed into the sea just off Weymouth with the loss of all thirteen people on board. The only clue was an eye-witness report of the crash in which it was said that, what appeared to be a wing fluttered down separately from the main aircraft. John was devastated by this news, especially as no cause for the crash had been established. The next year during an almost identical test another Bristol Freighter crashed in South Wales with the loss of all three crew. This time the wreckage was available and the cause determined. It appeared that in a climb with one engine stopped large amounts of rudder input were required to counteract the unbalanced thrust, resulting in a large yaw. With the fuselage shielding the airflow over the tail surfaces, this resulted in the rudder slamming hard over and overstressing its attachment. The result was that the fin and rudder sheared off, leaving the aircraft in an uncontrollable condition and causing it to spin in.

Edwin Shackleton, who is 79, holds the world record for flying in the largest number of aircraft types as a passenger. At the date of writing,

(September 2006), he has flown in eight hundred and thirty-eight types. In 1949 Edwin started work for Bristol Aeroplane Company as a Structural Test Engineer. He set up a low temperature test facility which was invaluable in Britannia development, later working on BAC1-11, BAe 146 and Concorde tests. He recalls a rear fuselage section of a Bristol Freighter and empennage in a test rig in the early 1950's. The tests were evidently successful and the solution, applied to all other aircraft of the type was to strengthen the fin attachment and to fit a strake to the front of the fin to prevent the rudder slamming hard over. This simple modification enabled the Bristol Freighter in all its variant forms to go on to be a workhorse for a large number of airlines and air forces. Silver City Airways carried many thousands of Britons together with their cars between Lydd and Calais (Plate 15-6), but few of them were aware of the considerable human cost that lay in the wreckage in the waters below.

Plate 15-6 Cross-Channel Silver Cities Bristol Freighter

In 1957 another member of the Redrup family went to work for the Bristol Aeroplane Company (BAC). Charles' brother Sidney had a son Ronald who started working as a messenger for British Overseas Airways Corporation (BOAC) during the Second World War, at their offices in the Spa Hotel in Clifton, Bristol. He moved firstly to their Whitchurch base where he worked on Dakotas before going to London Airport at Heathrow as a technical engineer. After about eight years with BOAC he moved back to Bristol and joined the Bristol Aeroplane Company at Filton as a design engineer. He worked on a wide range of BAC aircraft, including Concorde.

In October 1949, disillusioned with prospects in Britain, John and Joan Redrup emigrated to Canada where John hoped to arouse interest in the motorcycle concept. Meanwhile the radial-engined motorcycle was run by his brother Ray back in England. They travelled on the Ascania and in a flash of "déjà vu" experienced dreadful gales and heavy seas just as John's father had done fifty years earlier. They stayed in the Ford Hotel for a week then rented a self-contained top floor apartment in Armour Heights, Ontario, just outside Toronto. Within a week they bought furniture and had it delivered. Joan secured a Secretarial post and John obtained a job with A.V.Roe Canada working on the CF109 Starfighter. He found himself working with people from Dowty, as the CF109 had the patent Dowty "shrinking" undercarriage, which by a clever mechanism enabled the legs to shorten as they retracted, to fit into a compact undercarriage bay. (Plate 15-7).

Plate 15-7 "Shrinking" Undercarriage of the CF109 Starfighter

Whilst working for Avro Canada, John also hoped to kindle interest in the radial motorcycle concept but it soon became clear that motorcycling was not a high priority in Canada where winter conditions were not conducive to open-air travel. Reluctantly therefore they decided to return to England. This time however John was determined to travel on the biggest and most stable ship available and so they returned on the Queen Mary in August 1951. John quickly obtained a post with Simons Engineering once more but also went back to assisting his father on his engine developments.

Throughout his employment during World War Two Charles Redrup had tried to interest Roy Dobson in his large double-ended aero engine, but war work prevented any progress in this direction. Now in retirement he returned to the double-ended concept and working with John, devised and patented a much simpler, potentially more reliable version of the engine. Instead of using "Z" shafts and wobble plates, he arranged for the pistons to have dome-shaped ends which fitted into sinusoidal grooves in a cam. (Plate 15-8). This arrangement also had the advantage that it was self-centring and did not need stabiliser arms.

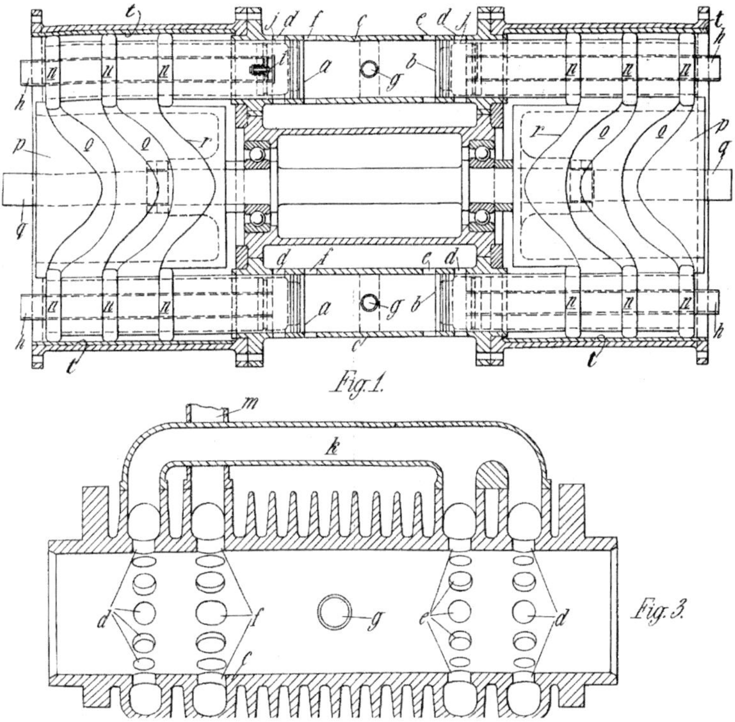

Plate 15-8 Air-Cooled Opposed-Piston Double Cam-Driven Two-Stroke Engine

Similar cam engines had been designed in the past but relied on shoes or rollers to couple the pistons to the cam. As with all axial engines good lubrication and low friction between pistons and drive shaft is essential

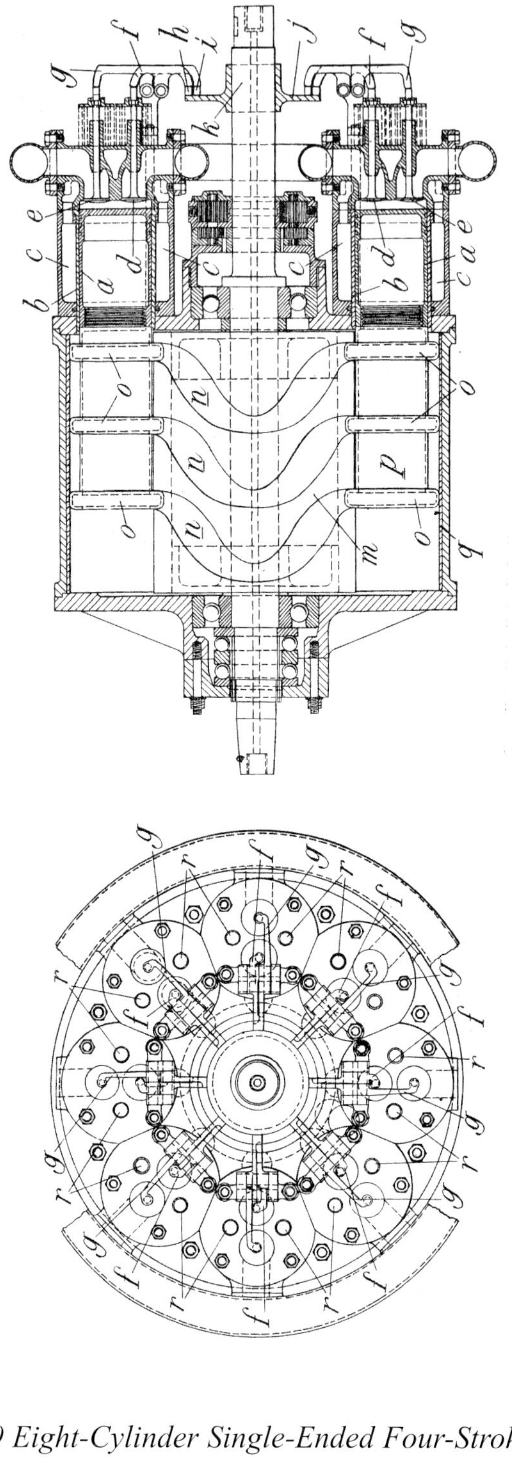

Plate 15-9 Eight-Cylinder Single-Ended Four-Stroke Cam Engine

and these earlier engines were not very reliable. Charles' design had several advantages over them. Because of the rotational symmetry of the pistons he was able to arrange for each cam to have three sinusoidal grooves in it and the pistons to have three corresponding circular bosses, thus increasing the bearing area and reducing friction. Because the pistons were not circumferentially restrained they could rotate and thus side loads were reduced and a continuous oil film could be maintained even at top-dead-centre and bottom-dead-centre. John and Charles patented two versions of this engine. These were a 500 horse-power single-ended version (Plate 15-9), and a one-thousand horse-power double-ended version, for petrol or diesel use. In addition either engine could be air or water-cooled.

Unlike the wobble-plate engine the cams could be arranged to have one or more cycles of motion around the periphery. With just one cycle per revolution the motion was similar to the wobble-plate engine, with one firing stroke per revolution. However by cutting the cam profile to give two or more axial motions of pistons per revolution the engine could in effect be geared down. Thus, for example, with a wobble-plate or cam engine with just one sinusoidal wave per revolution, with three thousand firing strokes per minute an engine would run at three thousand rpm. However by cutting a cam with two or three sinusoidal waves per revolution, the engine would run at fifteen hundred or a thousand rpm respectively. (Plate 15-10). This feature promised to be

Plate 15-10 Phosphor-Bronze Cam for Single-Ended Engine

Plate 15-11 Model of Opposed-Piston Double-Cam Engine

Plate 15-12 Drive-End of the Single-Cam 500 Horse-Power Engine

most useful in aero engine applications. Charles was most keen to see this engine go on test, but by this time in aero engine development the cost of setting up a test bed and undertaking engine development work was well beyond the scope of a single individual.

In 1951, with his patents applied for Charles wrote to Roy Dobson (now Sir Roy) at A.V.Roe with a copy of the patents and reminded him of the interest and enthusiasm that had been expressed from Mr Bucher of Armstrong Siddeley after his visit in 1942. He requested an interview and an opportunity to demonstrate the engine to the company. In a letter of reply which was very curt to someone who had been his colleague of over twenty-five years, Dobson replied that Avro were now concentrating on gas turbine engines and saw no future in piston engines. Charles wrote once more with documents to demonstrate the simplicity of construction and operation of his engine, but no further progress was made.

Over the next few years in Charles' workshop, he and John made a small demonstration model of the double-ended version with eight cylinders and a full-scale version of the 500 Horse-Power single-ended engine, also with eight cylinders, (Plates 15-11, 15-12 and colour plate C24). However by the late 1950's Charles' eyesight was failing and he was losing the ability to concentrate so none of these engines were completed.

John's sister Dorothy had become a theatre Sister at Frenchay hospital in Bristol by 1952 and a few years later she returned to the north-west to become a sister at Nab Top Sanatorium in Marple, Cheshire. (Plate 15-13). Florence was living in Bolton with her husband Tom, and Charles and Jessie moved to Southport to be near them. John and Charles wrote to several car and aircraft companies in America to try to rouse interest in the cam engines which had also been patented there. To try to market the concept directly John and Joan returned to Toronto in April 1957 with a view to Charles and Jessie eventually joining them. Dorothy also moved out to Canada to live with them and to help find Charles and Jessie a home. With Charles' failing health they thought a move would benefit him and sought permission for him and Jessie to emigrate to Canada. However the Canadian immigration authorities were tightening up on controls and required guarantees on housing and income which Charles was unable to meet. Also for elderly immigrants in poor health the authorities wanted proof of a substantial capital base. After several months the negotiations fell through and John and Joan returned again to England in November 1957 but Dorothy elected to stay in Toronto as she had settled in well and had a good job as a Staff Nurse in Toronto

Plate 15-13 Dorothy Redrup at Nab Top Sanatorium, Marple

General Hospital. One day whilst playing golf, she met a Canadian widower, Rudy Bache. They were married in 1964 and spent some very happy years together.

John and Joan (Plate 15-14), lived in Harlow, Essex for a short while, where John was working for the British Oxygen Company and Joan was secretary to the Office Manager. Eventually they bought a house in Dunmow and John went to work for another engineering company, Graveners, where he worked as a representative selling instrumentation. Florence used to visit John and Joan in Dunmow and liking the area, when her husband Tom died in 1958, she bought a house in nearby Frinton-on-Sea. Charles and Jessie went to live with her and as the family was still very close, John and Joan, who only lived about sixty miles away, saw much of his parents. (Plate 15-15).

Plate 15-14 John and Joan Redrup in the late 1950s

Plate 15-15 Charles, John and Jessie in 1958

Plate 15-16 Charles and Jessie with Aunt Rosie, 2nd from Left

Jessie's sister Rosie, who kept a post office in Tarling in Essex for many years was also a regular visitor to Frinton, (Plate 15-16, next to Charles), as was her other sister Libby. However Charles' health continued to decline and he was no longer able to work on his beloved engines. He died in August 1961 at the age of eighty-three years.

Despite having seven children Charles and Jessie only had three grandchildren. Peter and Jennifer Lake, Jessica's children, (Plate 15-17) were 13 and 10 when Charles died and he never met John and Joan's daughter Julia, who was born in August 1965, four years later.

In 1966 Graveners were taken over by another company and John became redundant. With a fourteen-month old daughter, in the November he and Joan set off once again to Canada. John secured an engineering post with Texas Instruments in Richmond Hill, Ontario on the basis of his instrumentation experience. They lived with Dorothy and Rudy who lived in Richmond Hill, until they found themselves a home. Dorothy doted on baby Julia and was very pleased to have some of her family close to her. John and Joan bought a large, split-level four-bedroomed house in Aurora, Ontario, close to the Texas Instruments works. John worked on developing automatic machinery for the manufacture of transistors and with the company patented a technique for increasing the yield. It was whilst they were living in Aurora that Dorothy became ill and died in January 1968 at the age of fifty-nine.

Plate 15-17 Two of Charles Grand-children, Peter and Jennifer Lake

Texas Instruments wanted John to move to their headquarters in Dallas and they offered him a substantial promotion but neither he nor Joan wanted to move to a much hotter climate with a small baby.

Joan's mother had recently died and they were both feeling homesick and so they returned to England in August 1968. John had always liked Devon and so they rented a small house by a stream in the village of Newton Poppleford just outside Sidmouth, whilst he found a job. He worked for a Bristol company, Robophone Ltd, one of the early start-up mobile telephone companies and was based in Exeter as a Communications Consultant. Robophone got into difficulties after about two years so John got a temporary job working for a car company in Exeter. Still hopeful of marketing the motor-cycle, he then decided to try his luck in Australia.

In June 1970 he, Joan and Julia flew out to Sidney where John had secured a job working for the engineering company Crookes, Michell, Peacock and Stewart. Coincidentally one of the founders of this company was the inventor of the Michell bearing, so widely used in swash-plate engines. The company paid their air fares and also for an apartment for three weeks whilst they found their own accommodation. They rented a bungalow in the grounds of the Christian Science Church in North Sidney. John worked in the design office and they made many friends in Australia. John's mother Jessie, still living with Florence, died in October 1971 and by 1973 they were thinking about what was best for Julia's education. (Plate 15-18).

Plate 15-18 Charles' Grand-daughter Julia

With great reluctance, as they were very happy in Sidney, they decided to return to England, and bought a house in Stroud, Gloucestershire. John went to work as a systems engineer for Redlers Engineering in Cainscross and he travelled around the area installing conveyors and other materials handling equipment. Julia went to Stroud High School for Girls and then took a three-year course in computer studies at the Gloucester College of Art and Technology. She then worked for McEvoys Oil Field Equipment Company as a computer Analyst. When John retired in 1987 the family moved back to Newton Poppleford in Devon and Julia worked for the London and Manchester Insurance Company in Exeter for eight years before moving for experience to Phoenix, Arizona for a year. She then returned to England and lived in London working freelance as an I T Consultant

Throughout his travels John tried to keep as many of his father's artefacts as possible, including machine tools, parts of engines and many drawings. He took all of this material with him when he travelled as he was always hopeful of re-kindling interest in the engines. When he retired he built himself a workshop where he kept his father's memorabilia and also continued to do his own work.

Until recently another of Charles Redrup's motor-cycles was in running order in England. It was a 1920 Redrup Radial, U4678, owned by Ken Blake the well-known motor cyclist. Ken had first heard of the machine round about 1952 when it was owned by Percy Clare. Fitted with two light alloy cylinder heads and one bronze one, it was a non-runner. Percy refused to sell and Ken forgot about it until in about 1984 he had a call from Jack Light, a well known collector. Jack was clearing out an old motor museum near Hampton Court. The museum, on Taggs Island in the River Thames had been closed for many years. Jack had realised that he would never get around to repairing the motor-cycle and asked Ken if he was interested. Ken went to see it and remarked that he would like to hear it run again. "So would I", said Jack, "and if you can let me hear it run again, you can have it!"

Ken stripped the machine down in his workshop at Parkstone in Dorset and realised that it had experienced a major mechanical breakdown the last time it had run. The bearings and pistons were all seized and a valve had stuck open and been struck by the piston. Various parts were missing, including the light alloy sump. Ken's story gives a good insight into the performance of this era of Charles Redrup's designs.

The two main weaknesses were the lubrication system and the carburettor. The original lubrication operated off two small plunger pumps in the sump but the engine orientation was such that the upper cylinder became starved of oil whilst the lower cylinders would be excessively oiled and the spark plugs would oil up, especially on shutdown when a partial vacuum formed in the cylinders. The carburettor problems arose from Charles' use of very fine jets which would soon clog up. Ken re-designed the oil system and fitted Triumph Tiger Cub plunger pumps to the scavenge side only, force-feeding their main bearings but with a supplementary hand-operated pump to supply the big-end bearing. This required some skill from the rider to remember to use it! The oil lines were now external to the casing and had adjustable restrictors.

Ken had to plate and re-grind the crankshaft and renew all nine bushes. He built patterns and cast a new sump and light alloy cylinder heads machined to take modern 14mm plugs to enable temperatures to be adjusted. The cylinder bores were opened up from 50.8mm to 51mm and Villiers pistons were machined to fit although the top ring had to be omitted. The original two-speed Burman gearbox was fitted as was the Verus frame. The magneto had long since disappeared but through a contact he obtained a 1919 Thompson-Bennett just like that fitted to original Redrup Radials. (Plate 6-9)

Ken Blake entered the rebuilt radial, painted in an attractive green colour scheme with cream and chocolate trim lines typical of the 1920s, into the *1986 Annual Banbury Run*. It performed well, struggling a little to climb Sunrising Hill but completed the course to be awarded the Jim Sheldon Trophy, awarded to the entry judged to be "Of Greatest Technical Interest". (See colour plate C11). According to John Redrup, The appearance of the Ken Blake restoration, whilst having an attractive colour scheme, did not do justice to the original. The carburettor was much larger and the fan was uglier than the lightweight longer-bladed fans fitted to the 1920's motor cycles.

Ken kept the Redrup Radial for many more years, eventually selling it via a third party to a Japanese collector for an undisclosed sum. Another 1920s Redrup Radial motor cycle surfaced again very recently. In the summer of 2006 David Earnshaw, a Yorkshire collector and restorer, purchased a rolling frame, minus engine from a Norwich collector. It is his intention to restore the machine and he is seeking an engine for it. It may be that there are still some of the Boyle and Redrup radial engines in existence in old factories and works around Leeds.

At the age of seventy-eight in the year 2000, John Redrup still had his 1948 Radial motor-cycle, but it was in poor condition by that time. Unable to carry out any more work on it, he decided to donate it to the Sammy Miller Museum Trust in Hampshire, on the condition that he could still take it for a spin occasionally. Sammy Miller was a legendary trials rider in the 1950s, 60s and 70s and went on to be a dealer and rider of motor-cycles for Ariel, Honda and the Spanish company Bultaco. His motor-cycle museum has about three hundred and fifty machines, all in working order and all run in public or at vintage race meets.

Sammy made a marvellous job of restoring the Redrup Radial motor-cycle, the only new component needed being the clutch, the original of which, with the primary drive gear had been lost during John's many moves around the world. This has resulted in a somewhat reduced performance as it adversely affects the gearing. As in earlier engines this one seemed to have suffered from poor lubrication and Sammy modified the oil system to give increased lubrication to the top of the engine and also includes a small amount of oil in the fuel. Sammy painted the machine in a rich red colour and John Redrup did an original design for a tank badge in silver. (See colour plate C25).

When the engine was started for the first time after about fifty years, Sammy was amazed at the rich exhaust sound. As the engine gives uniform firing strokes unlike modern twins, the three-into-two exhaust arrangement accounts for this sound. As soon as the throttle is opened the sound smoothes out and the engine revs much like a modern machine. With the perfect primary balance from the three cylinders the engine sound is very smooth although close-up there is a subsidiary whirring from all the auxiliary gearing, which is hidden by the exhaust note at any distance. John and Joan Redrup were guests of Sammy at the Museum and John had a chance to ride his old motor cycle. It was a great thrill for Sammy to see John riding it and says John was like a little boy with a new toy! (Plate 15-19 and colour plate C26). The machine featured in the April 2000 edition of *Classic Motor Cycle* magazine and can be seen in immaculate condition at Sammy's museum in Hampshire.

Plate 15-19 John Redrup on the 1948 Redrup Radial

John Redrup died in August 2004 at the age of eighty-two. He left a rich archive of his father's work which has been catalogued and maintained by his widow Joan Redrup. She also maintains in good order a few of Charles Redrup's engines and models and is seeking a good home for them. It is hoped to create a Redrup collection in a museum closely related to the places where he worked, either in Barry, Bristol or Manchester where the Avro archives are kept. It is only fitting that he should be remembered for the many contributions he made to many fields of engineering. The days are long gone when a single man could manufacture high quality engines of such innovative design as those of Charles Redrup, with little more than "A knife and fork".

Epilogue

The inventive genius of Charles Redrup covered such a wide span of activities that they are difficult to catalogue. They can however be divided into five broad categories and his legacy can be traced through them to the present day.

He was one of the very earliest pioneers of the rotary engine and applied these to motor-cycles, aircraft and cars. He was probably the first engineer to use the rotary engine in the contra-rotation mode and his brilliant application of this to the 1912 "Gyroscopic" motor-cycle and to his ten horse-power aero engine lives on in engines which survive to this day.

Charles tried several ways to overcome the disadvantages of poppet valves and his design and application of the sleeve-valve engine to circumvent the Knight and Argyll patents resulted in the very smooth double sleeve valve as used in the 1912 motor-cycle. The development to perfection by Roy Fedden of the sleeve-valve design for the huge family of engines produced by the Bristol Aeroplane Company testifies to the soundness of the concept. Redrup adapted the concept in developing the flat rotary valve with ports for his bus and aero engines of the 1930's.

When he turned his attention to stationary radial engines he was one of the very first to recognise the need for close-finning of the cylinders to improve cooling. His radial engines were ahead of their time and it is unfortunate that they did not see commercial success in the years of the First World War. The reasons for this are several but it seems clear that the development of his Hart engine was slower than expected and required greater commitment than was readily available. It was the first static radial engine to be fitted to a British aircraft and was not well suited to a pusher configuration. When installed in a tractor aircraft the lack of understanding of proper cowling arrangements worked to the disadvantage of the Hart engine. It is also clear that there was a dearth of enthusiasm in the War Department to continue development work with Vickers when there were several highly successful fighter aircraft available from other manufacturers.

In contrast the success of the Avro Alpha engine was self-evident, to the point where it was taken over and eliminated by the competition. The use of the Alpha in several highly-publicised and record-breaking flights, and its adoption in several flying club aircraft was testimony to its versatility. It is a great pity that no Alpha engine survives to this day.

Charles Redrup's small two and three-quarter horsepower radial engines had a short but successful life in industrial applications when manufactured by the Boyle and Redrup Company, but were most significant when installed as Redrup Radials in motor-cycles manufactured by a number of companies. He continued his interest in radial engines right up until the end of his life.

The most significant of his inventions was the "Wobble-plate" axial engine which was superior in many ways to the swash-plate engines which preceded it. The earliest application was in his marine engine, closely followed by the Fury aero engine as used in the Simmonds Spartan aircraft. Having solved the stabilisation problem for aircraft he was able to successfully implement the concept in the Bristol bus engines of the mid-1930s. His designs for powerful aircraft engines based on the principle were superseded by his involvement in aircraft armaments during the Second World War but he persevered after the war with his designs for two-thousand horse-power wobble-plate and cam engines working on a very similar principle. The advent of the gas turbine engine put paid to any significant use of large internal combustion engines thereafter for aircraft applications.

Charles Redrup's work on aircraft armaments during the Second World War was somewhat of a diversion from his real interests but he nevertheless made significant contributions to the performance of the Lancaster and its derivatives.

What then is the state of the art today in the fields where Charles Redrup worked? Rotary engines have ceased to play any part in the modern world, except at vintage air displays for aircraft such as the Shuttleworth Avro 504K fitted with a Gnome engine. The radial engine reached its peak in the late 1940s with the huge Wright multi-row radials used in such airliners as the Boeing Stratocruiser, (Plate E-1), but were rapidly superseded by the jet engine.

A characteristic of the axial drive in that if the drive-shaft is rotated, the friction between it and the pistons is low, whereas if the pistons drive the shaft, the mechanical advantage is reversed and the friction is much higher. This is similar to a worm and pinion gear drive as is used from time to time in steering mechanisms where the steering column has a worm wheel and the steering bar has a geared rack. The steering wheel can drive the steering bar very effectively but there is high friction if the road wheels try to centre the steering column. The author's 1938 Morris

Plate E-1 Wright Two-Row Cyclone Radial Engine of the 1950s

8 Tourer had this type of steering and wear on the worm wheel was very high. For this reason axial mechanisms are widely used for pumps in the form of swash-plate or cam designs but the application of axial prime-mover engines has drawn less interest and only a small number have been manufactured and put to use. The answer to this problem is to have low-friction drive couplings between pistons and wobble-plate or cam. Well-lubricated ball-joints and ball-bearings on the Z-shaft solved the problem with the wobble-plate engine, whilst for the cam engine the use of rollers is the best solution. Great care has to be taken to ensure the rollers are adequately supported as the impulse forces from combustion are very high and only line contact takes place between the moving surfaces

The most recent and successful application is the Dynacam engine, a twelve-cylinder petrol engine with double-ended pistons driving a single cam. (Plate E-2). This engine has been extensively test-flown in a Piper PA28 and is now going into production through a new company, Aero Marine Engine Inc. (See colour plate C27). The cost and difficulty of machining large cams had previously inhibited the development of this type of engine despite the fact that Charles Redrup was able to make high-precision cams of sinusoidal waveform on his home lathe using his proverbial "knife and fork". The availability of computer-aided design and machining (CAD-CAM) means that such cams can now be made in quantity to high accuracy. Furthermore the option becomes available to use more complex waveforms to optimise combustion control. Charles Redrup had the foresight to see that cam engines were well suited to diesel applications, especially where opposed pistons are used, as is evident from his patents. These balance out the combustion forces and reduce the stress on the crank-case enabling a much lighter engine to be manufactured.

Plate E-2 Cam and Pistons of Dynacam Engine

One such engine currently under development is the FairDiesel opposed-piston two-stroke diesel engine. Conventional diesel engines using the Diesel cycle cannot match the efficient fast combustion at top dead centre of Otto-Cycle petrol engines. In these diesels the fuel injection continues to take place during the combustion stroke and such engines therefore have to obtain their high efficiencies from the use of higher compression ratios. A conventional petrol engine has a thermal efficiency of about 33 percent and a diesel engine of about 43 percent. In the FairDiesel twin-cam engine the profiles are shaped to ensure that the pistons remain at top dead centre for the majority of the fuel injection and combustion period thereby following the Otto Cycle and a potential thermal efficiency in excess of 63 percent is possible. (See colour plate C28).

With the present concerns about carbon dioxide emissions this gives a large potential saving in overall emissions and it is likely that such engines will soon come back into favour. The development of electronically-controlled fuel injection for diesel engines has eliminated the characteristic "knock" which used to occur in engines with mechanical injection. By controlling the injection into a series of short bursts the combustion process can be smoothed out to ensure that the combustion pressure rises in an acceptable profile. The vested interests in the automotive industry have been very slow to take up such innovations but environmental pressures may soon force them to do so. It may well be that in small and medium-sized aircraft applications the axial cam engine could replace the propeller-turbine and pure jet engine, which have poor thermal efficiencies and are very thirsty compared to internal combustion engines. The cam engine has the further advantage of running very cool as waste heat is reduced and the cam can be profiled to ensure that combustion is completed before the exhaust ports are opened, reducing emissions of hydrocarbons and oxides of sulphur and nitrogen.

Many of Charles Redrup's ideas were far in advance of their time and he did not always receive the recognition he deserved. He was a shy man and not inclined to self-publicity and therefore suffered from the perennial problem of the small business, lack of sufficient development investment from backers with vision. What can be achieved when such investment is forthcoming is witnessed by the foresight of Alliott Verdon Roe and the success of the Avro Alpha engine, sadly cut short by the take-over of the company by John Siddeley. Similarly Charles Redrup's bus engines were showing how a marked increase in performance could be achieved with axial engines, when the Bristol Tramways Company experienced a take-over and the work was stopped. Although Charles did find backers for many of his other projects they rarely had the vision to see a project through the difficulties which inevitably beset any innovative venture.

Charles Redrup's qualities were many, but three predominate when reviewing his life. He was undoubtedly an outstanding engineer capable of tackling a wide range of problems in many fields of work. The quality of his work, whether it be design, drawing, pattern-making, casting or machining was consistently high and the engines which still exist possess a beauty and finish rarely seen in these days of mass production.

Secondly he had great stamina and persevered when everything seemed to be stacked up against him. He kept his independence through having his own workshop and could always fall back on his own resourcefulness. Despite having poor vision he did most of his own drawing and always had his next project lined up in readiness. Thirdly, he was a man of principles, with strong family values and a sense of obligation to his friends and colleagues. He also had a stubborn streak and this did not always go down well with his sponsors. He did not suffer fools gladly and this may have worked against him at times. His family was a close-knit one and all of his children acquired the sense of duty which he evidently possessed. He passed over a number of opportunities when he felt his colleagues might lose out. In this respect his commercial skills were not great but he was a bigger man because of it.

The works of Charles Benjamin Redrup have not been forgotten and his legacy carries on. Whilst his patents have now lapsed his concepts are still being pursued and will almost certainly experience a revival in the Twenty-first Century.

Appendix (i)

Known Redrup Engine Designs.

1896 (Circa) Steam engine.

1901 Single-cylinder motor cycle engine.

1903 The "Barry" two-cylinder two Horse-power Rotary motor cycle engine.

1906 Two-cylinder "Reactionless" aero engine.

1909 Ten-cylinder "Reactionless" aero engine.

1910 The "Barry" two-cylinder fifty Horse-power Car engine.

1911 Three-cylinder "Reactionless" aero engine with propeller.

1912 Three-cylinder "Reactionless" aero engine with contra-rotating propellers.

1912 Three-cylinder "Reactionless" motor cycle engine.

1912 Seven-cylinder 35 Horse-power Radial aero engine.

1913 Four-cylinder Sleeve-valve motor car engine.

1913 Nine-cylinder 150 Horse-power "Reactionless" aero engine.

1913 Single-cylinder 17 Horse-power test engine with Close finning.

1914 Nine-cylinder 150 Horse-power Hart Radial engine.

1917 Double-ended Wobble-plate axial engine patent.

1918 Five-cylinder Radial engine with Exhaust-valve induction.

1919 309cc Boyle and Redrup General purpose three-cylinder side-valve Radial engine.

1920 "Redrup Radial" side-valve motor cycle.

1921 "Redrup Six" six-cylinder Radial-engined motor cycle.

1922 Six-cylinder double-ended two-stroke Axial marine engine.

1924 Six-cylinder single-ended two-stroke Axial marine engine.

1926 Five-cylinder 100 Horse-power "Alpha I" Radial engine for A.V.Roe.

1927 Five-cylinder 100 Horse-power "Alpha II" Radial engine for A.V.Roe.

1927Five-cylinder Water-cooled Axial car engine for Crossley Motors.

1928 Seven-cylinder 100 Horse-power "Fury I" Axial engine.

1929 Seven-cylinder 100 Horse-power "Fury II" Axial engine.

1931 Nine-cylinder Seven-litre poppet-valve RR1 Axial bus engine.

1932 Nine-cylinder Seven-litre poppet-valve RR2 Axial bus engine.

1933 Nine-cylinder Seven-litre Rotary-valve RR3 bus engine.

1935 Seven-cylinder 120 Horse-power "Fury III" Axial engine.

1936 Nine-cylinder Seven-litre Rotary-valve RR4/1 and 4/2 bus engines.

1936 Nine-cylinder Radial engine with parallel-action motion of connecting-rods.

1936 Eight-cylinder opposed-piston 2000 Horse-power Axial engine.

1940 6.3 Horse-power 1500 psi double-ended wobble-plate hydraulic pump for Cannon drive.

1940 83 gpm single-ended wobble-plate hydraulic motor for Cannon drive.

1941 Winch for loading of bombs into aircraft.

1942 Aero-hydraulic drive for Gun-turret operation.

1943 200 gpm 2,000 psi double-ended wobble-plate hydraulic pump for Bomb-spinning drive.

1946 309cc three-cylinder Axial wobble-plate motor cycle engine.

1948 248cc three-cylinder overhead-valve Radial motor cycle engine.

1952 Eight-cylinder 2,000 Horse-power opposed-piston Axial Cam aero engine

1953 Eight-cylinder 1,000 Horse-power single-ended Axial Cam aero engine.

Appendix (ii)

Known Surviving Redrup Engines

A Three-cylinder “Reactionless” 1912 Aero engine.

Private Collector in Holland.

B Three-cylinder 1922 Redrup Radial engine and motor cycle

A private Japanese collector.

C Three-cylinder 309cc 1946 Axial wobble-plate motor cycle engine.

Mrs Joan Redrup

D Three-cylinder 248cc 1948 overhead-valve Radial engine and motor cycle.

The Sammy Miller Trust Museum.

E Eight-cylinder 1,000 Horse-power single-ended Axial aero engine.

Mrs Joan Redrup.

F Model of eight-cylinder 2,000 Horse-power opposed-piston Axial aero Engine.

Mrs Joan Redrup.